AF633073

DEDICATED TO........

—MY PARENTS—

—Dr. Racharla Ganapathi

CONTENTS

Foreword (*ix*)
Acknowledgements (*xi*)
Abbreviations (*xiii*)

CHAPTER-I
Introduction 01-28

CHAPTER-II
Political History of the Subordinate Rulers of the Kākatīyas (Early Phase) 29-72

CHAPTER-III
Political History of the Subordinate Rulers of the Kakatiyas (Later Phase) 73-129

CHAPTER-IV
Military Administration: Nayankara System 130-144

CHAPTER-V
Socio-Economic and Religious condition under the Subordinate Rulers 145-176

CHAPER-VI
Contribution of Subordinate Rulers towards Literature, Art and Architecture 177-201

CHAPTER-VII
Conclusion 202-215

Bibliography 216-224

FOREWORD

Dr.R. Ganapathi as a native of the area once ruled by the Subordinates of Kakatiyas and Kakatiyas, has rightly choosen the topic. His love towards his native soil might inspired him to work on the Subordinate rulers in order to present a detailed account which will be useful to the research scholars and professionals working in history Departments. Earlier, P.V.P. Sastry has worked on the Kakatiyas of Warangal wherein a brief account on the place of subordinate rulers was presented.

The present work deals with the Political relations of the Subordinate families with the overlords i.e., the Kakatiyas who left an indelible mark in the annals of the Medieval Deccan History. The author is successful in his attempts in putting forth all the available materials in one volume by collecting data from inscriptions and literature of the period, he made a thorough survey based on epigraphs and analysed the Policies of taxation and revenue. His arguments about the rule of the Subordinates under the royal sanctions and thought provoking.

The contributions made by Dr. R. Ganapathi are commandable in gleaming information and offering interpretations pertaining to the aspects of economic prospority, social solidarity, literature, sculpture and temple building activity of the Subordinate rulers under the Kakatiyas of Warangal. His study also reveals that even the Subordinate rulers also possessed titles like their overlords, and the systems of both military and civil administration.

I feel that the book is indispansable for all Scholars engaged in medieval studies particularly of South India. I congratulate Dr. R. Ganapathi for his indepth study and analysis on the topic.

Dr. E. SIVA NAGI REDDY

ACKNOWLEDGEMENTS

I express my deep sense of gratitude to Prof.Mrs. K. Sarojini Devi, Department of Hisotry, Osmania University, Hyderabad, for her valuable guidance in bringing out this Volume.

I am grateful to Dr. S. Bhanumati Ranga Rao, and Dr. V. Sadanandam, Department of History, Osmania University, Hyderabad, who offered useful suggestions at various levels.

I wish to acknowledge the moral support extended to me by Prof. M. Radhakrishna Sarma and Prof. R. Soma Reddy of the Osmania University for their constant support during the course of writing this book.

I place on record my sincere thanks to Dr. G. Venkatrajam, Mrs. R. Varalakshmi and Dr. A. Sathyanarayana, Readers, Department of History, Osmania University, Hyderabad for giving me moral support during the period of my reseach.

I express my sincere thanks to Late Prof. T. Vasudev, Former Vice-Chancellor, Kakatiya University, Warangal and Prof. G. Laxminarayana, Former Vice-Chancellor, J.N.T. University Hyderabad, for their help and encouragement throughout my research.

I am grateful to Prof. Y. Vaikuntham, Former Vice-Chancellor, Kakatiya University, Warangal, who made many valuable suggestions for improving the final presentation of the main arguments.

I am grateful to Dr. P.V. Parabrahma Sastry, Dy. Director (Retd.), Department of Archaeology and Museums, Government of Andhra Pradesh, Shri B.N. Sastry, Epigraphist, Hyderabad, and also Sri D. Someshwar Rao, Retd. Principal, A.V.V. Junior College, Warangal, for their valuable suggestions made on the topic.

I express my profound thanks to Prof. G.Krishna Murthy, Principal and Dr. G. Bhaskar, Lecturer, Department of Economics, P.G. College, Subedari, Kakatiya University, Warangal for their constant support and affection.

I cannot adequately thank Dr. E. Sivanagi Reddy, Asst. Sthapati, Department of Archaeology and Museums, A.P. Hyderabad who helped me in many a way while carrying out the research work by offering scholarly advise. I also take this opportunity to thank Dr. B. Subrahmanyam, Smt. M. Varalakshmi, Librarian, Shri S. Rangachari, Astt. Director and Shri S. Brahmanandam of the same Department for their co-operation.

I am also thankful to Dr. G. Meeneshwar Rao, Head Department of History, and Dr. K. Mohan Rao, Head, Department of Public Administration, C.K.M. College, Warangal, for their unstinted encouragement.

I thank the authorities of the Libraries of Osmania University, Telugu University and State Archives and Research Institute, Hyderabad who helped me by providing access to the sources pertaining to my research work.

I would like to place on record my heartfelt thanks to My wife Mrs. Padma Pravallika for her understanding and also for relieving me from household botherations. Similarly I cannot forget the help I received from my brother Mr. R. Narahari in finalising this work.

I am also grateful to the officials of the Indian Council of Historical Research, New Delhi for awarding me fellowship for completion of this research work.

It is a great pleasure to record my sincere thanks to Sri C.P. Goutham, of Bharatiya Kala Prakashan, New Delhi for bringing out this book very neatly.

Finally, I thank one and all who have direectly or indirectly extended their co-operation in completion of this Volume.

01-05-2000
WARANGAL **Dr. RACHARLA GANAPATHI**

ABBREVIATIONS

A.P.R.E	:	Andhra Pradesh Government Report on Epigraphy
A.R.E.	:	Annual Report of South Indian Epigraphy
Corpus	:	Corpus of Inscriptions in the Telengana Districts
E.A.	:	Epigraphia Andhrica
E.H.D.	:	Early History of the Deccan, Ed. Dr. G. Yazdani
E.I.	:	Epigraphia Indica
I.A.P.Cd.	:	Inscriptions of Andhra Pradesh- Cuddapah District
I.A.P.Kn.	:	Inscriptions of Andhra Pradesh-Karimnagar District
I.A.P.Ng.	:	Inscriptions of Andhra Pradesh- Nalgonda District
I.A.P.Wg.	:	Inscriptions of Andhra Pradesh- Warangal District
J.A.H.R.S.	:	Journal of Andhra Historical Research Society
N.D.I.	:	Nellore District Inscriptions
P.A.P.H.C.	:	Proceedings of Andhra Pradesh History Congress
S.E.A.P.	:	Select Epigraphs of Andhra Pradesh
S.I.I	:	South Indian Inscriptions

Chapter-I

INTRODUCTION

The Kākatīyas were one of the major rulers of Andhra desa for about three hundred and twenty three years from A.D. 1000 to A.D. 1323. During the period of their rule, they creditably shaped the political and cultural destinies of the Andhra people. In the beginning they were the feudatories of the Rāshṭrakūṭas and later shifted their loyalty to the Western Chālukyas of Kalyāṇi. Taking advantage of the political turmoil in the 11th century, the Kākatīyas established their power at Orugallu by about A.D. 1000. Gradually they brought the present Andhra Pradesh, parts of Orissa and Tamilnadu under their sway.

The origin of the Kākatīyas has been highly debated. Several theories are putforward regarding the early chiefs, the derivation of the name Kākatīya and the caste of the Kākatīyas.

The Kākatīya chiefs in their early records are represented as Sāmantas or feudatory chiefs as Sāmanta vishṭi vaṁśa oṛ Sāmanta Voddi Saṁjñaṁ Kulaṁ. Sāmantas governed feudal estates or fiefs and enjoyed certain rights. They lead armies in wars along with their overlords. The Kākatīya chiefs were not mere Rāshṭrakūṭa officers as some scholars believed. On the other hand it was also mentioned that these Sāmantas "ruled the earth from the town Kākati". They also possessed the Garuḍa banner befitting their status of Sāmantas. Garuḍa is the divine vehicle of lord Vishṇu.

"Garuḍa which means the mythical eagle or the divine vehicle of god Vishṇu, was adopted as a royal insignia by the Rāshṭrakūṭas and some other allied dynasties of the Deccan, who generally trace their descent from a *puranic Vrishṇi- Vaṁśa* of lord Krishna. It is not improbable that the Kākatīyas who were called Rāshṭrakūṭas in the Māṅgallu grant, bore the family name like *Rāya-Garuḍa-Kula* after their royal insignia".[1] The feudatories of the Kākatīya rulers adopted the *Garuḍa* banner like their overlords. The Palampet epigraph[2] states that the shafts containing the arrows of the Kākatīya general Recharla Rudra were decorated with Garuḍa symbols. Some Kākatiya rulers like Beta II claimed to belong to the family of *Sāmanta Viṣṭi* or *Vṛishṇi* to which clan lord Krishṇa belonged. There are different opinions regarding the family name Kākatīya. Literary evidence suggest that the Kākatīyas worshipped the goddess Kākati, one of the forms of Durga, on account of which they attained the name Kākati. Some scholars are of the view that Kākati refers to a place which was probably the capital or headquarters of the early Kākatīya rulers.[3] K. Lakshminārāyana Rao accepting this identified the place Kākati with it's namesake situated in Belgaum.[4] It is possible that the Kākatīyas who were associated with the Rāshṭrakūṭas as their subordinates hailed from Kākati in Karnāṭaka. For any chief or ruler the original home is dear and the memories of its association are always cherished. Venna, the founder of the family proudly recalled that the ruled the earth with his residence at Kākati.[5] Though this aspect needs further investigation, it appears that affiliations to original homes are stronger than religious affiliations.

It is also difficult to identify the caste of the Kākatīya rulers. The Malkapuram inscription[6] of Viśvēśvara Śivāchārya and the Moṭupalli inscription[7] of Gaṇapatideva suggest that the *Kākatīya* rulers belonged to the *Kshatriya* caste of the solar race. They claimed descent from Manu, Ikshvāku, Māndhāta, Bhagīratha, Raghu, Daśaratha and Rāma. Obviously all these kings were Kṣhatriyas of the solar race. Manu, a great king of solar race is said to have built the city of Ayodhya, capital of Kosala ruled by Daśaratha.[8] However, most of the Kākatīya inscriptions do not mention the caste or the gotra of the rulers. Vidyānātha, the author of *Pratāparudrīyam* says that the Kākatīyas were superior to the solar and lunar race of the Kshatriyas.[9] This may be interpreted that the Kākatīyas were *Kshatriyas* but, far greater than the well known solar and lunar races. In fact Vidyānātha stated in his work that when Brahma created Pratāparudra out of his shoulders, he felt immense satisfaction that He justified His role as the creator.

According to *Purushasūkta* theory, the *Kshatriyas* originated from the arms of Brahma. Some scholars believe that this need not be interpreted as a reference to the caste of Pratāparudra. It merely referes to the Kshātra or valour of the king and not the caste, that is the *Kshatriya* caste. However, it is not known why Vidyānātha referred to the creation of Pratāparudra from the shoulders of Brahma and not other limbs. It is well known that the *Brahmins, Kshatriyas, Vaisyas* and *Śūdras* were created from the head, arms, thighs and feet of Brahma. Probably the Kākatīyas originally *Kshatriyas* suffered Varṇa *Sānkarya* on account of their marriages with the chiefs belonging to different castes including the *chaturthakula* and lost their identity. In this connection M.Somasekhara Sarma's valuable observations are worth noting: He stated on the basis of a chatuverse, called the *Kshatriya gōtra Sisamālika* in Telugu, that the Rāchavāru or Rājus of the Telugu country were the descendents of four major primary *Kshatriya* houses namely the Kākatīyas, the Kōṭas, the Parichedis, and the Varnaṭakas of the Kāśyapa, Dhananjaya, Vaśishta and Kauṇḍinya gōtras respectively. The Kshatriyas of the Andhra country were popularly known as Rāchavāru or Rajus.[10] Thus literary evidence indicates that the Kākatīyas were *Kshatriyas*. Inscriptional evidence like the Malkāpuram inscription of Viśveśvara Śivāchārya specifically states that the Kākatīyas belonged to the *Sūryavaṁśa-Kshatriya* caste.[11]

One reason why the other inscripions and literary works do not specifically mention the caste of the Kākatīya rulers is the emergence of the mixed castes on account of matrimonial alliances for political reasons between the rulers and their feudatoreis as will be noted later. The problem of the identification of the caste of the Kākatīyas need further investigation.

Most of the ruling families in 12th and13th centuries after attaining political authority aspired for corresponding social status. The spread of Kālāmukha Śaivism in Andhra opened before the Śūdras the gates of religious and secular training. The ritual status of the Śūdra ruling families came to be recognised. Gradually the Śūdras conscious of their status put themselves in a separate category as Sat Śūdras very much different from the peasants and peasant warriors. The titles mentioned in the inscriptions like *Chaturtha kulavanaja marthaṇḍa, Śūdras sathima, Chaturtha vaṁśa Chathuranana* suggest that these *Sat śūdras* claimed equally with Kshatriyas and even with brahmans. The *Kshatriya* families like the Haihayas, the Chālukyas of Niḍadavole, in order to maintain their authority entered into matrimonial alliances with the powerful Śūdra ruling families. Thus the marriage alliances gave rise to mixed castes and the identity of individual caste was lost in the bargain. The same might have happened in the case of the Kākatīyas whether they were *Kshatriyas* or Śūdras.

It is necessary to make a brief survey of the political history of the Kākatīyas to a better understanding of the relations with the subordinates. According to some epigraphs, the founder of the family was Venna who belonged to Durjaya family. Durjaya perhaps was powerful chieftain since some other chiefs also trace their origin to Durjaya. Venna claims to have hailed from Kākati. He was followed by Gunḍa I, Gunḍa II and Gunḍa III. Eṟra son of Gunḍa III was raised to the status of a feudatory by the Rāshṭ rakūṭas who conferred on him the Koravi region and Mānukoṭa. Gunḍa IV or Pinḍi Gunḍa helped Dānārṇava, the ruler of Vengi in regaining his throne. Dānārṇava isued the Māṅgallu edict in A.D. 956 acknowledging the help received from Pinḍi Gunḍa.[12] However, when Tailapa II over threw the Rāshṭrakūṭas and established the hegemony of the Western Chalukyas of Kalyāṇi, Gunḍa IV, taking adventage of the political confusion proclaimed his independence. After the death of Gunḍa IV, his young son Beta or Garuḍa Beta became the ward of Kāmavasāni, wife of the Viriyāla chief Erra. She took pity on Beta and prevailed upon her husband to use his influence with the Western Chālukyas to secure the fief of Anumakoṇḍa *vishaya* included parts of present Warangal district and Sanigaram region of Karimnagar district. Beta ruled from A.D. 1000-A.D. 1052.[13] His son and successor Prolarāja I (A.D. 1030-1075) who was a far-sighted diplomat, acknowledged the suzerainty of the Western Chālukya ruler, Someśwara I and secured his support in fulfilling his ambitions and also the permanent possession of the principality of Anumakoṇḍa *vishaya,* He was not only a great general but also an efficient administrator who carved for the prosperity of his people. He is credited with the construction of an irrigation tank called Kēsari or Jagatikēsari, so named after one of his *birudus*. His son and successor Betarāja II (A.D. 1075-1110) obtained *Sabbimanḍala* from VikramādityaVI. Prolarāja II, son and successor of Beta II took active part in the Kālachuri revolution at Kalyāṇi and after the overthrow of Tailapa II proclaimed independance. Though he made extenive connquests in Telengana, his endeavour to carry the banner of victory upto the east coast proved futile and he lost his life at the hands of the rulers of Velanāḍu.

Prolarāja was succeeded by his eldest son Rudradeva (A.D. 1150-1196) under whom the Kākatīya dynasty reached great heights of glory. He avenged his father's death by defeating the rulers of Velanāḍu and annexing large portions of their kingdom. Rudradeva's kingdom extended from the Godāvari in the North to Śrīśailam in the South, to the Eastern ghats in the East and to Kalyāṇi in the west. He entered into matrimonial relations with powerful chieftains and enlisted their support. The example of the Kākatīya rulers was taken as a good precedent and followed by their feudatories later. The military achievements of Rudra were eqalled by his contribution to Hinduism. He constructed many temples among which the temple of Rudreśvara popularly known as Thousand Pillars temple at Anumakoṇḍa is prominent. Even today it attracts many Indians and foreign tourists. Unfortunately Rudra was defeated and killed by Yadava ruler Juitugi who looked at the rising power of Kākatīyas as a great threat to his existence Rudra's death lost his in battle in A.D. 1198.[14]

Gaṇapatideva, son of Mahadeva ascended the Kākatīya throne in A.D. 1209. Gaṇapatideva, was the greatest of the Kākatīya kings and his reign constituted the most brilliant epoch in his history of the dynasty. During his long reign he was continuously engaged in wars. He not only conquered the petty kingdoms between the river Goḍavari and Pennār, but also succeeded in occupying a large portion of Kalinga. The Telugu Choḍa kingdom of Nellore was subjugated and Kāñchi was made the Southern outpost of the Kākatīyas. The Yādavas under the leadership of Singhana who underestimated the power of Gaṇapatideva invaded the Kākatīya kingdom. But Ganapatideva defeated and forced him to surrender a portion of his kingdom on the Godavari region. He established matrimonial alliances with the Yadavas and strengthened his position. He changed his capital from Anumakoṇḍa to Orugallu in about A.D. 1254. Thus Ganapatideva succeeded in bringing under his control the whole of the Telugu country and his empire extended from the Godavari district upto Chengalpat in the Tamilnadu and from Yelgandal to the Bay of Bengal. He encouraged trade and commerce and ensured protection to merchants engaged in foreign trade. The Motupalli inscription[15] dated A.D. 1244-45 is an eloquent testimony of the *abḥaya* or security to the merchants.

Gaṇapatideva was succeeded by his daughter Rudramadevi or Rudrāmba in A.D.1262. She ruled upto A.D. 1296 under the name of Rudradeva Mahārāja. She was a brave and capable ruler well trained in martial arts and statecraft. She successfully repulsed the invasions of Yādava Mahadeva in the North and the Chōḷas and Pāṇḍyas in the South. Rudramāmba kept infact the integrity of the kingdom and won the admiration of even the foreign travellers who paid glowing tributes to her efficient rule and the prosperity of her kingdom.[16]

Rudramāmba was succeeded by her grandson, Pratāparudra (A.D.1296-1323). At the time of his accession, the Kākatīya kingdom was in disturbed condition. So Pratāparudra entrusted the task of restoring order in the kingdom to the Padmanāyaka chieftains. It is stated that the special favour shown to the Velama officers incurred the displeasure and jealousy of the Reddi lieutenants of Pratāparudra which resulted in disloyalty among the rank and file of the armed forces and subordinate chiefs. However, Pratāparudra suppressed the revolt of the Telugu Chōḍas and the Reḍḍis of Gaṇḍikōṭa. Later he inflicted a crushing defeat on the Pāṇḍyan forces and re-established his authority at Kāñchi.

Thus for a little more than a century the Kākatīyas were able to maintain their hold on almost the entire Andhra country with the exception of Kalinga. Bidar and Kaulas in the West, Simhachalam and Mahur in the North and Kāñchi and Vallur near Gaṇḍikōṭa in the South were the boundaries of their kingdom.[17]

However, the Kākatīya kingdom became the target of the Muslim invasions from A.D.1303. Muslim directed against Telengāna. But the valuable copper plate grants of Vilasa and Kaluvacheru informs that the emperors of Delhi led eight invasions against the Kākatīya kingdom and not five as stated by the Muslim chronicles. In seven out of the eight invasions Pratāparudra is creditably stated to have defeated and driven out of the forces of Delhi. But as observed by M.S.Sarma, the often repeated invasions, no doubt, broke the morale of the Hindus and paved the way for the success of the Muslims. The kingdom of Orugallu was finally conquerred in A.D. 1323.[18]

The Kākatīya rulers seemed to have given preference to decentralized type of administration and gave autocracy to their feudatories in administering their territories. They were however careful not to allow the feudatories to meddle with the military matters. The benevolent attitude of the rulers towards the *sāmantas* is reflected in the following factors: The Kākatīyas did not bear any high sounding titles indicative of their soverign power. The title *mahāmaṇḍalēś*vara only figures in their *praśastis*. Obviously they did not exert any sovereignity over the feudatories and saved them from a sense of humiliation and subordination. Like the Rāshṭrakūṭas, the Kākatīya overlords did not alienate the village in the dominions of their vassels.[19] In some of the epigraphs of the feudatories the names of the Kākatīya overlords donot find mention. The Kākatīyas honoured the local traditions in the conquered areas. The disloyal feudatories in medieval India were generally subjected to various indiginities like sweeping the stables of his victor. For instance the ruler of Veṇgi had to sweep the stables of his victor Govinda II.[20] Feudatories had to surrender their precious gems, treasures, dancing girls, horses and elephants to the imperial powers as punishment to their disloyalty. Even their wives were taken captives. In some cases the defeated feudatories were deprived of their property and territories.[21] However, in the history of the Kākatīyas instances of ill treatement and humiliation of the feudatories are not forthcoming.

The Kākatīyas exhibited great political sagacity in dealing with *māṇḍalikas* like the Kōṇa chiefs of the Haihaya family and the Chālukya chiefs of Pithapuram, who exercised some power in Godavari region. These chiefs still owed allegiance to the Chōḷas though the imperial authority of the Cholas in the Telugu country declined. Gaṇapatideva followed a policy of 'live and let live' towards these *māṇḍalikas* who were also apprehensive of the mighty power of the rulers. They did not try to assert their independence for the simple reason that they were conscious of their inferior strength. The Kākatīya rulers undertook conquest and annexation under unavoidable circumstances. For example, the conquest and annexation of Coastal Andhra was unavoidable. The coastal Andhra from Godavari to Penna was of strategic importance and always posed a threat to the Kākatīya rulers. Their objective in the conquerred regions was not impostion of sovereign authority but that of peaceful co-existence. The *māṇḍalikas* were allowed to enjoy their freedom. For example Gaṇapatideva allowed the Ayya chiefs of Divi to rule their land as his subordinates without annexing the conquerred territory. This was in sharp contrast with the policies of the Chālukyas and Chōḷas. It may be recalled in this connection that the Chalukyas fought with the Chōḷas, the successors of the Pallavas and prevented their expansion into the Deccan. The Chōḷas followed an aggressive policy and compelled many rulers in the South to acknowledge their supremacy.

The Kākatīya rulers did not assume high sounding titles or hyperbolical *praśastis* tracing descent from mythological heroes. Their records simply state that while a particular king is ruling the earth etc,[22] surprisingly in an age when the insignificant chiefs and even the merchants of the guilds adopted lengthy *praśastis*. They did not view seriously the indifference of the *māṇḍalikas* in mentioning the names of their overlords in their records. For instance there is no reference to Pratāparudradeva in the Durgi epigraph[23] dated A.D. 1297 belonging to Rudradeva, the trusted commander-in-chief of Pratāparudra. This does not mean that the *māṇḍalikas* had no respect for their overlords. They were very much loyal to the rulers till the fall of the empire. The Kākatīyas followed a policy of decentralisation of power instead of centralisation of power in their hands amounting to administrative suffocation of the subordinates.

The subordinate rulers under the Kākatīyas can be broadly divided into four categories as mentioned below :

1. The subordinate rulers who were associated with the early Kākatīyas, when they were subordinates of the Chālukyas of Kalyāṇa: Under this category come the two subordinate families viz., Viriyala and Natavāḍi, who were the earliest associates of the Kākatīyas. They were earlier subordinates of the Rāshṭrakūṭas, and later the Chālukyas of Kalyāṇa. Their common interests were further promoted by matrimonial alliances which survived for a long period to the benefit of the Kākatīya rulers in their political aspirations.

   The subordinate rulers by way of appointment to rulership over a particular region under their control: The Recharla Reḍḍis, were appointed by the Kākatīyas as rulers of Āmanagallu and Pillalamarri regions of the present Nalgonda District. Bamma *Sēnāni* a subordinate chief of the early Kākatīyas served his successors upto the period of Gaṇapatideva. Another such family was the Malyāla chiefs. They were associated with the Kākatīyas from around A.D. 1076 to A.D. 1276 as testified by their inscriptions. Next come the Cheruku chiefs who were great warriors and faithful subordinates of the Kākatīyas. The earliest known member of Cheruku family was Kāṭa I who entered the service of Kākati Beta II, and he was initially given the region around Cheruku-12 in recongnition of his services and served the Kākatīyas loyalty upto 1323.A.D. The Kāyasthas who were the most powerful subordinates of the Kākatīyas come under this catagory as independent rulers and subordinate to the Kākatīyas. They ruled over a land in Andhra from Panugal to Marjavāḍi. One more such family was of the Induluri chiefs. The earliest known member was Nana Goura who entered the service of Kākatīyas during the reign of Prola II. His sons Peda Malla and *Pina* Malla served Kakati Rudra. The Recherla Velama chiefs were appoointed as the rulers of Pillalamarri and Āmanagallu during the reign of Kākati Ganapatideva. Betala Nāyaka or Chevvi Reddi was the founder of the family. Perhaps after the Recharla reḍḍis had lost their prominance at the imperial court, they entered the service of the Kākatīyas around A.D. 1210 and served them until the end in A.D.1323. Then come Gona chiefs who entered the service of the Kākatīyas around A.D. 1290 i.e., during the rule of Kākati Rudramma and also served under Pratāpa Rudra. The Raichur doab which was under their control with dense forests was cleared and reclaimed for cultivation by these feudatories. These chiefs lost their prominance after the fall of the Kākatīya Kingdom.

3. The subordinates were subjugated by war and by annexation of territories: Under this category comes Kōṭa family who ruled over *shaṭ sahasrāvanī* in Velanaḍu-6000 country lying to the southern bank of river Krishṇa beginning as independent rulers. They acknowledged the Chālukya Chōḷas as their overlords, and later on became subordinates of the Kākatīyas.

4. The subordinates by way of matrimonial alliances: There is a solitary example of this king i.e., the Chālukyas of Niḍadavole. The Kākatīyas tried serval times to penetrate into the Kalinga region but were forced to retreat to the south of Godavari at the hands of the Ganga king Ananga Bhima III. In order to strengthen his hold over the coastal region Gaṇapatideva sought to secure this political allegiance of the Chālukyas of Niḍadavolve by offering, his daughter Rudrama to the Chālukya prince, Virabhadra, the younger son of Induśekhara, probably in A.D. 1259 as evidenced by the Juttiga epigrapy of the same date. This family also withered away along with the Kākatīyas.

The Kākatīyas had marital relations with five families viz., Viriyāla, Natavādi, Kōṭa, the Chālukyas of Niḍadavole and Indulūri. Some of the feudatories became relatives by entering into marital alliances among themselves. For example Viriyāla Mailama married Malyāla Chaunḍa Senāpati, Malyāla Gunḍa *danḍadhisa* married Gona Kuppāmbika, daughter of Gona Buddhaya, and Kōṭa Keta III married Bayyaladevi, daughter of Naṭavādi Pakkidi Rudra or Rudra II. Such close relationship remained a strong bond which enabled the Kākatīyas to grow into a major power. It may be noted that there are only two exceptions i.e., Recherla Reḍḍis and Velamas, who did not have any marital alliances either with the family of their overlords or with the other feudatories.

The role played by subordinate chiefs in the Kākatīya polity was significant and should be properly studied. Almost all the earlier members of the subordinate families were taken into the service of the Kākatīya rulers because of their military prowess. Some of them were initially made the Chiefs of principalities who later rose to the status of *Sāmantas*, *Mahasāmantas* and then to *Mānḍalikas* and *Mahāmānḍalēśvaras*.

The Kākatiya subordinates who assisted their overlords assumed titles such as Nāyaka, *Sāmanta, Mahsāmanta*, *Māndalika*, *Mahāmanḍalika* and *Mahāmanḍalēśwara* etc. Which are defined hereunder. In order to appreciate the role of the feudatories in the Kākatīya polity it is necessary to understand the meaning and significance of the titles of the feuatories, their functions and responsibilities.

Nāyaka was a military functionary or military leader.[24] According to *Pratāpacharitra*, Prātaparudra entrusted the defence of the seventy seven bastions of his fort to seventy seven *Nāyakas* of the Velama community alloting them one fort of his kingdom as estate to enable them to maintain the stipulated army. It is not possible to ascertain whether all the seventy seven were Velama *Nāyakas* or not. Because *Nāyakas* of other castes are also noticed inscriptions. The *lemkas* who seem to be equal to *Nāyakas* include Reḍḍis and other castes. Juttiya lemka Goṇka Reḍḍi, Dachaya lemka, Pinnaya lemka were not Velamas.[25]

R.S. Sharma opines that the smaller chiefs who were reduced to subordinations and reinstated in their positions by the king paid regular tributes and did homage to the king. Such feudatories were called *Sāmantas*.[26] Normally an important duty of the *sāmanta* was to render military aid[27] and supply forces to the ruler.[28] Gradually the term *sāmanta* was extended from defeated chiefs to royal officials.[29] Although the *sāmanta* appear as a feudal vassal from the 6th century A.D. onwards, we have no idea of their rights and obligations except that they had to furnish soliders to their overlords.[30] *Mahāsāmanta* was a higher post than that of *sāmanta*. A graded relationship possibly, regulated by grant of land and extent of supply of military to the overlord, existed between *sāmanta* and *mahasāmanta*.[31]

Aparājitha priçÇha of Bhaṭṭa Bhuvanadēva, a work of 12th century enumerates in descending order nine categories of rulers known as *mahipati, rāja, naradhipa, mahāmanḍalēśwara, mānḍalika, mahāsāmanta sāmanta, laghu sāmanta* and *chaturāsika*. In each case the extent of territory held is specified and it ranges from the whole earth in respect of the *mahipati* and 1000 villages in respect of *chaturāsika*. The work also describes the composition of a typical feudal court. It recommends that the emperor (sāmrat) who held the title of *mahārājādhirāja Paramēśwara* should have in his court 4 *manḍalēśwaras*, 12 *manḍalikas*, 32 *sāmantas*, 160 *laghu sāmantas*, and 400 *chaturāsikas*. It also lay down that the income of the *laghu sāmanta* should amount of 5,000 of the *sāmanta* to 10,000 and of the *mahāsāmanta* to 20,000 in ascending order. Thus the work provides many instances of graded subordinate relations linked up with tribute and service. The text however does not fix the rate of revenue to be collected by those chiefs from their subjects, but it provides a systematised hierarchy in terms of political and economic power.[32] The chief obligation of all the vassals was to render military service to their lords.[33] As Bhaṭṭa Bhuvanadēva's work belongs to 12th century, it may be assumed that the Kākatīya feudatories followed the same gradations linked up with military service and tribute. The feudatories were permitted to use a feudal throne, fly whisk, palamquins and elephants. Under the Rāshṭrakūṭas vassals were permitted to use these symbols of royal insignia. As the Kākatīyas were the feudatories of the Rāshṭrakūṭas.[34]

Recherla Rudra acquired *Simhāsanam* and *Mānḍalikābhidhanam* (The office of *mānḍalika* and throne) from Gaṇapatideva.[35] The early members of this family, namely Bamma, Mucha, Kata I and Kama served their overlords as *Danḍanāyakas* and *Chamupatis*. But during the time of Rudra, the Recherla chiefs became *Mānḍalikas*. When the great general Rudra removed the throne that lay in the way of the feet of the Kākatīya king and restored the kingdom, as a reward, his soverign Gaṇapatideva presented him a throne and the paraphernalia of a *Mānḍalika*. Of the two branches of Recherla Reḍḍis only the Elkurti branch of Rudra Sēnāni is credited with the distinction of *Mānḍalika* status as noticed in his Palampet, Dicchakunta epigraphs. In contrast to this the chiefs of Pillalamarri branch remained in *mahāsāmanta* position.[37] In the Rāshṭrakūṭa records the *mahāsāmanta* is represented as a breaker of the hair-parting of the dames of hostile barons, a gallant dear to the courtesans of warriors., a wind dissipating the clouds (of) opponent barons, a furious elephant to Nāgaladevi, a time of world dissolution to enemy barons, a Gopāla to the worthiest of barons, a heroic Kumāra to the demon Tāra's rival barons, a awful rutting elephant to the beds of lotuses (who are) the barons of Tondai, (a) rod for the skillful right hand of king Gandaraditya....crest gem of barons....'' Though this description of the *mahāsāmanta* may appear hyperbolical, it certainly indicates position and the obligation of a *mahāsāmanta* to suppress the hostile and protect the friendly *sāmantas*.[37A]

Even before the rise of the Kākatīyas, the Viriyāla family held the status of *mānḍalika*. We know from the Gūduru inscription dated A.D. 1124 that Poramti Venna of Viriyāla family was a *mānḍalika*.[38] The Pammi inscription dated A.D. 1234[39] speaks of *mahāsāmanta* Viriyāla Nāgāsanamma. Malyāla Kāṭa Sēnāni was stated to be a *mahāsāmanta*.[40] Natavāḍi Durga held the epithet *mānḍalika*.[41]

It seems that the sons of Keṭa I of Cheruku family Keṭa II, Māra I, Eṛra I, Eṛra II renderd military assistance to Kākati Rudra in his conflict with the Chōḍa chiefs and were conferred the status of *mahāsāmantas.*[42] Cheruku Bollaya Reḍḍi another *mahāsāmanta*[43] under Kākatīya Ganapatideva ruled the areas around Amarabad, Vanguru seema and parts of Kurnool *manḍala*. The Cheruku chiefs were elevated to the position of the *mahāsāmanta* status by Kākati Rudra. The Jammulūru branch of Cheruku chiefs also enjoyed the *mahāsāmanta* status.[44]

In contrast the Kōṭa chiefs enjoyed a higher position of *mahāmaṇḍalēśvaras*. For instance, the Kolluru inscription dated 1233[45] mentions Kōṭa Bhima III as *mahāmaṇḍalēśvaras*. Kōta Keta III is mentioned in Amarāvati inscription dated A.D. 1235[46] as *mahāmaṇḍalēśvaras* Manma Keṭarāja. Even the later rulers of Dhanyavati who were neither prominent nor powerful retained the same *mahāmaṇḍalēśvara* status. Kōta Gaṇapatideva was a *mahāmaṇḍalēśvara* styled as Gaṇapatideva rāja.[47] Kōṭa Bhima IV, son of Keṭa III who ruled for a brief period of six years was *mahāmaṇḍalēśvaras.*[48] Kota Devarāja and Mummaḍirāja were referred to as *mahāmaṇḍalēśvaras.*[49] Gaṇapāmba, daughter of Kākati Gaṇapatideva, and wife of Kōṭa Beṭa was referred as *mahāmaṇḍalēśvara* Gaṇapamadeva *yammangāru.*[50] The *mahāmaṇḍalēśvaras* often bore the title of rāja or rāsa (Canarese).[51]

The Kāyashta chiefs were also mentioned as *Mahāmaṇḍa-lēśvaras*. The Satrasāla record of A.D. 1244[52] mentions *Mahā-maṇḍalēśvaras* Ambayyadeva, brother-in-law of Gangaya Sāhini. Gangaya Sāhini was not only a *Mahāmaṇḍalēśvaras* but also *bāhattāri niyōgādhipati,* the chief of 72 branches of administration in Kākaṭīya kingdom.[53] Jannigadeva was also *Mahāmaṇḍalē-śvaras.*[54] and Gaṇapatideva dakshiṇa bhujadaṇḍa.[55] Ambadeva was referred to as *Mahāmaṇḍalēśvaras.*[56] The Chālukyas of Nidadavole were described as *Mahāmaṇḍalēśvaras.*[57] The following table shows the status of different feudatory families.

Staus	*Subordinate Rules*
Mahāsāmanta	Cheruku, Malyāla.
Māṇḍalikas	Recharla, Viriyāla, Natavādi
Mahāmāṇḍalika/ Mahāmaṇḍalēśvara	Kōṭa, Kāyastha, Chālukyas of Niḍadavole

The above table shows that Cheruku and Malyāla chiefs enjoyed the status of *mahāsāmantas*, where as Recharla, Viriyala and Natavādi were *māṇḍalikas*. The *mahāmāndalika* or *mahāmaṇḍalēśvara* status was enjoyed only by the Kōtas, Kāyasthas and Chālukyas of Niḍadavole even before they entered the service of Kākatiyas, who allowed them to retain the titles. The other families which in their *praśasti* did not bear any of these titles must have been *Sāmantas* in this regard G. Yazadani rightly pointed out "How the *Sāmantas* and *mahāsāmantas* differed, and what their status, privilages and functions were cannot be accuretely determined at present."[58] The same applies to the *Māṇḍalika* and *mahāmāṇḍalika* statuses as well. However, their hierarchical status might have been, greatly honoured and rewarded by the Kākatiyas. It is interesting to note that though the Velama chiefs did not adopt any of these status symbols, they were given greater importance ignoring some times the Reḍḍi chiefs was one of the reasons for the fall of Kākatīyas.

It is equally interesting to note that the epithets found in the *praśastis* of Kākatīya rulers in their epigraphs such as *mahārājadhirāja paramēśvara* etc., were borne by their feudatories too. This might be interpreted as a poetic exaggeration of the composers of the records who were mostly scholars and poets.[59] For instance, the Kotas, Kāyasthas and Chālukyas of Niḍadavole styled themselves *mahāmandalēśvaras,* though they were not equal to their overlords. Obviously the Kākatiya overlords gave freedom to their feudatories in other to please their whims and fancies. In this connection Dr. P.V. Parabramha Sāstry observes: "The subordinate Chiefs were allowed to have their freedom in all respects except military matters. The only concern for the king was to check their overgrowth in power".[60] The maximum freedom thus allowed to the subordinate Chiefs endeared the Kākatīya rulers to them and the Chiefs could play a better role in the affairs of the empire. The appointment of *sāmantas*, *mahāsāmantas*, *māṇḍalikas* or *mahāmanḍalēś*varas was invariably accompanied with *simhāsanam* (throne) besides other royal paraphernalia. This gave a feudatories a feeling a sharing the royal power and glory that went with royalty.

The terms *mahāpradhana*, *pradhāna*, *preggaḍa, amātya,* and *mantri* are mentioned in the inscriptions and also in contemporary literature. No other inforamtion is available about the monarch in transacting the state craft. A *mantri* was recognised from very ancient times as one of the saptāngas (the seven constituent members) of the body politic. A king who has no minister to advice him to compared to an elephant without it's trunk. The king is required to exercise great caution in the choice of his minister and the delegation of powers to them. He should, according to the *Nitisāstra Muktāvali* of Baddena, avoid an ignorant man though he may happen to be a personal friend of the king and should appoint a wise and trust worthy person as the minister. He should place confidence in people noted for their wisdom and loyalty and should avoid fickle minded individuals who are likely to divulge the secrets of council. He should not make any minister head of the govrnment of the state; for a minsiter entrusted with such unlimited authority would become too powerful and wealthy. The respective positions of the king and the minister in a state should not be reversed, for the excessive growth of powers of any single member of body politic would destroy the majesty of the regnal state and ruin the kingdom.[61]

The *Rājanīti* requires the king to appoint his ministers from brahmins who were well versed in *Vēdas,* the *Śāstras* and Political Science. But the Kākatīya rulers did not restrict their choice of minister to any single community. The instances of Malyāla Hemādri Reddi and of Muppiḍināyaka a Velama who held the office of *Mahāpradhāna* respectively under Ganapatideva and Pratparudra show that they selected their minister from all the principal castes of subjects. Merit was probably the criterion while making appointments to public officers. For example Vellanki Gangādhara, who started his career as an official in the royal palace under Prola II, was subsequently promoted to the office of an *amātya* or minister by his son and successor. Rudra on account of his loyalty and his efficient discharge of duties. This indicates that great importance was given by the king to pure merit when filling ministerial positions. The appointment of a person to the officer of a minister was invariably accompanied by the conferment of special insignia such as palanquin, the white umbrella and a special dress and besides the grant of *Jivita* or *Vritti* pertaining to the *niyōga* (office) and presents of valuable ornaments and costly perfumes.[62]

It is a general phenomenon of ancient Indian administration that, the subordinates were to assist and follow the orders of their overlords during military compaigns. The *sāmantas* are advised to help their overlord in war and to mobilise his allies and auxilliaries according to *Agnipurāna* a work of about the tenth eleventh century.[63] In accordance with this the feudatories of the Kākatīyas not only supplied armies but also acted as *Sēnāpatis*, *Chamupatis*, *Daṇḍanāyakas* and *Māndāḍis*.[64]

The military officers of the Kākatīyas known as *Sāhinis* were employed for training the horses and elephants for the purpose of war. The Officer-incharge of horse was the *Aśvasāhini*. The Kāyastha chief Gangaya was a *sāhin*i in-charge of royal cavalry under Gaṇapatideva. All the members of his family enjoyed the previleged position of *sāhinis*. They were praised as *ativishama hāyaruḍuha proudha rēkha rēvanta*.[65] Bendapudi Annaya was the chief of elephant forces of the Kākatīya king (*Mahāraya Gajasāhini*)[66] one Pradakshinamu Mahadevamanchi was the keeper of horse (*Māndāḍi*) of the Recherla chief Kata IV.[67]

All of the foregoing suggest that irrespective of their appellations, all the subordinate chiefs were participants in military enterprise. The fact that the latter chiefs associated with the Kākatīya rulers like Kōṭa, Velama, Chālukyas, Gona chiefs donot bear any of these appellations suggests that some of them were already *māṇḍalikas* even before they entered the service of Kākatiya rulers and even the Kākatīya king were not interested to give such inferior status to their subordinate chiefs.

In the present state of knowledge it may be assumed that the civil and military administration of the feudatories was carried out on the same lines of that Kākatīya kings.

SCOPE OF THE STUDY

The theme of the present research work is to study the 'place of the subordinate rulers in the Kākatīya polity'. The area of investigation comprises not only the present Andhra Pradesh but also the non Telugu speaking regions of contiguous parts. The present work attempts to study the role of the subordinate rulers with reference to their origin, geneogoy, political history and their relationship with the Kākatīyas. The socio-economic, religious conditions and their contribution in the fields of art and architecture are also considered in the study. The period of study is from the foundation of Kākatīya rule in A.D. 1000-A.D. 1323 to fall of the kingdom. During this period the feudatories not only played an important role but also made significant contribution to the history of the Kākatīyas.

SOURCES OF THE STUDY

The sources of the present study can be divided into two kinds, viz., Epigraphical and Literary. The epigraphical sources are of two kinds: copper plate grants and lithic records.

Epigraphical Sources : The history of the Kākatīyas is largely based on epigraphical evidence as is the case of their overlords. There are several lithic records, a mention of which becomes too unwiedly to list out here. Much of the information regarding the political as well as socio-economic history of the subordinate rulers is contained in the stone inscriptions.

The Dicçḥakunṭa epigraph mentions *mānḍalika* Rudrareḍḍi and his son Kāṭreḍḍi. The Elkurti inscription mentions Rudra Senāpati and his sons.[68] If *mānḍalika* Rudrareḍḍi mentioned in Dicçḥakunṭa inscription and Elkurti inscriptions are considered to be identical, it may be assumed that Rudra Senāpati had three sons Kāṭa, Loka and Gaṇapati, The Yadlapalli inscriptions and the Palampet record throw light on the Recharla chiefs[69] Regarding the Viriyāla chiefs recrods from Gūduru, Kaṭakūru, Sambhuniguḍi and Koṭagiri copper plates furnish information about the role of the chiefs in establishing the Kākatīyas and extending their authority in the early stages.[70] The Malyāla chiefs were represented by the

Koṇḍaparti and Bothapur records. The composer of these records was Iśvara Sūri, an eminent scholar in various branches of learning.[71] The earliest record of the Natavāḍi chiefs was found at Narsampet dated A.D.1101. The Niḍigoṇḍa epigraph is helpful in tracing the origin of the Natavāḍi chiefs. The Bayyaram tank inscription of Mailama and Tripurantakam temple inscriptions speak of the Natavāḍi chiefs.[72] The Jammuluṛu epigraph, the Vollala inscription of Mallikārjuna Chōḍa, Goruvankapalli grant from Acchampet taluq throw valuable light on the relations of the Cheraku chiefs with the Kākatiya rulers.[73] The stone inscriptions of the Kōṭa chiefs noticed in the Amarēśvara temple at Amaravati, the Ramalingēśvara temple at Velpuru and the Moguluṭla copper plate grant give geneological account of the Kōṭa chiefs. The Eḍavalli copper plate grant furnished a lengthy geneology of the Kōṭa chiefs.[74] About the great Gangaya Sāhini, inscriptions from Gundluru dated A.D. 1239 credits him with the title *Gaṇḍa peṇḍera*. The Tripurantakam inscription of Ambadeva, datable to A.D. 1290 is a historical document which records besides the geneological account of the Kāyasthas, several outstanding military victories of Ambadeva.[75] The Chandupaṭla epigraph datable to A.D. 1289 furnishes the clue that Rudrama devi might have died in a battle fought with Ambadeva.[76] The Attirala epigraph dated A.D. 1287 refers to the areas under the control of Ambadeva.[77] The unpublished Visunuru epigraph datable to A.D.1280 establishes the identity of Rudranayaka, brother of Prasāditya, the Velama chief.

Literary Sources: There are various works which depict the political, social, economic and cultural conditions of the Kākatīya period.

SANSKRIT

Pratāparudrīyam or Pratāparudra Yashōbhūshanam: This a treatise on rhetorics in Sanskrit language composed by Vidyānātha the renowned court poet of Pratāparudra, the last Kākatīya ruler. As the title sugest the work was dedicated to Pratāparudra, the patron lord of Vidyānātha. It is helpful in knowing about the race and the relationship of Rudramadevi to

Gaṇapatideva and Pratāparudra. Though the work deals mainly with the history of the Kākatīya rulers, it no doubt is helpful in assessing the relations of the feudatories with the Kākatīya overlords.

Nrittaratnāvaḷi: Jāyapa Sēnāni, the general and minister of Gaṇapatideva composed the work illustrating various styles of *nritta* and *nātya*. The work is of gret value in understanding the dance forms of the period. The feudatories emulated the rulers in promoting dance and drama. The Kākatīya rulers and their feudatories attained great fame on account of their contribution to culutre.

TELUGU

Telugu literature is a very important source for reconstructing the history of Kākatīya rulers and their feudatories.

Krīdābhirāmamu: The authorship of this work is attributed to Vinukoṇḍa Vallabharāya. Some scholars are of the opinion that it was composed by Srinadha. As both the authors belong to the same period A.D. 14th and 15th centuries, the value of the work is beyond controversy. The theme of the book centres round the conversation between two friends Manchana Śarma and Tiṭṭibhaśetti who exchange notes of individual experiences in the capital Orugallu. Thus the work throws valuable light on the physical, social and economic conditions of the Kākatīya period.

Panḍitārādhya Charitramu: Pālkuriki Somanātha, a contemporary of Pratāparudra was the author of this famous work. It is a voluminous work in *divipada* style of composition. Somanātha established the greatness of Panḍitārādhya, a great Śaiva saint and also the superiority of Śaivism. He furnished a good deal of inforamtion about the religious conditions in the regions ruled by the feudatories in particular and of the Andhra country in general.

Śivayōgasāramu: Kolani Gaṇapatideva composed this work highlightinᵍ the greatness of Śaivism. It gives us the history of the Induluri chiefs who served the Kākatīyas from the time of Gaṇapatideva. Annaya, one of the Indulūri chiefs married the third daughter of Rudramadevi and rendered yeomen service to Rudramadevi and Pratāparudra as general and minister. Though the entire work is not avaible, the extant portion provides the geneology of the Indulūri chiefs and their relations with the Kākatīya rulers. Thus *Śivayōgasāramu* is a very valuable source to understand the part played by the Indulūri chiefs in the history of Kākatīyas.

Nītiśāstramuktāvaḷi: Baddena, a Telugu Chōḷa chief composed this work. He described the position and powers of the king, ministers, defence of the kingdom, anarchy, evils of unloyal officers and either in politics and administration.

Ranganātha Rāmāyana: It was composed by Buddharāja of Gona family, Buddharāja traced his descent from Vithala, Buddha and Rudra, his father, grand father and great grand father respectively of the Gona family. *Ranganātha Rāmāyana* considered to be the best of the Telugu *dvipada* poems is valuable to understand the contribution of the members of the Gona family to literature. In this connection it may be noted that during Kākatīya period more than one Rāmāyana were composed in Telugu.

CHRONICLES:

Chronicles from an important sources in reconstructing the history of the feudatories during the Kākatīya period.

Pratāpa Charitra: This is a work in Telugu prose composed by Ekāmranātha.

Siddhēśvara Charitra: This is in Telugu *dvipada* type of the verse written by Kāse Sarvappa. Though it belonged to the 17th century, it however contains a good deal of information about the Viriyāla chiefs corroborated by the inscriptional evidence.

Palnati Veera Charitra: It is a ballad in *dvipada* metre describing the family feud of the Haihaya chiefs of Palnāḍu. But the central theme is the story of Nalagāmarāja and his step brother Mallidevarāja contempory to Kākatīya Rudradeva. It not only gives useful inforamtion about the political conditons of Andhra regions during the early part of Ruddra's reign but also the social and religious conditions of the period in the Telugu country. This work is of great help to understand the political, social and religious conditons in the fiefs of the feudatories during the period under review.

Velugōṭivāri Vaṁśāvaḷi and Velugōtivāri Vaṁśa Charitra: These two are very important works in Telugu to reconstruct the history of the Velama Chiefs particularly the early chiefs of the family. The Velama chiefs first served Gaṇapatideva as his military generals. They continued to serve Rudramadevi and Pratāparudra. Though both the works are of late origin, the value of the works as sources of the history of the feudatories cannot be under estimated. *Velugōṭivāri Vaṁśāvali* gives the important information that Prasāditya, an early member of the Velama Chiefs installed Rudramadevi on the throne putting down the rebels who opposed the accession of Rudramadevi.

Monuments: The temples constructed by the feudatories are living examples of their contribution to art and architecture. In *Trikūṭa* temples the Kākatīyas followed the architecture of the Chālukyas. The temple at Palampet in Mulugu Taluq was constructed by Recherla Rudra, the famous general of Gaṇapatideva in about A.D. 1213 as stated in inscription found at the place. Thus the monuments form an important source for a study of the contribution of the feudatories to art and architecture. This becomes significant as the contribution of any ruler or feudatory to culture is more valued than his political achievements.

HISTORIOGRAPHICAL STUDY

Despite the fact that the subordinate chiefs occupied an important place and played a vital role in the Polity of Kākatīya kingdom, thorough investigation has not been made on the history of the subordinate families. Several writers dealt extensively about the Kākatīya rulers but none of them attempted to make an exhaustive study of the subordinate families as whole. The inforamtion available on the feudatories of the *Kākatīya sanchika* in Telugu language (1936) edited by M.Rama Rao contains a number of articles throwing valuable light on the Kākatīyas but there are only some references to the subordinate chiefs in the article published in it.

Chilukuri Veerabhadra Rao's *Kākatīyāndhra Rājayuga Charitramu* (1938) mainly dwells on the history of the Kākatīyas and is not helpful to glean the history of their subordinate chiefs. Similarly another work edited by G.Yazdani namely *The Early History of the Deccan* (1960) deals with the Kākatīyas of Warangal. Dr. N. Venkataramanayya and M. Somaśekhara Śarma contributed a well documented article on the Kākatīyas history. However, the objective of the part IX of this book, being the Kākatīya rulers, their administration, religious conditions and growth of literature during that period etc., It could not throw light on the subordinate rulers of the Kākatīyas. It provides only scattered information regarding them and did not give a full fledged and coherent picutre. Dr. P.V. Parabrahma Śāstry's The *Kākatīyas of Warangal* (1978) is a detailed study of the Kākatīyas. It deals with the political history, administration, economic, soçial and religious conditions, literature, art and architecture. There is only one chapter entitled *Feudatories and Subordinate officers* which is a birds eye view of their history. This is understandable as the main theme of the work is related to Kākatiya rulers. B.N. Śāstri's *Āndhradeśa Charitra Saṁskriti*, Parts I & II (1990) deals with the families of the Recharla, Cheruku, Kāyastha, Malyāla, Viriyāla, Natavāḍi and Velama besides other feudatories and dynasties. This work more or less presents a brief account on these families. Text of the inscriptions are given instead of drawing purposeful inferences from them. It is incomplete and also maintain silence regarding the gaps in chronology.

A Study of *History and Culture of the Āndhras*, Vol.II (1983) by K.Satyanarāyana gave an account of Agriculture, Society, Industries, Religion, Art and Architecture of the Kākatīya period. As the main objective of the book being the history of Andhras there was no scope for the author to dwell upon the Kākatīya subordinate rulers. The monumental work, *The History of Āndhra Country* (1000A.D.- 1500A.D) (1993) by Smt. V. Yashodadevi gives a detailed account of the subsidary dynasties of the period and it is the only one of its kind, in which she prsents purely political history of each family basing on epigraphs. However most of them pertained to the Coastal belt excepting the Natavāḍi, Kāyastha and Kōṭa chiefs.

In view of the above facts putforth, the present study is undertaken aimed at bringing out a comprehensive history of the subordinate rulers of Kākatīyas drawing relevant informtion from the original and secondary sources and also supplementing it by other evidences, and filling the gaps in chronology. This study is aimed to explore the origin, geneology, political history of the subordinate rulers, the socio-economic and religious conditions, art and architecture in their fiefs during the period under review. This study helps us to understand the various aspects of the minor dynasties and their role in the Kākatīya polity.

METHODOLOGY

For carrying out the present study both historical and empirical methods are adopted. This study is based on the data collected from different sources mainly original and to some extent on the secondary sources. The material from primary sources comprising the inscriptions both lithic records and copper plates and the contemporary literary works have been carefully analysed. An extensive field work is undertaken with in the ruling area of the subordinate chiefs to cull information from architectual and cultural remains.

The study comprises of the following chapters:

Chapter I: It is the introductory chapter dealing with origin, political history of the Kākatīyas, historiographial survey, sources of study, aims and objectives.

Chapter II: It deals with political history of the subordinate rulers who served the Kākatīyas in their early phase of rule viz., Viriyāla, Natavāḍi, Recherla, Cheruku and Indulūri chiefs.

Chapter III: It deals with the subordinate chiefs who served the Kākatīyas in the later phase of their rule viz., Malyāla, Kōṭa, Kāyastha, Chālukyas of Niḍadavole, Velama and Gona families. In both the chapter II and III, the aspects of the origin, geneology and political history of each family is discussed thoroughly. Geographical locales of each family are also delineated as mentioned in their inscriptions.

Chapter IV: This chapter deals with military administration and Nāyankara system which is an important aspect of the administrative organization of the Kākatīya rulers.

Chapter V: In this chapter the socio-economic and religious conditions under the rule of the subordinate are discussed. The social structure, agriculture, taxation, prominent religions are described in detail.

Chapter VI: This chapter highlights the contribution of the subordinate rulers to literature, art and architecture which is significant. The feudatories were not mere sources of political power but were distinguished promoters of culture.

Chapter VII: The concluding chapter sums up the major results of the study.

REFERENCES

1. P.V.P. Sastry, *The Kākatīyas*, Hyderabad, 1978, p.19.
2. *I.A.P.* Wg. No.50.
3. *Pratāparudriya,* p. 12.
4. P.V.P. Sastry, op. cit.,p.23.
5. *E.I.I*, pp.71.
6. *S.I.I.*, X, No. 340.
7. *E.I.* XII, pp.188 ff.
8. *Rāmāyana,* p.17.
9. *Pratāparudrīya,* Nataka,-1, V,23.
10. M. Somasekhara Sarma, *History of the Reddi kingdom* Vishakapatnam, 1993,p.267
11. *S.I.I.* X, 395, Lines 11-12; *E.I.I*, pp. 57ft.

12. *E.I.I*, pp.57ft.
13. *I.A.P.* Wg. p.81; *Ibid.*, kn, No.14
14. B.S.L. Hanumantha Rao, *Indian History and Culture*, Guntur, pp.422-423;
15. *E.I.*, XII, pp.188 ff.
16. S. Natarajan, *Political and Cultural History of India*, Vol.I, Hyderabad, 1993, pp. 281-83; P.R. Rao, *History and Culture of Andhra Pradesh*, Reprint, New Delhi, 1995, pp. 69-71.
17. M.Soma sekhara Sarma, *A Forgotten Chapter of Andhra History*, Waltair, 1945, p. 4
18. *Ibid*, Appendix-I, II.
19. *E.I.I*, II, 33-5.
20. *Ibid.*, XVIII, 26, Verses 43-6.
21. A.S. Altekar, *State and Government in Ancient India*, Delhi.1958, p. 267
22. B.S.L. Hanmantha Rao, op, cit., pp.
23. *S.I.I.* X, 482,483.
24. R.S. Sarma, *Indian Feudalism*, Delhi, II ed. 1980, p.134
25. P.V.P. Sastry, op. cit., p. 195
26. R.S. Sarma, op. cit., p. 19.
27. *Ibid.*,
28. *Ibid.*, p. 132.
29. *Ibid.*, p. 20
30. *Ibid.*, p. 61
31. *Ibid.*, p. 228
32. *Ibid.*, pp. 167-168.
33. *Ibid.*, p. 216
34. A.S. Altekar, op. cit., p. 263.
35. *I.A.P.*Wg., No. 52.
36. *J.A.H.R.S.*, V, Pt. III, pp. 143-144.
37. P.V.P. Sastry, op. cit., p. 145.

37(A). R.S. Sarma, op. cit., pp.82-83.

38. *I.A.P.* Wg., No. 27.

39. M. Rama Rao (ed), op. cit., p. 398.
40. *I.A.P.* Kn., No. 29.
41. *I.A.P.* Wg., No. 49.
42. B.N. Sastry, op. cit., 1991, p.713.
43. *Ibid.*
44. B.N. Sastry, *Cheruku Vamśa Charita Śāsanamulu*, Hyderabad, 1981, No.13.
45. *A.R.E.*, 299 of 1934-35.
46. *A.R.E.*, 484 of 1913.
47. *A.R.E.*, 302 of 1932-33.
48. *A.R.E.*, 565 of 1915.
49. *A.R.E.*, 301 of 1934-35.
50. *A.R.E.*, 535 of 1913.
51. A.S. Alteker, op. cit., p. 173.
52. *A.R.E.*, 314 of 1930-31.
53. B.N. Sastry, *Kāyastha Rājulu*, Hyderabad, 1981, Ins. No. 1.
54. *Ibid.*, No. 8.
55. *Ibid.*, No. 11.
56. *Ibid.*, No. 22.
57. *S.I.I*, IV, No. 735.
58. *E.H.D.*, pp. 640-641.
59. P.V.P. Sastry, op. cit., pp. 175-176.
60. *Ibid.*, p. 175.
61. *E.H.D.*, p. 672.
62. *Ibid.*, pp. 672-673.
63. M.N. Dutt, *Agnipurana*, Culcutta, 1903-4, Vol. II, pp.226, 865.
64. *I.A.P.*, Wg., Nos. 55-56.
65. *S.I.I.*X, 334.
66. Srīnādha, *Bheemeśvarapurāna*, I, 48.
67. *I.A.P.*, Wg., Nos. 55,56.
68. P.V.P. Sastry, op. cit., 1978, p. 144.
69. *I.A.P.* Wg. No. 50.

70. *J.A.H.R.S.*, XXXVI, I, Appendix-6-A; *I.A.P.* Wg. Nos. 27,59.
71. *Corpus*, Nos. 50, 52
72. *I.A.P.* Wg. No. 17; E.A.I, pp.71.
73- *A.P.R.E.*, 1966, Nos. 133, 147; N. Ramesan, *Copper plate Inscriptions of* Hyderabad Museums. I, pp. 98 ff.
74. *E.A.* IV, pp. 100ff.; *A.R.S.E.* 1915, pp. 137-138.
75. *S.I.I.* X, 465.
76. *Sudies in Indian Epigraphy* I, No. 9.
77. *S.I.I.* X, 448.
78. *Bharati*, 1977, pp.56ff.

Chapter-II

POLITICAL HISTORY OF THE SUBORDINATE RULERS OF THE KĀKATĪYAS (EARLY PHASE)

The Kākatīyas who started their political career as subordinates to the later Chālukyas had asserted independence from the time of Kākatīya king Rudra. A few minor families ruling certain principalities along the Kākatīyas upto that time became subordinates to the latter. In this part of dissertation aspects of geographical area, the origin, geneology, political history of the subordinate rulers is taken into consideration for discussion. The subordinate chiefs viz., Viriyāla, Natavāḍi, Recherla, Cheruku and finally Induluri families are discussed in this chapter.

Notable contribution of these chiefs include Viriyala Kāmavasāni's intervention in the troublesome and tough times of the early Kākatīyas when they were subordinates of the Kalyāṇi Chālukyas. But for her efforts Kākatīyas would not have survived and carved out a kingdom. Similarly the valour of Recherla Rudra Reḍḍi as the military general under reign of Kākatiya Gaṇpatideva cannot be ignored. Another important events was the marriage of Ruyyama, the daughter of Rudramadevi with Annayadeva of the Kākatīya administration. He gave a strong resistance to the rebel Ambadeva of the Kāyastha family and stood by the side of the Kākatīya king. Thus the subordinate rulers had played a vital role during the Kākatīya rule. We begin our discussion with the Viriyāla chiefs.

THE VIRIYĀLA CHIEFS

The Viriyāla Chiefs who served the Kākatīyas ruled the area comprising some parts of the present day Janagaon and Warangal taluqs of the Warangal district and important villages under their rule as mentioned in their inscriptions are given below :

Inscriptional Toponyms	*Identifications*
Gummuḍūru, Mogaḍupalli-12 Vēlpugonda, Mada- 30, Nereḍubotipaḍu	Gūḍuru, Koḍakanḍla Tq. Warangal Dist.[1]
Kaṭukuru	Kaṭukuru, Huzurabad Tq. Karimnagar Dist.[2]
Kollipāka	Moripirala, Wardhannapet Tq., Warangal Dist.[3]
Rēmbarti	Pammi, Jangaon Tq., Warangal Distt.[4]
Rāyaparti	Rāyaparti, Wardhannapet Tq., Warangal Dist.[5]
Konḍapallināḍu	Māmillagūḍa, Suryapet Tq., Nalgonḍa Dist.[6]

The Gūḍuru inscription[7] dated 1124 A.D. issued by Chālukya Ganga Perammaḍi Kumāra Someśvaradeva, son of Chālukya emperor Tribhuvana malladeva (Vikramaditya VI) furnishes valuable information on the geneology of the Viriyāla family. The inscriptions states that Sūra was the son of Eṛṛa of the Viriyāla family. Viriyāla Eṛṛabhūpati's son was Bhima, who like Bhima, the *madhyama* among the *pānḍavas* was the the destroyer of the kings and to him was born Eṛṛa Narendra, the ornament of the *mānḍalikas*. He espoused the cause of Boṭṭu Beta and having destroyed his enemy in battle established him in the Koravi country and obtained from him the Mogaḍupalli.

The Gūḍuru epigraph furnishes the following geneology of the Viriyāla chiefs.

Poraṁṭi Venna

↓

son-Eṛṛa Bhūpati

↓

son-Viriyāla Bhima

↓

son-Eṛṛa-narendra
m.Kāmavasāni
↓
Sūra
↓
Beta
↓
Malla (A.D. 1124)

The Viriyāla chiefs appear to have begun their career as military generals under the Rāshṭrakūṭas and continued to serve the Western Chālukyas also.

Eṛṛa Narendra

Kākati Gunda IV, father of Beta I continued as a loyal subordinate of Rāshṭrakūṭas till their collapse in A.D. 972. Gunda with his Rāshṭrakūṭa affiliations was in a dilemma whether to surrender himself to the new Chālukya king Tailapa II of the Jata Choḍa Bhima who seized the Vengi kingdom after killing its ruler Dānarnava. He did not choose either of the two, but preferred to remain independent with his small principality in the Koravi region. With much ambition and determination he drove away the Mudigoṇḍa Chālukya chiefs from Koravi his capital. Since then Chālukya chiefs had shifted to a place southwards called Boṭṭu and consequently the family came to be called after the name of the place. The Mudigoṇḍa chiefs must have transferred their loyalty to Tailapa II, who at the appeal of Boṭṭu Beta, the ousted feudatory, sent his loyal general Viriyāla Eṛṛa to reinstate Boṭṭu Beta at Koravi. According to the Gūḍuru epigraph[8] Gunda IV was killed in the battle and his son Garuḍa Beta was too young to fight with the enemies. The date of this event, though not precisely known, must be sometime around the last decade of the tenth century A.D. The same epigraph[9] states that Kāmavasāni, wife of Viriyāla Eṛṛa took up the cause of the young Garuḍa Beta and having approached the emperor established the line of Kākati, securing him the Anumakoṇḍa *vishaya* as fief.

The contemporary literary works like Sri *Siddhēśvara Charitramu* and *Pratāparudra Charitramu* are helpful in reconstructing the history of the Viriyāla Chiefs. The first Sri *Siddhēśwara Charitramu* written by Kāse Sarvappa who lived in the fourteenth century[10] and Ekāmranātha's *Pratāparudra Charitramu*[11] which was composed during the last decade of 15th century or the first decade of 16th century, contain several anachronisms. Yet it is possible to glean some historical facts from these two works. According to them, Vennama Raju was succeeded by Pendli Gunḍama Rāju, supposed to be Garuḍa Beta or Beta I. At the time of his death his son Yeruka Deva Rāja was still a child. So his aunt Kuntala Devi became the regent of the kingdom for a period of 19 years according to Sri *Siddhēśvara Charitramu* and 9 years according to the *Pratāparudra Charitramu*. She was a woman of great valour and defeated a number of kings and received tributes from them. With the help of Kuntaladevi, Yerukadeva Rāja wielded kingly power.[12] If the personal names Kāmavasāni and Garuḍa Beta of Gūḍuru inscription are equated to Kuntaladevi and Erukadeva Rāja respectively, the events in both the narrations tally with each other.

In this connection, Dr. P.V. Parabrahma Sastry says that Kāmavasāni most likely being related to the Kākatīya family strove hard to compensate the loss done by her husband. It is not unreasonable to assume that Viriyāla Eṛṛa's wife Kāmavasāni out of relationship took up the cause of Guruḍa Beta and helped him through her husband who had already won the favour of the king by reinstating Boṭṭu Beta at Koravi.[13] It seems Eṛṛa Narendra did not live long after making Garuḍa Beta, the feudatory of Anumakoṇḍa *vishaya*. In the absence of any other evidence, we may believe the narration of the chronicles and we have to assume that Kāmavasāni assumed regency upto A.D. 1000 when Garuḍa Beta ascended the throne. If Eṛṛa Narendra was alive he would have taken care of Garuḍa Beta. So, Eṛṛa Narendra might have died by either A.D. 981 or A.D. 991 soon after restoring Boṭṭu Beta the feudatory of Koravi.

Sūra I

The Gūḍuru inscription[14] describes the achievements of certain Sūra whose connection with the Viriyālas is not very clear.

He is said to have killed Kāṭayanāyaka of Velpugoṇḍa established Ravva nṛipa at Velpugonda and obtained from him Mogadupalli, Mada 30, Nareḍiboṭipāḍu, Māvidlu and also secured the friendship of Garuḍa Rāja. Dr. P.V. Parabrahma Sastry assumes that Sūra I was the son of Eṛṛa Narendra.[15] However in the absence of clear evidence it cannot be definitely established that Sūra was the son of Eṛṛa Narendra. He might also be his brother. In this connection scholars like P.V. Prabrahma Sastry state that Sūra helped Garuḍa Beta when he was in political distress and was favoured by him with the grant of some villages mentioned in Gūḍuru inscription. But it is stated that Sūra installed certain Ravva nṛipa at Velpugoṇḍa, which is identified with the modern Jaffarghad, a hill fort situated about twenty miles south-east of Warangal belonging to the Rāshṭrakūṭa and later periods. K. Harsha Vardhana sarma identified Ravva nṛipa with young Kākatiya chief Beta I that is Garuḍa Beta and concluded that Sūra after killing Kāḍaya nāyaka of Velpugoṇḍa, installed in his place the Kākatiya chief Beta, It may be assumed that Sūra helped Beta I in strengthening his position and to rule from his temporary capital Velpugoṇḍa.[16]

Prola I, Malla I and Beta

The Kaṭukūru inscription[17] of Mailama, wife of Malyāla Chaunḍa Senāni dated A.D. 1202 refers to the genealogy of Viriyāla family as follows:

Sūra (Sūra I)
↓
Prola I m. Nāgasāni | Malla I | Beta m. Bejjamāmba
↓ (Beta)
Sūra II | Malla II | Prola II | Komma
↓ (Malla II)
Annaya m. Aitama
↓
Mailama (daughter) m. Malyāla Chounda

We cannot give more details of the sons of Sūra with the meagre information available. Beta had a wife by name Bejjimambika. B.N. Sastry, states that the Moripirala inscription dated A.D. 1181 refers to one Beta,[18] who is other Viriyāla family member.

Sūra II, Malla II, Prola II and Komma

According to Kaṭukūru inscription[19] these were the sons of Beta. Sūra is stated to have built a temple for god Śiva and excavated a tank Ayyanapura. Malla II bore the title *Kaṭaka Mannīruva* and built a temple dedicated to *Malleśvara*. He is also stated to have excavated a tank and dug wells at Gumuduru.[20] It is well known that these counted among the seven great services to the community.

Annaya

Annaya was the son of Malla II whose wife was Aitama. They had a daughter Mailama, the wife of Malyāla Chaunḍa Senāni of Konḍaparti.

Rudraya Raja

The Pammi inscription[21] dated A.D. 1234 states that *Mahāsāmanta* the Viriyāla Nāgasānamma came to Pammi from Rembarti along with her sons Malrāju and Mummadirāju. Nāgasāni is said to be the wife of Prola (Prola I), son of Sūra I, who was the feudatory ruler of Rembarti area. After his death, his sons Malraju and Mummadi Rāju being young. Nāgasāni might have looked after the affairs of the fief. To this family belong Rudraya Rāja for whom some *settis* made gifts for the merit of the Viriyāla Rudrarāya.[22] Another inscription from Śambuniguḍi dated A.D. 1245 records that the king Kākati Gaṇapatideva and his subordinate Rudra of the Viriyāla family granted thirty cows for the maintenance of a perpetual lamp to the god Svayambhuvadeva.[23] B.N. Sastry considers him to be the son of Malrāju.[24] Rudra might belong to the generation of Mailamma the son of Malrāju.[25]

Ganapati I and Sūra III

The Kotagiri copper plates dated A.D. 1273[26] speak of

Viriyāla Sūra, son of Gaṇapati and grand son of Rudra. Rudra of this grant could be identified with the donor Rudra of the Sambhuniguḍi epigraph.[27]

Thus there were marital relations between these two families and the association of the family with the Kākatīyas as close friends, relatives and subordinates is an undenible fact. This alliance continued from the time of Kākati Gunda IV upto the time of Rudrama Devi.

Geneology of the Viriyāla Chiefs

Poraṁti Venna
↓
Eṛṛa Bhūpati
↓
Bhima
↓
Eṛṛa Narendra
m. Kāmavasāni
↓

Prola I m. Nāgasāni	Malla I	Beta m. Bejjāmbika

Prola I m. Nāgasāni ↓

Malrāju	Mummadi Rāju
↓	
Rudraraya rāja	
↓	
Ganapati	
↓	
Sūra III	

Beta m. Bejjāmbika ↓

Sūra II	Malla II	Prola II	Komma
	↓		
	Annayam m. Aitama		
	↓		
	Mailama (daughter) m. Malyāla Chounḍasenāni		

THE NATAVĀDI CHIEFS

The Natavāḍi chiefs who ruled over the Natavāḍi *vishaya* for a century and half from A.D. 1101 with its capital at Maḍapalli, played an important role in the history of Andhradeśa. Their records are found at Narsampet, Niḍigonḍa, Kundavaram (Jangoan

Taluq), Kundavaram (Chennur Taluq) Bayyaram, Inugurti and Tripurantakam. The rulers owed allegiance to the Chālukyas of Kalyāṇi in the beginning of their career and shifted their loyalty to the Kākatīyas after they became independent. Though the Natavāḍi chiefs attained prominence on account of their marriage alliance with the Kākatīyas on the one hand and the Kōṭas on the other they however could not claim independent status.

The records of Chālukyas of Veṇgi mention Tonka *Natavāḍi vishaya*, *Pennatavāḍi vishaya*, and *Natavāḍi vishaya*, whereas Natavāḍi records mention only Natavāḍi vishaya. Natavāḍi vishaya is identical with the correspond to the modern Nandigāma taluq of Kri̇shṇa district, where as Pennatavāḍi refers to a bigger Natavāḍi and Tonkanatavāḍi to a part of it towards one end. They were described as the lords of *Maḍapallipura* a village near Madhira. During the region of Kākati Gaṇapatideva these chiefs shifted their capital from Maḍapalli to Inugurti in the present Mahabubabad taluq in Warangal district.[28] The earliest record of this family is found at Narsampet in the Warangal district, dated A.D. 1101.[29] It registers a grant of the village, named Indrapura to a Brahmin sabha, a corporate body, by Buddha raja of the Natavāḍi family. His son was Durgabhupala who is represented by an epigraph of A.D. 1104, found at Niḍigoṇḍa in the same district.[30] In both the records they are stated to be the subordinate of the Western Chālukya king. Tribhuvanamalla Deva (Vikramaditya VI). The Natavāḍi chiefs ruled *Natavāḍi vishaya* as the Kākatiya feudatories between A.D. 1104 and A.D. 1269.

The *Natavāḍi vishaya* comprised of the area of Nandigāma taluq in Krishṇa district, Madhira taluq in Khammam district, Mahabubabad and Jangaon taluqs in Warangal district.[31] The inscriptional evidence testify to the inclusion of Narsampet taluq also.

Inscriptional Toponyms	*Identifications*
Indrapura	Narsampet, Narsampet Tq., Warangal Dist.[32]
Bayyāram	Bayyāram, Yellandu Tq., Khammam Dist.[33]

Dharmakirthipura	Kotagadda, Yellandu Tq., Khammam Dist.[34]
Namulapadu	Namulapadu Yellandu Tq., Khammam Dist.[35]
Chitapalli	Inugurti, Mahabubabad Tq., Warangal Dist.[36]
Kundapura	Chennuru, Chennur Tq., Adilabad Dist.[37]
Jeedikallu	Niḍigonda, Janagoan Tq., Warangal Dist.,[38]
Vemulatonṭa	Kundaram, Jangaon Tq.,
Danujapuri, Kundapuram	Warangal Dist.[39]
Dittalu	Tripuranthakam, Yeṟṟagondapalem Tq., Prakasham Distt.[40]
Konakanchi	Nandigama Tq.,
Guḍimetta	Krishna Dist[41]

The Bayyāram tank inscription[42] of Kākati Mailama, the daughter-in-law of Buddharāja states that both th families Natavāḍi and Kākatiya belonged to the same caste. The Niḍigonḍa epigraph[43] reveals that Durgarāja, son of Beta was a *Ratta,* which denotes his Rāshṭrakūṭa origin, on account of which a tank was called as *Duggarāsaratta-Samudra,* obviously constructed by *Duggrāsa-ratta*. It is possible that though these Natavāḍi chiefs served under the Western Chālukyas, they could not forget their Rāshṭrakūṭa affiliations.

Beta

Beta *Kshōṇipālaka* figuring in the Inugurti inscription[44] dated A.D. 1050 was probably the earliest Natavāḍi chief known so far, who was the father of Durgarāja. Besides a son, Natavāḍi Durga, Beta had a daughter by name Muppāmbika whom he married to the Kākatīya ruler Prola II (A.D. 1116-1157) thus strengthening his position.

Durga

Durga was considered to be the real founder of the Natavāḍi family as it attained prominence during his period. His earliest inscription from Niḍigonḍa[45] dated to A.D. 1104 mentions him as Dugga, Duggarāsa and Duggabhūpati and refers to his titles such as *Māṇḍalika* and *Natavāṭidhātrināṭha*. In A.D. 1157 as seen from a record at Nave Potavaram,[46] Prolamadevi, wife of Durga made grants for the merit of her husband Durgarāja or Natavāḍi Durga whose reign probably lasted upto A.D. 1157.

The Narsampet epigraph dated A.D. 1101 was issued by his son Buddha. So it is not possible to suppose that Durga's rule began from A.D. 1104.[47] There is an attempt to explain that Buddharāja issued the grant of Narsampet dated A.D. 1101, while his father, perhaps very old still alive and ruling with the assistance of the former.[48] It is possible that Durgarāja made his son Buddha as the ruler of the area around Narsampet and Niḍigonḍa situated far away from Maḍapalle, his capital. His rule might have started earlier, to the Niḍigonḍa inscription dated 1104 A.D. Buddha, is said to have ruled upto A.D. 1201, till his son Rudra I ascended the throne.

The Niḍigonḍa inscription suggests that Durga was the subordinate of Vikramaditya VI of the Chālukyas of Kalyāni, whom he served faithfully and was bestowed with the rulership of Natavāḍi chiefs maintained friendly relations with their neighbouring subordinates such as Chāgis or Konda Paḍumatis though they had to fight occasionally with the Kōnakanḍravāḍis. Durga seems to have lost his life in the hands of a Kōnakanḍravāḍi ruler. For an inscription dated A.D. 1213 credits Kōnakanḍravāḍi Bhima with the title of *Satrundripāla Dugganarēndrachura*. The battle that took place between the Natavāḍis and the Kōnakanḍravāḍis sometime prior to A.D. 1157 resulted in the death of Durgaraja.[49]

Buddha

Buddha was the son and successor of Durga and ruled from A.D. 1157 to 1201. According to his Inugurti inscription,[50] which gives inforamtion about the genealogy of the Natavāḍi chiefs, Beta had a son Durga whose son was Buddha. During this period, some of the principalities in Vengi were under the control of the Kotas, the Konḍapaḍumatis, the Kōnakanḍravāḍis, and the Chāgis besides Velanādu Chōḍas and the Telugu Chōḍas. Among these only the Chāgis claim to be overlords of Natavāḍi *vishaya* as is evident from their inscriptions. However, Buddha acknowledged the supremacy of the Kākatīyas under Rudradeva which is attested by his Inugurti inscription. The political alliance of Buddha and Mahadeva lasted till the end of the Natavāḍi rule.[51]

Buddha was succeeded by his son Rudra I in A.D. 1201. The Tripurantakam epigraph clearly states that Pakkidi Rudra was the second son of Buddha.[52] He may be identified with Rudra II and the husband of Mailama, the daughter of Mahadeva.[53] This fact is also attested by the Inugurti inscription dated A.D. 1266.[54] The Bezawada inscription dated A.D. 1201[55] describes Rudra I as the brother-in-law of Mahadeva. Another Bezawada inscription dated A.D. 1205[56] describes him as the son of Natavaḍi Buddharāja. The Kundavaram inscription dated A.D. 1210[57] describes Rudra, as the husband of Kundama, sister of Gaṇapatideva. This fact is attested by Niḍigonḍa inscription dated A.D. 1219.[58]

Obviously, Buddha had two sons Rudra I and Rudra II, the later known as Pakkiidi Rudra. They married the daughter of Kākati Mahadeva or sister of Kākati Gaṇapatideva. The eldest Kundāmba was married to Rudra I and the youngest Mailāmbika to Rudra II. By these matrimonial relations Buddha became a close relative of the Kākatīyas.

Rudra I

A record at Mudunur mentions king Rudra, as lord of Natavāḍi, his queen Kundāmba, daughter of Mahadeva of the Kākatīyas, their son Mahadeva or Mādhava and his queen Mahadevi.[59] The Kundavaram (Jangaon Taluq) inscription[60] dated A.D. 1210 states that Kundamāmba, the sister of Kākatiya Gaṇapatidevaand wife of Natavāḍi Rudra gifted the village Vemulatonṭa renaming it as Kundavaram. The Niḍigonḍa inscription[61] dated A.D. 1219, mentions some endowments made by Kundamāmba. She consecreted the god Rudresa after her husband's name god Mahadeva, after her father's name (Kākati Mahadeva), Sūrya and Gaṇapati after her brother Gaṇapatideva. The inscription also states that Kundamamba had a son named Mahadeva or Madhava. Another inscription of Kundamāmba was also noticed at Kundavaram (Chennur Taluq, Adilabad district) which[62] contains the same genealogical details. The Kundavaram (Jangaon Taluq, Warangal district) inscription[63] dated A.D. 1291 speaks of the descent of Natavāḍi family from lord Danujapuri, his son Buddha, his son Rudra to whom king Mahadeva had given Kundaladevi in marriage. Their son was Mahadeva known as Mādhava. Kundamāmba is stated to have given lands in the village of Kundapuram, for the conduct of worship in the temple of Kundesvara. The village of Kundavaram is said to be called Vemulatoṇṭa earlier and was presented to her by her father at the time of her marriage as *haridramanya*. Besides being the brother-in-law of Gaṇapatdeva, Rudra enjoyed the position of a *sāmanta* of Gaṇapatideva, whom he accompanied in his Velanāḍu expedition.

Mahadeva or Madhava

We do not know much of Madhava, except that he was the son of Rudra I and Kundāmba. Kundāmba lived long after her husband's death as is recorded by her Kundavaram inscription. Mādhava must have become insignificant because the fief of Natavāḍi *Vishaya* passed under the control of his uncle Rudra II or Pakkidi Rudra. Madhava must have died before his mother Kundāmba as is indicated by the Kundavaram inscription.[64]

Rudra II or Pakkidi Rudra

According to the information contained in the Inugurti inscriptions dated A.D. 1206 and A.D. 1221 Rudra married Mailama, the daughter of Kākatiya Mahadeva and sister of Gaṇapatideva.[65] She was known as *Dharmakīrti*. The Tripurantakam inscription dated A.D. 1209 mentions that Pakkidi Rudra was the second son of Buddha whose queen was Mailāmbika.[66] Since there were no records issued by Rudra after A.D. 1242 it can be said that he ruled up to A.D. 1248, from which year the earliest inscription of his sons are available.

Amarāvati inscription dated A.D. 1234 refers to Bayyaladevi, wife of Kōṭa III,[67] daughter of Natavāḍi Rudra and Mailāmba, who might have named her daughter after her mother Bayyāmba, wife of Kākati Mahadeva. Rudra II's epithets *Vakkaḍimalla*,

Doḍḍappadevi Ganḍa-bhairava and *Parabala Sadhaka* show that he was a great warrior. He styled himself as *Maḍapalle Purādhiśvara* or the lord of Maḍapalli.[68]

Rudradeva III

Rudra III, Mahadeva and Mummaḍi Gaṇapati or Kumāra Gaṇapatideva *Mahārāja* were the three sons of Rudra II and Mailama, according to Tripurantakam inscription,[69] dated 1248 A.D. Rudra III, the eldest son of Rudra II succeeded his father to the throne. Rudra's reign lasted upto A.D. 1259 being the last regnal year of Gaṇapatideva of the Kākatīyas.

Mummadi Gaṇapati

Rudra III was succeeded by his brother Gaṇapati,[70] who styled himself as Kumāra Gaṇapatideva Mahārāja in the Tripurantakam inscription,[71] issued in the 61st regnal year of Kākati Gaṇapatideva which also attests the subordination of the Natavāḍis to the Kākatīyas. As we do not hear of Natavāḍi chiefs after A.D. 1259, we may conclude that after Mummaḍi Gaṇapati the Natavāḍi territories were ruled by the Kākatiya kings from the time of Rudramadevi.

Genealogy of the Natavāḍi chiefs

- Beta
  - Durgarāja m. Prolamadevi
    - Buddha Rāja
      - Rudra I m.Kākati Kundamba
        - Mahadeva or Mādhava
      - Rudra II (Pakkidi Rudra) m.Kākati Mailama
        - Rudra III
        - Mahadeva
        - Mummaḍi Gaṇapati or Kumāra Gaṇapati Deva Mahārāja
  - Muppāmba m. Kākati Prola II

THE RECHERLA CHIEFS

While writing on Recherla chiefs P.V.P. Sastry observes, "of the many subordinate families of the Kākatīyas, the Recherla Chiefs deserve particular mention. They were Reḍḍis by caste and distinguished from the other family of the same name belonging to the Velama chiefs. The former name seems to have originated from the village *Recheruvula* whereas the latter from the founder of the family Rechaḍi or Rechaḍla. With unfailing loyalty the Recherla chiefs served the Kākatīyas for many generations as military commanders".[72]

The areas under the political control of the Recherla chiefs could be ascertained from their inscriptions as they mention the towns and villages belonging to them given away as gifts. The Recherla family his two branches who operated from Elkurti and Amanagallu. The Elkurti principality consisted of the places like Machapur, Goḍisala, Elkurti, Dichchakuṇta, Dharmarāopet, Rāmannapet, Chityalampāḍu and Pālampet. The Āmanagallu principality consisted of places like Āmanagallu, Pillalamarri, Nāgulapāḍu, Tāḍuvai, Vāḍapalli, Burugugaḍḍa, Somavaram, Sirikoṇḍa and Chilkur.

The following is the list of the toponyms found in the inscriptions of Recherala chiefs.[73] This would enable us to assess the extent of the area ruled by these chiefs.

Inscriptions Toponyms	*Identification*
Gollakōṭa	Elkurti Haveli Warangal Tq., and Dist.[74]
Rasaveedhi	Dharmarāopet (Ramakrishnanpuram) Narsampet Tq., Warangal Dist.[75]
Gollakota	Dichchakuṇṭa, Narsampet Tq., Warangal Dist.[76]
Nekkoṇḍa, Upparapalli, Bolapalli, Naḍikudi	Palampet, Mulugu Tq., Warangal Dist.[77]

Bommakallu, Pincharapalli	Goḍisala, Huzurabad Tq., Karimnangar Dist.[78]
Boḍupatu, Padanipalli, Boḍukoḍuru	Machāpūr, Mulugu Tq., Warangal Dist.[79]
Upparapalli, Maratūru, Katyaboyinimetta	Rāmannapet, Warangal Tq., Warangal Distt.[80]
Kuḍukuḍi, Erakavaram, Upparipādu, Chillapalli, Kalluru, Neretla Cheruvu, Guntipalli, Erukapuram, Kropolu, Mrontukuru	Pillalamarri, Suryapet Tq., Nalgonda Dist.[81]
Nāgapura	Musampalli, Miryalagūda Tq., Nalgonda Dist.[82]
Bommakallu, Jupalli Bhimarājupalli (Eruva-bhumi)	Yedlapalli, Sūryapet Tq., Nalgonda Distt.[83]
Pinadevalapalli Nāgulapāḍu, Marrepāḍu	Nāgulapāḍu, Sūryapet Tq., Nalgonda Distt.[84]
Utlapalli	Vutlapalli, Devarakinda Tq., Nalgonda Distt.[85]
Bikkamale, Chintapalli Catla Cheruvu	Somavaram, Huzurnagar Tq., Nalgonda Dist.[86]
Taduvai	Taḍuvai, Huzunagar Tq., Nalgonda Dist.[87]

The inscriptions show the geographical extent of the fief of the Recherla family. The Elkurti family ruled over the areas comprising the present day Mulug, Narsampet and Warangal Taluqs in Warangal district and some parts of Huzurabad Taluq in Karimnagar district. The Amanagallu family ruled over the area consisting of some part of Sūryapet, Huzurnagar and Niḍamanuru Taluqs of Nalgonda district.

The following is the origin and history of the Recherla chiefs. The Palampet[88] and Machapur[89] inscriptions of Rudra Senāni provide the geneological details of the Recherla family in addition to the Pillalamarri[90] inscription dated A.D. 1202 of Recherla Nāmi Reḍḍi which says "In the large family which originated from the lotus feet of *Brahma*, there was a great man named Bamma, who delighted in terrific battles and uprooted the tree of the dignity of the Chōḍa king carrying away the gate of the city of Kāñchi".[91] This suggests that the Recherla chiefs claimed descent from Brahma the creator of the universe and Bamma senapati was the first member of the family. He is credited with the capture of Kāñchi. Obviously Beta I, referred to as *Kākativallabha* captured the city of Kāñchi by the active assistance of Bamma senani.[92] scholars like B.N. Sastry opine that Bamma might have entered into the service of his lord in A.D. 1035 and lived upto 1055 A.D..[93]

Muchcha Sēnāni

The Pillalamarri inscription[94] furnishes valuable information on the personality of Mucha Sēnāni, a notable chief of the line. It describes, "in the family (*Kulu*) appered Mucha of great qualities, whose fame was heard all over the world, and who was efficient in removing the misery of those in suffering in great battles, and in giving uncommon gifts." He was further described as *āyoto-bhujo* (of long arms), a great warrior and a generous person.[95]

Kata Sēnāni I

Kāṭa I, son of Muchcha Sēnāi was not only a great warrior but also a scholar.[96] He was the commander of armies of the Kākatīya King, Beta II who ruled from 1076 to A.D. 1108,[97] and who is credited with the title *Sriman Vikrama-Chakri Sri Beta-Manḍalikōttamah*, as a mark of reward conferred on him by Vikramaditya VI for the support given by Beta against Someshwara II. It can fairly be surmised that Beta II could not have achieved this distinction without the support of Kāṭa I.

Kāma I

Kāma or Kāma *Chamupati* was the son of Kāṭa I. He served

as the commander of forces during the reign of Beta II and continued to serve Tribhuvanamalla Durgarāja (A.D. 1108- 1115) and Prola II (A.D. 1116-1157) also. The Pillalamarri inscription[98] describes him, as a great warrior.[99] Kāma had three sons and a daughter. viz, Kata II, Beti Reḍḍi, Nāmi Reḍḍi and Vallasani. Kāma *Chamupati* actively participated in all the exploits of his overlord Prola II, as mentioned in the Anumakoṇḍa inscription[100] of Rudra dated A.D 1163. The Pālampet inscription[101] records that Kāma, son of Kāṭa was powrful general and led King Prola's army against Manthyena Gunda and beheaded him. Guṇḍa may be identfied with the brother of Medarāja, the king of Polavāsa and Chitrakūta.

Kāṭa II

Kāṭa II was the eldest son of Kāma, who served the Kākatīya rulers Rudra and Mahadeva. Kākati Rudra made him his feudatory and lord of Elkurti consisting of Narsampet, Mulugu, Huzurabad, Machapur and sorrounding area of Orugallu in recognition of his services.[102] According to the Chityalampāḍu inscription he acquired *Simhāsanam* and *Mānḍalikābhi dhanam* (The office of Mānḍalika and a throne from the king).[103] His brothers Beti Reḍḍi and Nami Reḍḍi were made the *danḍanayakas* in the service of Rudra. He got for them the area consisting of Amanagallu, Pillalamarri and Nāgulapādu as a fief, while he and his sons become the feudatory lords of Elkurti.[104] The expression *Āmanaganti puravareśwara* which find mention in some of the inscriptions indicates that Āmanagallu was another headquarter of Recherla family.[105]

Beta or Beti Reḍḍi

He was the second son of Kāma and brother of Kāṭa II. The Pillalamarri inscription refers to him as *Recharla Pillalamarri Beti Reḍḍi*. His wife was Erukasāni described as *Srimatu Recherla Pillalamarri Beti Reḍḍi pendlāmu Sakala gunālankritayaina Erukasānamma gāru*[106] in very respectable terms. But Reḍḍi built the town of Pillalamarri and shifted his headquarters to that town from Āmanagallu and his brother Nāmi Reḍḍi was entrusted with the responsibility of looking after the affairs of Nāgulapādu. Basing on his Somavaram inscription[107] B.N. Sastry explains that Beti

Reḍḍi stayed at Orugallu until his nephew Recharla Rudra senāni destroyed the enemies of Kākati Gaṇapatideva, strengthened the position of Gaṇapatideva and then only returned to Pillalamarri.[108]

Nami Reḍḍi

Nāmi Reḍḍi was the third son of Kama, who ruled the area around Āmanagallu. He participated in various expeditions of Kākati Rudra along with his brother Beti Reḍḍi. His wife was Aitāmbika. The Pillalamarri inscription[109] dated A.D. 1195 credits him with the establishment of political supremacy in Telengana. When Kākati Rudra turned his attention to the coastal *Andhradesa*, and set out with an army accompanied by his subordinate chiefs on the pretext of the appeal for help made by Palnati chief Nalagāma. He defeated Kōṭa chief Doḍḍa Bhima and captured his town Dharanikōṭa. But he installed Keṭa II son of Doḍḍa Bhima on the throne as his vassel. Later he proceeded against the Velanati chief and subjugated Kondapaḍumati chiefs. He died in the battle fought against the Yādavas in A.D. 1195. It appears that Nāmi Reḍḍi did not exercise control over the regions of Āmanagallu and hence it is pertinent to assume that he served his master loyally in all the expeditions.

The Elkurti Family

A branch of the Recherla family consisted of the chiefs of Elkurti.

Muchcha II

The founder of the Elkurti family was Muchcha II, eldest son of Keta II. His brother the famous Rudra Senani, known as the *Elkurti Puravaradheesvara* was totally engaged in imperial affairs and the defence of the Kākatiya kingdom. So the task of ruling over the Elkurti area was taken up by Muchcha Sēnāni. He is stated to have dug a tank at the village Kammepalli.[110]

Rudra Sēnāni

Redrasēnāni was the great commander-in-chief of the illustrious Kākatīya king Gaṇapati Deva. He was the greatest member of the family and was one of the supporting pillars of the kingdom of Gaṇapati Deva. He occupied such a prominent place in the kingdom that he was described as having "brone with success, the burden of the Kākatīya realm" *(Kākati-rājya bhāra dhoureyunḍu)*.[111] Accoridng to Rudra's Pālampet inscription[112] dated 1213, after the death of Rudradeva the nobles of the royal family and the enemy kings of the neighbouring states who probably did not approve Mahadeva's succession rose in revolt. Among those enemies certain Nāgatirāja is stated to have been put to flight by Rudra the Celebrated Kākatīya general. Nāgatirāja was the younger brother of Boṭṭu Kusumāḍitya of the Mudigonḍa Chālukya family ruling Visurunāḍu, comprising the region of the present Khammam district. Recherla Rudra inflicted a crushing defeat on Nāgati who fled the battle field. The other enemies of the Kākatīyas in the coastal Andhra were also defeated by Rudra during his eastern campaign in about A.D. 1185. The Kōṭa chiefs, the Konḍapaḍumaties and the Velanāti chiefs tried to exploit the situation. But it was due to the untiring efforts of Recherla Rudra, that Kākatīya kingdom was saved from disintegration. The Rāmakrishnāpuram epigraph[113] of the same period further states that Rudrasēnāni reinstated Gaṇapatideva on the throne. He has also played an important role in securing freedom for his master Gaṇapatideva who was made captive by Jaitgi, the Yādava cheif. Rudra was not only a great minister but also an able administrator as indicated by the titles *sanmantri* and *Kākatī-rājya-samartha* associated with his name in the Drāksharāmam inscription.[114]

Rudra played an equally important role in Gaṇpatideva's campaign against Divi Island, situated at the mouth of river Krishṇa. The Island fortress was siezed by the Kākatīya force and celebrated general Recherla Rudra plundered the whole Divi Island and enriched the treasury of Gaṇapatideva with the precious diamonds acquired during the compaign. Then he waged a war against Velanāḍu and the Velanâti King was killed in battle field. He also assisted Gaṇapatideva in annexing Kalinga region and penetrated up to Aska in the Ganjām district.[115] As a reward for his meritorious services Gaṇpatideva presented Rudra a throne and the paraphernalia of a *mānḍalika*. Thus Rudra sēnāni rendered meritorious services to Gaṇapatideva along with his sons and his subordinates. He had three sons Lōka, Gaṇapati and Kata IV but none of them proved worthy successors of Rudra, who proved himself a great commander.

Loka Chamupati, Elder Gaṇapati and Kata IV

The eldest son of Recherla Rudra sēnāni was Lōka. The Elkurti inscription[116] says that Rudrasēnāni built a temple after the name of his son Lōka Reḍḍi who is described in the inscription as *Rudra senāpate varaputro*. He might have participated in one of the expeditions of Kākati Gaṇapatideva along with his illustious father. Elder Gaṇapati was the second son of Rudra *senāni* according to the Elkurti inscription.[117] He also served as commander-in-chief (*Sakala Senādhipati*) of Kākati Gaṇapatideva. Rudrasenāni's third son was Kāṭa IV, who served Gaṇapatideva as *Mandāḍi* or officer incharge of royal cavalry forces. An undated inscription[118] from Machapur describes him as a conquerer of many countries such as Chōḍa, Gouḍa, Magadha, Anga, Kalinga, Vanga, Kashmira and also Karnaṭa, Laṭa, Kuru, Kosala, Mastya, Sindhu and Panḍya kingdom besides giving the geneology of the Recherla family. Much of the praise may be hyperbolical but his participation in the wars waged by king Gaṇapatideva cannot be ruled out. According to Maṭṭevāda inscription[119] dated A.D. 1228. He might had also participated in Gaṇapati's Southern expedition in which Kāñchi was occupied. The Dichakunṭa inscription[120] dated 1217 A.D. states that Kāṭa IV, the *Mandaḍi* of Gaṇapatideva gifted some lands to certain Mahadeva Manchi and God Yeleśvaradeva of Gollakōta probably as thanks offering for the victory of his master. The third inscription[121] which speaks about Kāṭa IV is again from Dichakunṭa. This undated inscription mention some gifts made by Mahadeva Manchi from the grants he received from Kāṭa IV. The last inscription[122] is from Machapur dated A.D. 1217 which mentions Kāṭa IV, the *mandaḍi* of Kākati Gaṇapatideva *Mahārāja*.

Gaṇapati Chamupati

He was the son of Lōka *Chamupati* and grand son of Rudra senāni. The Elkurti inscription[123] states that Rudra senāpati built four temples to Rudreśvara, Anyeśvara, Lokeśvara and Gaṇeśvara after the names of his son and cousins. The inscription stated that Gaṇapati provided for the worship and festivals of the dieties. We have no more details pertaining to him.

Pasāyita Chamunātha

The Dharmarāopet undated epigraph[124] issued by Soma mantri speaks about Pasāyita Chamupati belonging to Elkurti, as the sucessor of Kāta IV. Pasāyita exercised control over the areas of the present day. Machapur, Narsampet, Mulug and Huzurabad.

Vīrapasāyita Chamupati

Vīrapasāyita Chamupati is known from the undated Dharmarāopet inscription[125] as son of Pasāyita, grand-son of Kāṭaya and the great-grand son of Rudra senāni. According to it, he made a gift of the entire tank Appāmbudhi, constructed by him in the name of his father in the village of Rājavīdhi to the Maheśvaras, built the temples of Appeśvara Mahadeva named after his father, Iśvara Mahadeva named after his grand father, and another in the name of his master and granted for their maintenance Padala tank and six *nivartanas* of land under it. Thus, Chamupati appear to be a follower of Śaivism and devotee of Iśvara or Śiva. It can be said that Vīrapasāyita was the last ruler of Elkurti family of Recherla chiefs and his rule ended during the regnal period of Gaṇapatideva.

The Families of Amangallu and Pillalamarri

The history of the family of Beti Reḍḍi and Nāmi Reḍḍi, son of Kāmi Reḍḍi whose seat of power was centred at Āmanagallu and Pillalamarri deserve attention. Beti Reḍḍi had two wives Erukasāni and Kamasāni. Erukasāni's son was Malla Reḍḍi and Kamasāni's son was Lōk Reḍḍi. Beti Reḍḍi's hereditary titles were transferred to his brother Nāmi Reḍḍi in A.D. 1202, though he was alive upto A.D. 1213. So the sons of Beti Reḍḍi were no longer the lords of Āmanagallu but might have been held in esteem by their uncle Nāmi Reḍḍi and served the Kākatīyas.

Malla Reḍḍi and Loki Reḍḍi

Erukasāni's Pillalamarri inscription[126] dated A.D. 1208

describes Mallā Reḍḍi as a virtuous, generous and valiant man. The only available inscription[127] of Lōki Reḍḍi states that he has excavated a tank called Lōka *samudra* at Uṭukūr situated in the present day Nalgonda disrict.

Kata III

Nāmi Reḍḍi had two sons namely Kata III and Kāma II. Kāṭa III's Nāgulapāḍu inscription[128] described him as *Āmanikanṭi Puravarādhiśvara*. He is credited with the consecration of gods Nāmeśvara, Aytēsvara and Kāteśwara for the merit of his parents and himself. Kāṭa III was obviously a devotee of Śiva. He must have been very active in the imperial affairs and was not simply contended with his principality of Āmangallu, as is evident from his close association with Kanvayuḍu, the bodyguard of Rudramadevi, with whose collaboration he donated land for the worship of Taḍuvai Mallikārjuna Devara and also for the merit of Gaṇapatideva as recorded in the undated Taḍuvai inscription[129] He appears to have ruled over this principality between A.D. 1234-1258, as the *Sāmanta* of Gaṇpatideva which extended to Taḍuvai of the present Huzuranagar Taluq, besides Nāgulapāḍu area.

Kāma II

We have two inscriptions of Kāma II dated 1258 A.D. found at Annavaram[130] and Nāgulapādu.[131] The former records the installation of god Kāmeśwara in Nāgulapāḍu and grant of his halfshare of land by *Āmaniganṭi puravareśwara, Rēcherulvula* Kāmi Reḍḍi, son of Aytāmbika. The Nāgulapāḍu inscription records Kāmi Reḍḍi's donation of his share of land, lying east of *Nāmasamudram* to Trikuteśwarālayam built by his brother Kāṭ-Reḍḍi. At the end of the inscription, the donor invokes blessings for the merit of his glorious king Kākati Gaṇapatideva which speaks of his *Prabhubhakti* and also his gratitude. Kāma became feudatory chief of Āmanagallu after his brother's death. The above two inscriptions of Kāma II reveal that Nāmi Reḍḍi's sons Kat Reḍḍi and Kami Reḍḍi have divided that principality of Amanagallu into two equal parts and ruled over their respective regions. Kama ruled over his principality from A.D. 1258 to 1264.[132]

Nāmaya, Kāmaya and Mallaya

The Nāgulapāḍu inscription dated A.D. 1264[133] informs that Nāmaya, Kāmaya and Mallaya were the sons of Parasāni and Kāṭ Reḍḍi.

Ganapi Reḍḍi and Mal Reḍḍi

According to the above mentioned inscription[134] Ganapi Reḍḍi and Māl Reḍḍi were the sons of Kāma II.

Th foregoing study leads us to conclude that the Recherla chiefs ruled over their principalities of Elkurti and Āmanagallu for about 250 years from about 1000 A.D. and very faithfully served the Kākatīyas as feudatories upto the regnal period of Gaṇapatideva. The Elkurti family of Rudra sēnāpati is credited with the distinction of *Māṇḍalika* status as mentioned in the Pālampet record and one of Dichakunta epigraphs where in the Pillalamarri branch is credited with *Mahāsāmanthaship.*[135] Thus it is clear that the Recherla chiefs maintained good relations with the Kākatīyas and were rewarded suitably with positions like to commander-in-chief and inturn they maintained law and order in the country under the instruction of the imperial kings. They also acknowledged the kings in all their inscriptions though they were issued to records some grants made by the Recherla families. These subordinate chiefs acted like bridges between the kings and the subjects.

Genealogy of the Recherla chiefs

- Bamma Senāni
  - Muchcha I
    - Kāta I
      - Kāma I m. Kachamāmba
        - The family of Elkurti
          - Kāṭa II m. Bejjamāmba
            - Muchcha II m. Kāmasāni
              - Lōka
                - Gaṇapati
              - Elder Gaṇapati
              - Kāta IV
                - Pasayita
                  - Veera Pasāyita
            - Rudraśenāni
        - The family of Āmanagallu and Pillalamarri
          - Beti Reḍḍi m.Erukasāni, and Kāmasāni
            - Mallā Reḍḍi
            - Lōki Reḍḍi
          - Nāmi Reḍḍi m. Aitāmba
            - Kāṭa III m. Parasāni
              - Nāmaya
              - Kāmaya
              - Mallaya
            - Kāma II
              - Gaṇapi Reḍḍi
              - Māl Reḍḍi
          - Vallasāni m. Prolaya

THE CHERUKU CHIEFS

The Cheruku chiefs were regarded as the most loyal subordinates of the Kākatiya rulers. Some scholars hold that the name of the family was derived after a small town called Cheruku, originally consisting of twelve villages situated in the *Ēruva* region, extending on both sides of the river Krishṇa in the Nalgonda and Prakasam districts.[136]

The first capital of the Cheruku rulers was Jammulūru situated in Tirumalgiri taluq of Nalgonda district.. In recognition of the valour of Kāṭa I of this family, Kākatiya king Beta II gave him an area called Cheruku-12. The numerical suffix 12 suggests the number of villages like Gunḍiyapūḍi and Gottiparti could be identified with the village Gunḍepuri and Gottiparti could be identified with the village Gunḍepuri and Gottiparti respectively which are situated near could be identified with Torrur, at present a manḍal head quarters in Warangal district. The Cheruku chiefs became *Mahāsāmantapatis* and were styled *Jammulūru Puravarādhīśvaras* in their inscriptions. The Jalālpur family ruled the areas of Tāḍuvai, Palakaveedu, Kurella all situated in Nalgonda district. Bolla II's son Peda Devaya and his successors ruled from Veluru which included Velūru and some areas of Nandikotkuru taluq in Kurnool district.

The following table shows the epigraphical evidence of the geographical locales of Cheruku chiefs.

Inscriptional Toponyms	*Identifications*
Jammulūrupura, Regpundi, Ganimetta, Lenjitta, Surepalli, Srigiri (Alampur), Rajavrolu, Doddapalli, Gottipasumdla, Gunḍiyapunḍi, Thorruru, Rupurala, Marikunta.	Jalālpur, Suryapet Tq., Nalgonda Dist.[138]
Nalladampelli	Devarakonda Tq., Nalgonda Distt.[139]
Tāḍuvai, Nelamarri	Tāḍuvai, Huzurnagar Tq., Nalgonda Dist.[140]
Amarābād	Amarābād, Achchampet Tq., Mahabubnagar Dist.[141]
Iruvennu	Irvin, Kalvakurthi Tq., Mahabubnagar Dist.[142]
Mellacheruvu	Dondapādu, Kodad Tq., Nalgonda Dist.[143]
Goruvankapalli	Goruvankapalli, Nakrekal Tq., Nalgonda Dist.[144]

Cheruku rulers of Jammulūru have an area comprising of Tungaturti Devarakoṇḍa, Huzurnagar, Nakrekal, Motkur, Kodaḍ, and Miryalagūḍa taluqs of Nalgonda district. Another branch of this family which ruled from Velūru had Goruvankapalli and Kurulla under their control as suggested by the inscriptions found at the above two places. The Amarābād family must have governed the area around Achampet and Ālampur taluqs touching the present Kurnool district.

The Cheruku chiefs of Velūru branch ruled over some part of Nandikotkur taluq of Kurnool district. Cheruku Rājarudra's records from Malayāla and Lingāla villages in Nandikotkur and Achampet taluq prove that some parts of Kurnool and Mahabubnagar districts were under his control.

The Cheruku chiefs belonging to the forth caste claimed divine origin i.e., from the lotus feet of lord Brahma.[145] The Cheruku chiefs seem to belong to the Reḍḍi caste as suggested by the names Bollaya Reḍḍi, Vishvanatha Reḍḍi of the later generation. According to the Jalālapuram epigraph,[146] Kāṭa the earliest Cheruku *Prabhu* born of the fourth caste killed Kongoṇḍa Dhavala like a tiger with ferocity and valour and got Cheruku-12 from Kākati Beta. On the other hand the Rapur[147] inscription states that Kāṭa was the founder of the family and was said to have obtained Cheruku-12 included in *Ēruva manḍala* from king Bhima (Telugu Chōla chief) on account of which they got their family name as Cheruku.

Kāṭa was the earliest ruler of the Cheruku family and he had three sons namely, Kēta, Sūra and Bolla I. These borthers gave unstinted support to Kākati Rudra by supplying military contingents in his conflict with the Telugu Chōḍa chief.

Kata I

Kāṭa was succeeded by his son Keta I. The earliest record of Cheruku family from Jalālpuram dated A.D. 1202.[148] and A.D. 1253[149] provides the following geneology.

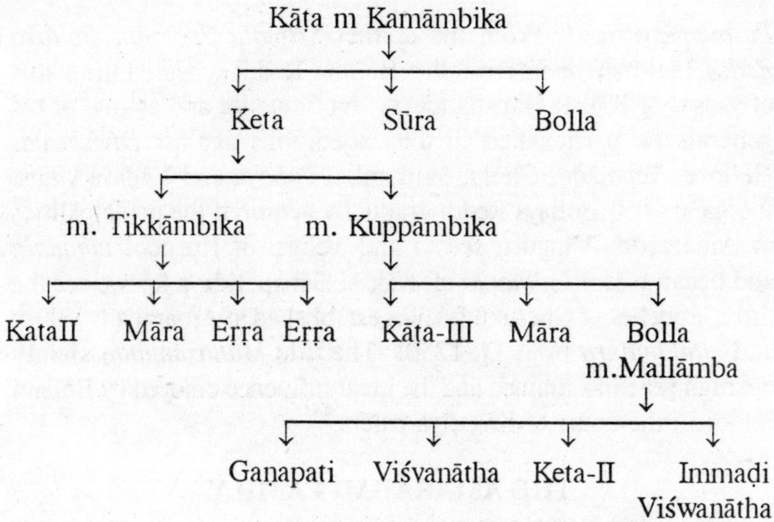

Keta had two wives Tikkāmbika and Kuppāmbika. He had four sons Kāṭa II, Māra I, Eṛra I and Eṛra II by his first wife Tikkāmbika. The Cheruku chiefs according to *Jammulūru* epigraph[150] dated A.D. 1202 rendered millitary assistance to Kākati Rudra in his conflict with the Chōḍa chiefs their earstwhile masters. Obviously, they shifted their loyalty from Chōḍa chiefs to the rising Kākatīyas who elevated them to the position of *Mahāsāmantas* with control over the present Achampet taluq. The same inscription states that Kākati Rudra with the support of the Cheruku chiefs marched on Udaya Chōḍa's capital Panugallu and over powered him. There upon Udaya Chōḍa sued for peace offering his daughter to Rudra. This expedition must have taken place in between A.D. 1157 and A.D. 1162.[152] Kākati Rudra in recognition of the services rendered by the chiefs made a gift of Gunḍiyapūḍi (Gundepuri) Berapūḍi, Gottipalli (Gottiparti), Pasupala Thorruru and other villages situated in the present Nalgonda and Warangal districts. From his second wife Kuppāmbika Keta got three sons viz., Kāṭa III, Māra II and Bolla II.[152]

Bolla II or Bollaya Reḍḍi

Bollaya Reḍḍi ascended the throne as *Jammulūri*

Puravarēśvara.[153] From the epithet *Srīmatu Sāmanta Bollaya Reḍḍi,*[154] it may be inferred that Bollaya Reḍḍi accepted the status of vassal of Kākati Gaṇapatideva. As *Sāmanta* and as one of his generals he participated in the expeditions against *Diviseema,* Nellore, Velanāḍu, Chōla, Vaidumba, Panḍya and Yādava kings. It appears that Bollaya Reḍḍi gradually acquired the principalities of Amarabād, Vanguru *seema* and Veluru of Kurnool *manḍala* and became *Mahāsāmanta* of Kākati Gaṇapatideva for we see the three branches of Cheruku familes established at Amarabād, Velūru and *Jammulūru* by A.D. 1250. The title *Mahāsāmanta* signify the high position attained and the great influence enjoyed by Bollaya Reḍḍi in the court of Kākatīya rulers.[155]

THE AMARABAD FAMILY

Immadi Viśvanātha

Immaḍi Viśvanātha was the fourth son of Cheruku Bollaya Reḍḍi and Mallāmba. The Jalāpūr inscription[156] dated A.D. 1253 records the installation of gods, Bolleśvara, Malleśvara and Gaṇapeśvara, probably in honour and memory of his deceased parents and eldest brother Gaṇapati. We also have no information about his two elder brothers Viśvanātha and Keta II. Immadi Viśvanātha was a great warrior and was held in high esteem by his overlord Kākati Gaṇapatideva. As he was totally involved in the imperial affairs and spent most of his time at Orugallu, the principality of Jammulūru was looked after by his cousin Māraya Gaṇapati Reḍḍi. So the Jammulūr fief has gradually gone into the hands of the descendents of Māra II, while the sons of Immaḍi Viśvanātha ruled over Amarabād.

Immaḍi Devaya and Immaḍi Bollaya Reḍḍi

Immaḍi Viśvanātha had two sons Immaḍi Devaya or Devaya II and Immaḍi Bollaya Reḍḍi. Immaḍi Devaya was referred to in his father's Jalālpur inscription[157] of A.D. 1253 and again in Amarabād inscription[158] dated A.D. 1264. It appears that he was killed in some battle and hence the fief of Amarabād passed into the hands of his brother Immaḍi Bollaya Reḍḍi.

Immaḍi Bollaya Reḍḍi was a great General. He entered into matrimonial alliances with the Vavilāla chiefs and married Rudrasāni, sister of Vavilāla Rudraya Reḍḍi, as mentioned in the Irvin epigraph.[159] The Amarabād inscription[160] of A.D. 1290 refers to the reign of Immaḍi Jeti Bollaya Reḍḍi (*Sriman Mahāsāmanta Immaḍi jeti Bollaya Reḍḍi vāru Prithvirājyamu sēyanganu*). Obviosly, the rule of Bollaya Reḍḍi ended by A.D. 1290 as his records are not available after that date.

Immaḍi Jeti Bollaya Reḍḍi

Immaḍi Bollaya Reḍḍi was succeeded by his nephew Immaḍi Jeti Bollaya Reḍḍi. It seems that Immaḍi Jeti Bollaya Reḍḍi took an active part in the affairs of the state as is evident from the Amarabād inscription dated A.D. 1286 during the reign of his uncle Immaḍi Bollaya Reḍḍi, on whose death he became the *mahāsāmanta* by A.D. 1290. After the death of the Kākatīya ruler Rudramadevi, Ambadeva the Kāyastha chief became powerful and vanquished all the Kākati *Nāyankaras*. Ambadeva entered into matrimonial alliances with Cheruku family. Ambadeva offered his daughter to Rajanna, son of Bollayapati along with the town Nandapura as dowry. Following the line tread by Cheruku Rāja Rudra of Velūru, Cheruku Immadi Jeti Bollaya Reḍḍi did not obey the overlordship of the Kākatīya rulers. This is evident from the Amarabād epigraph[161] dated A.D. 1290 which merely refers to the rule of Cheruku Immadi Jeti Bollaya. Nothing was mentioned about the Kākatīya overlords in this record.

Pratāparudra who ascended the throne of Orugallu in A.D. 1289 vanquished Ambadeva and suppressed all the rebel *sāmantas*. Along with others, Immaḍi Jeti Bollaya Reḍḍi who betryed the trust of the overlords must also have lost his principality by A.D. 1293. Thus, he had a very short span of reign for just 3 years from A.D. 1290 to 1293. Immaḍi Jeti Bollaya Reḍḍi had a brother by name Prolaya. The Kaluvakolanu inscription of A.D. 1321 refers to him.[162] It appears that Prolaya regained the favour of Kākati Prataparudra and ruled Kaluvakolanu area. Evidence of the rule of Cheruku chiefs after the fall of Kākatīya empire is not forthcoming.

The Velūru Family

The descendents of Immaḍi Viśvanātha made Amarabād their capital. Peda Devaya *vāhinisa* or Devaya I, son of Bolla II and his son Veluru Bolla ruled Nandikotur area in Kurnool district and the areas lying south of the river Tungabhadra with head quarters at Velūru, as the *sāmantas* of Kākatīya rulers. The Goruvankapalli inscription[163] provides the genealogy of the Cheruku chifs. The Kurella inscription[164] speaks of Cheruku Velūri Bollaya and his son Rudra.

Peda Devaya or Devaya I

Peda Devaya's title *Vāhinisa* denotes that he was a general in the service of Kākati Gaṇapatideva. It appears that he acquired the control of the region of Velūru around A.D. 1250 along with the step brother Immadi Viśvandha, who because of his intimacy with Kākati Gaṇapatideva, maintained close relations with the imperial family.

Veluri Bolla or Manuma Bolla

It appears Veluri Bolla Prabhu had been loyal to Kākati Rudramadevi in the initial period of her rule. The rise and revolt of Kāyastha Ambadeva, who established a vast Kāyastha kingdom in A.D. 1272 and ruled up to A.D. 1291 might have influenced Velūri Bolla to change loyalty. It is well known that Kāyastha Ambadeva ignored his overlord Rudramadevi and maintained close and friendly relations with Pāṇḍyas and Yādavas of Devagiri. Ambadeva's Tripurantakam inscription dated A.D. 1290 gives a lengthy account of his victories over several *māṇḍalikas* who were all subordinates of the Kākatīya queen Rudramadevi.[165] In A.D. 1288, Rudramadevi led an expedition against Ambadeva and she lost her life in the battle field along with her bodygurd Mallikārjuna *nāyaka*.[166] Pratāpa Rudra who ascended the Kākatīya throne after Rudrama, addressed himself to the task of suppressing the Kāyastha chief Ambadeva. In the war waged at Valluru, the capital of

Ambadeva, he was defeated along with his twelve *sāmanta māṇḍalikas*. Velūri Bollaya who also participated in the battle must have also been killed along with him. Thus ended the rule of Velūri Bolla by A.D. 1289, which is also attested by the Malayala, Lingala inscriptions and also Rājarudra's Goruvankapalli copper plate grant. From these inscriptions it may be assumed the Velūri Bolla died some time in A.D. 1289.

Rāja Rudra

Pratāparudra who remembered the services rendered by Cheruku Bollaya Reḍḍi and his brothers must have pardoned his great grandson Rājarudra and accepted him as his *Sāmanta*. For we find Rājaruda paid obeisance to his overlords Kākati Mahadeva, Gaṇapatideva, Rudrama and Pratāparudra as *sāmanta* mentioned in the Goruvankapalli copper plates[167] as well as the Kurella stone inscription.[168] According to the contemporary literary works like the *Dvipada Bhāgavata* and *Rāmarājiyam* Tatapinnama vanquished Rājarudra[169] and assumed the title *Samasta durāchāra Cheruku rāchanāyaka rāja saptānga harana*.[170] Later Rājarudra showed loyalty to Pratāparudra and rendered valuable service to him. With his death, the Cheruku family also lost its feifdom to the Muslims and we hear nothing of Cheruku chiefs after that.

The Jammalūru Family

After the death of his borther Māra II, Bolla II took care of his nephews and gave them the seat of Jammalūru which included Taḍuvāi and Palakaveedu areas.

Māraya Gaṇapati Reḍḍi

Māraya Gaṇapati Reḍḍi was the eldest son of Māra II The following inscriptions give information about Gaṇapati Reḍḍi. For instance Palakaveedu inscription dated A.D. 1269,[171] records the grant of land by Gaṇapati Reḍḍi for the merit of his father Māraya Reḍḍi. According to Tāḍuvāi inscription[172] dated A.D. 1300 some people of Tāḍuvāi made a grant for the merit of Cheruku *Jagaddālu Māraya Gaṇapati*. The Kaluvakolanu inscription dated A.D. 1286 praises the exploits of Gaṇapati Senāni. Gaṇapati Reḍḍi seem to have ruled from A.D. 1250 upto A.D. 1298.

Annaya Reḍḍi

Annaya Reḍḍi was the second son of Māra II, who came to power after his borther's death in A.D. 1298. The Tāḍuvai inscription[173] dated A.D. 1306 refer to the reign of *Mahāsāmanta* Cheruku Jagadālu Annaya Reḍḍi in the words *Svasti srīman māha sāmanta Cheraku Jagadālu Annaya Reḍḍi vāru rājyam sēyu-chundaganu* and records the grant for god Chennamallikārjuna. Another inscription[174] dated A.D. 1314, from the same place records the regnal period of Kākati Pratāparudra and *Mahāsāmanta* Cherku Jagadālu Annaya Reḍḍi who provided for the *angaranga bhōga* of god Mailādēvara in the village. Annaya Reḍḍi obtained the permission of *Samastha prajā* of the Tāḍuvai, collected contributions and made a gift to the god Mailāraḍēvara from the villagers on various items.[175] Thus, Annaya expressed his devotion to Mailāradēva.

Nāmi Reḍḍi

Nāmi Reḍḍi son of Annaya Reḍḍi was mentioned only in the Tāḍuvāi inscription of A.D. 1314.[176]

Nāgi Reḍḍi Bollaya Reḍḍi

There are two inscriptions of his regnal period. The Donḍapāḍu inscription dated A.D. 1312,[177] records that during the regnal period of Pratāparudra, Cherku Nāgi Reḍḍi Bollaya Reḍḍi who was under the *Nāyaṇkara* of Bommarāja Eṛṛaya Preggaḍa gave grants for the *anga ranga bhōga* of the god Chenna Malnādhadēvara.The Mēllacheruvu inscription dated A.D. 1312,[178] informs that during the rule of Pratāparudra, Nāgi Reḍḍi Bollaya Reḍḍi who was under the *Nāyaṁkara* of Bommarāju Eṛṛaya Preggada provided for the *ranga bhōga* of Mūlasthānēśvara Śri Svayambhūdevara of Mēllacheruvu. It seems Nāgi Reḍḍi Bollaya Reḍḍi ruled over the area consisting of Donḍapāḍu and Mēllacheurvu even during the time of his father's life. It can be assumed that even this branch of Cheruku family also did not survive the Muslim onslaughts and must have disappeared by A.D. 1323.

The Cheruku chiefs particularly the Velūru branch rebelled

against their overlords which resulted in the subjugation of the area under their control. Commenting on the role of the Cheruku chiefs P.V. Parabrahma Sastry does not agree with the view that Cheruku chiefs turned traitors and betrayed the Kākatīya rulers. In this connection he observes: "In the military undertakings of Kākatīya kings, participation of these chiefs was always accompaigned by victory. There arises a serious objection that, the age long loyalty of the Cheruku family is to be believed to have been at stake and consequently the members of the family were to branded as traitors, because the conflict between the Kākatīyas and Ambadeva which resulted in the death of queen Rudramadevi was not a trifling event to be condoned. But the Goruvankapalli grant issued by a Rāja Rudra in A.D. 1293 and the Kurella grant issued by the same chief in A.D. 1290 declare in unmistakable terms that Rājarudra was showing unmistakable loyalty to Pratāparudra. Had it been otherwise, the later would not have pardoned and retained him in the same subordinate postion. There were only few subordinates of the Kākatīyas who were empowered with the authority of issuing copper plate grants. We notice Viriyāla Rudra, Yādava Yellana and the present Rājarudra among those who issued copper plate grants and village grants. Rājarudra's loyalty was therefore unquestionable".[179]

Geneology of the Cheruku chiefs

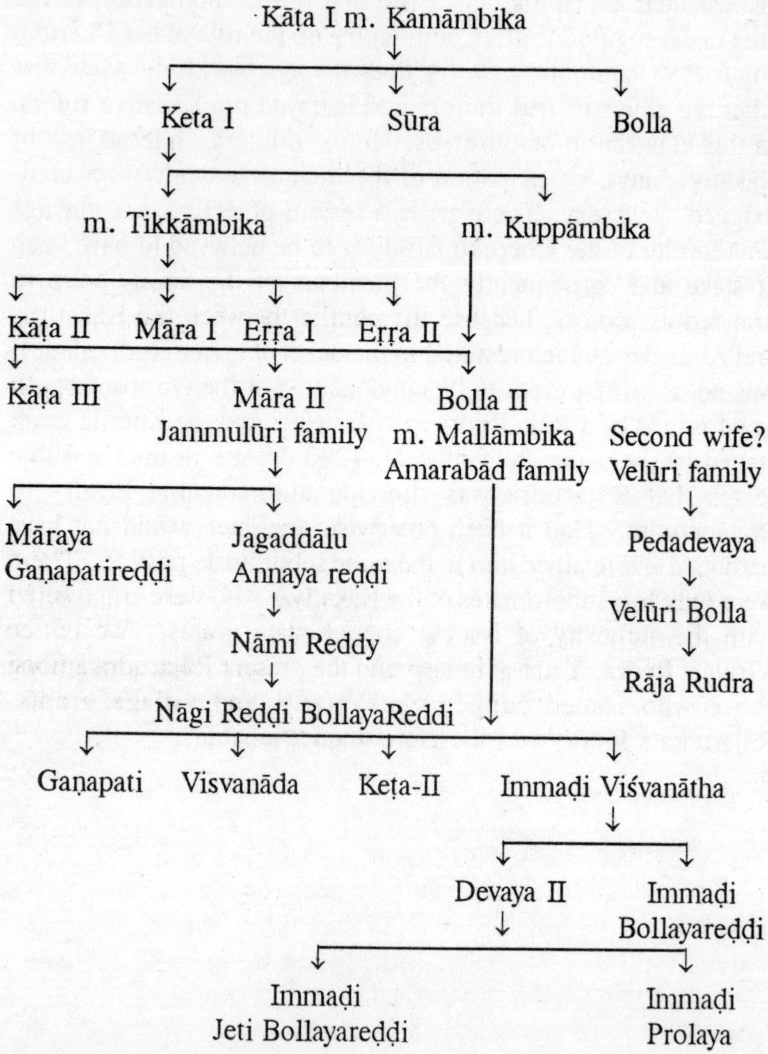

THE INDULŪRI CHIEFS

The Indulūri chiefs ruled over the area of Kolanuvidu and Kolanu in Telugu means lake. It refers to the lake Kolleru in West Godavari district. Kolanavīdu is a *Jaladurga*. Kolanu *seema* comprised of Ēluru, Bhimavaram and Tanuku taluqs of West

Godavari district.[180] The Indulūri chiefs might have expanded this original region into East Godavari and Vizag districts in the North and tracts of Bhadrāchalam in the West. The main source of information on the Indulūri chiefs is a Telugu work called Śivayōgasāram[181] by Kolani Gaṇapati, the last member of the Induluri family. It is believed that the author flourished during the 15th century A.D. While describing his ancestors the author gives us an interesting account of his fore fathers as detailed below.

Nāna Gaura

The family belonged to the *Kouṇḍinya gōtra* of the *Ārādhya* sect. Nāna gaura, the earliest known member of the family was a devotee of Śiva. He is described as *Indulūri Vibhudu* (The lord of Indulūru), perhaps a petty principality in Warangal district, which gave the family name. It is likely that Nāna Gaura migrated to Anumakoṇḍa and entered the service of the Kākatīya during the reign of Prola II (A.D. 116-1157).[182]

Peda Malla and Pina Malla

Nāna Gaura had two sons peda Malla and Pina Malla who served king Rurdadeva as ministers. When the king shifted his capital from Anumakoṇḍa to Orugallu, he made Peda Malla the *nāyaka* or commander of the armies and Pina Malla the chief accountant (Peda samprati). Pedamalla had two sons *Somamantri* and Peda Gaṇapati.

Soma Mantri

Soma mantri an illustrious member of the family entered the service of Kākatīya Rudradeva during the last phase of his rule and continued to serve Mahadeva and his son Gaṇapatideva also. The *Śivayōgasāram* gave detailed account of his exploits. It is stated that some *mantri* led an expedition with a huge army into the regions east of Orugallu, annexed the lands and vanquished the *Māṇḍalikas* of Gogulanāḍu, Kolanivīḍu and beyond the river Godavari, the two *Maḍiyas,* the twelve *Manniyas* and the territory included in Kalinga seema. But contrary to this the Kākatīya conquest of the Costal Andhra and Kalinga appears, to have been effected in a phased manner, but not in a single campaign, as the

Śivayōgasāram projected. Kākati Gaṇapati, is stated to have sent in army to the Kalinga region under the command of Soma mantri and Rājanāyaka, the general of Recherla Rudra. The Upparapalli inscription[183] of Katenāyaka, son of Rajanāyaka dated A.D. 1236, credit them with the victories at Bokkera, killing of the chief bearing the title *Godhumarati*, capture of Udayagiri and putting to flight certain Padiraya. The identify of Padiraya is not known. Bokkera is identified with a place of that name in the Aska taluq of the Ganjam district. It may be assumed that the Kākatīya forces under the leadership of Soma mantri penetrated into Kalinga though it did not fetch much of material benefit to Kākati Gaṇapatideva. The Kalinga king Ananga Bhima III subsequently forced the Kākatiya forces to retreat to the south of the Godavari. It seems these compaigns were conducted between A.D. 1212 and A.D. 1217-18, the dates of Rājanāyaka's and Ananga Bhima's recors at Bhīmeśvara temple in Drāksharāmam.[184]

Conquest of Kolanu region by Indulūri Soma mantri might have taken place sometime before A.D. 1240, that is after the death of Kolanu Kesava deva Mahārāja whose inscriptions are noticeable upto A.D. 1231 and the retreat of Ganga forces. Indulūri *Somamantri* who effectd in the conquest of Vengi was made the lord of Kolanu.[185] Subsequently he became famous as Kolani Soma. Kolanu or Sarasipuri likely to be Saripalle situated in the West Godavari district.

Manuma Ganna and Peda Ganna

Soma mantri and his wife Appāmba got a son named Manuma Ganna. He served Rudramadevi as commander of her forces. The *Śivayōgasāram* praising his military exploits state that Manuma disbursed the armies of the enemy and captured 72 *Bāhattara* forts because of the encouragement and moral support give by Rudramadevi. It is well known that Rudrama was a valiant and bold fighter and capable of leading her soldiers in war. Two inscriptions from Tripurantakam dated A.D. 1259[186] and A.D. 1261[187] refer to one Gannaya, son of Indulūri Ganapaya. The former inscription refers Gannaya as the *Mahāpradhāni* and the *Bāhattaraniyōgādhipati*. In the present state of knowledge it is difficult to identify this Indulūri Ganapaya. Manuma Ganna is credited witht he capture of all the forts of Ambadeva who was the *Bahattara Durgādhipati* of Rudramadevi and who setup the standard of revolt in the last part of the reign of the queen. Peda Ganna, son of Peda Malla and younger brother of Soma mantri seem to have enjoyed the position of *Bāhattaraniyōgādhipati*. The *Śivayōgasāramu* is silent as to the military enterprises of Peda Ganna.

Kolani Rudra

Manuma Ganna had three sons, namely Rudra, Immaḍi Rudra and Mummaḍi Rudra by his wife Mallamāmba. Of them, the first know as Kolani Rudra was an illustrious member of the family. He was not only a great general but also a learned scholar and efficient administrator. He served the Kākatīya king Prataparudra as *Mudrāpaka* or the officer incharge of the royal seal. He was also the governor of the region between Orugallu and Simhachala in the east with capital at Kolanuvīḍu. The forts of Chebrolu, Undi, Paḍinapuramu, Devapuram, Jayavādi, Enamadala, Kamcharla, Podili, Poḍikanuru, Ulacharla, Āduru, Nujella, Sūravaram, Rājamahendravaramu, Goḍikuru, Turukoṭa, Chamalakoṭa, Boḍisakuru, Benḍapūdi, and others are said to have been included in his province. Some of these seem to be the forts actually conquered by Kolani Rudra.[188]

The *Śivayōgasāramu* also states that he was made the *Bāhattari Durganāyaka* by Pratāpa Rudra. He is also credited with the victory over the *Pancha Pāṇḍyas* or the five Paṇḍya Kings; obviously it refers to the military campaign conducted by Pratāparudra over the Pāṇḍyas in A.D. 1316, when Sundara Pandya was reinstated on the Pandya throne. He possessed the titles *Rāya Chouhattamalla, Mānḍalika chouhattamalla, Iruvattaganda, Kalingarāya Vibhāla*, and *Pancha Pāṇḍyarāja Mānamarda, Rājarudriya* credits him with the designation of *Pradhāna* of Pratāparudra and incharge of *Mudrāpaka* or custodian of royal seal.[189] Kolani Rudra survived the Muslim onslaught on the Kākatīya kingdom and lived even after A.D. 1326.[190]

Annaya Deva

Peda Ganna, younger brother of Kolani Soma, had a son named Indulūri Annaya by his wife Gourama. Being impressed with his good qualities and valour queen Rudramadevi offered her third daughter Ruyyama in marriage to this chief. Apart from Ruyyama, he had two more wives, named Adrija and Lakumāmba. He was one of the loyal ministers of Pratāparudra, and command the fifth battalion of the Kākatiya military cadets, consisting of one lakh foot soldiers and 12000 cavalry. He was entrusted with the defence of the stone fort of Orugallu during the Muslim invasions. Annayadeva play an important role as military commander of Pratāparudra when he sent an army in A.D. 1291 to Tripurantakam to subjugate Kāyastha Ambadeva under the command of Annayadeva and his cousin Manuma Gannaya. Ambadeva was defeated and was forced to retreat southwards i.e., Mulikināḍu.[191] Annayadeva succeeded in seizing the 72 forts of the enemy. He also defeated the chief of Mopuru in Mārjavāḍi and assumed the titles *Rāya- chouhattamalla* and *Iruvattu-ganda*. He ruled the Vengi region with his capital at Śuravaramu and entrusted Rājamahendra to his nephew Parvata Mallu and the fort of Racherala to the son-in-law of Manuma Ganna. He had also the titles of *Mururāyara Jagadadiganda*, and *Jagamartya ganda* according to the records at Tripurantakam dated A.D. 1291[192] and Drākshārāmam dated A.D. 1293.[193] The Khandavalli plates[194] dated A.D. 1289 of Pratāparudra contain the *Dāyagaja Kesari* seal which was issued by Indulūri Annayadeva. In this connection it may be noted that an epigraph set up in the Siddhēśvara temple at Terala (Guntur dist.) by Rudraya Peddi in A.D. 1292 contains the king's *praśasti*. It refers inter alia to the title *dāyagaja kesari lānchana* of Prataparudra.

Geneology of the Indulūri chiefs

Nāna Goura
↓
- Peda Malla m. Pochamāmbika
  ↓
  - Soma Mantri m. Appāmba
    ↓
    Manuma Ganna m. Mallamamaba
    ↓
    - Kolani Rudra m. Gouramba
    - Immadi Rudra
    - Mummaḍi Rudra
  - Peda Ganna m.Gourama
    ↓
    Annayadeva m. Ruyyama d/o Kākati Rudramadevi
- Pina Malla

REFERENCES

1. *I.A.P.* Wg. No. 27
2. *I.A.P.* Kn. No. 29
3. *I.A.P.* Wg. No. 40
4. M. Rama Rao (ed), *Kākatiya Sanchika*, Hyderabad, 1991, pp. 398-399
5. *I.A.P.* Wg. No. 83
6. *I.A.P.* Ng. II, No. 41.
7. *I.A.P.* Wg. No. 27
8. P.V.P. Sastry, *The Kākatīyas of Warangal*, Hyderabad, 1978, pp. 41-42.
9. *I.A.P.* Wg. No. 27
10. K. Laxmiranjanam (ed) *Sri Siddhēśvara Charitramu,* Kāse Sarvapppa, Intrdocution. p. IV.
11. C.V. Ramachandra Rao (ed) *Pratāapa Charitrammu*, Ekāmranātha, Peethika, pp. 11-12.
12. K. Laxmiranjanam (ed) *op. cit,* Intrduction. pp. XXII-XXIV.
13. P.V.P. Sastry, *op cit.*, p. 43
14. *I.A.P.* Wg. No. 27
15. P.V.P. Sastry, op. cit., p. 147

16. *Ibid.*, pp. 43-44.
17. *I.A.P.* Kn. No. 29
18. B.N. Sastry, *Ahdhradesa Charitra Samskriti*, pt-II, Hyderabad, 1992, p. 242.
19. *I.A.P.* Kn. No. 29
20. *I.A.P.* Wg. No. 27
21. M. Rama Rao (ed). *op. cit.*, p. 398.
22. *I.A.P.* Wg. No. 83.
23. *I.A.P.* Wg. No. 65
24. B.N. Sastry, *op. cit.*, p. 236
25. P.V.P. Sastry, op. cit., p. 147
26. *Corpus*, pp. 114 ff.
27. P.V.P. Sastry, op. cit., p. 148
28. B.N. Sastry, op. cit., p. 256.
29. *I.A.P.* Wg. No. 16.
30. *I.A.P.* Wg. No. 17.
31. B.N. Sastry, *op. cit.*, p.257.
32. *I.A.P.* Wg. No. 16
33. *E.A.*, I, pp. 87-89; *A.P.R.E.* 1965, Nos. 193 & 194.
34. *A.P.R.E.* 1965, Nos. 196 & 197.
35. *A.P.R.E.* 1965, No. 198.
36. *A.P.R.E.* 1965, Nos. 356 & 358.
37. *A.P.R.E.* 1965, No. 5.
38. *A.P.R.E.* 1966, No. 325.; I.A.P. Wg. No. 57
39. *A.P.R.E.* 1966, No. 326.; *I.A.P.* Wg. No. 58.; Corpus-IV, No.27.
40. *S.I.I.* X, No. 254.
41. *S.I.I.* X, No. 544.
42. *Epigraphia Andhrica*, I, pp. 87-89.
43. *I.A.P.* Wg. No. 57.
44. *I.A.P.* Wg. No. 49.
45. *I.A.P.* Wg. No. 57.
46. *J.A.H.R.S.* XX, p. 124.
47. *Ibid.*; *I.A.P.* Wg. No. 16.
48. *A.P.R.E.* 1965, p. 99.: I.A.P. Wg. No. 16.
49. *J.A.H.R.S.* XX, p. 125.
50. *I.A.P.* Wg. No. 49.
51. *Ibid.*, *J.A.H.R.S.* XX, pp. 125-126.
52. B.N. Sastry, *Tripurāthakadēvālaya Śāsanamulu*, Hyderabad, 1984, No. 11.
53. *Ibid.*

54. *I.A.P.* Wg. No. 49.
55. *Epigraphia Indica,* VI, p. 159.
56. *Ibid.,*
57. *I.A.P.* Wg. No. 58.
58. *I.A.P.* Wg. No. 57.
59. Cited in *J.A.H.R.S.* XX, P. 127.
60. *I.A.P.* Wg. No. 58.
61. *I.A.P.* Wg. No. 57.
62. *Ibid.,*
63. *Corpus* IV, No. 27.
64. *Ibid.,*
65. *I.A.P.* Wg. No. 49 & 59.
66. B.N. Sastry, *op. cit.*, 1984, No 11.
67. B.N. Sastry, *op.* cit., 1992, p. 262.
68. *J.A.H.R.S.,* XX, p. 127.
69. B.N. Sastry, *op. cit.*, 1984, Nos 26, 27 & 28.
70. *J.A.H.R.S.*, XX, p. 129.
71. B.N. Sastry, *op. cit.*, 1984, No. 49.
72. P.V.P. Sastry, *op. cit.*, p. 143.
73. B.N. Sastry, *Recherla Reḍḍi Vamshacharita Śāsanamulu,* Hyderabad, 1989, pp. 42-43.
74. *A.P.R.E.*, 1965, No. 329.; *I.A.P.*, Wg. No. 91
75. *A.P.R.E.*, 1965, No. 353.; *I.A.P.*, Wg. No. 69.; *Corpus* IV, No. 33.
76. *A.P.R.E.*, 1966, No. 354.; *I.A.P.,* Wg. No. 55.; *Corpus* IV, No. 28.
77. *A.P.R.E.*, 1966, No. 344.; *I.A.P.*, Wg. No. 50.
78. B.N. Sastry, *op. cit.*, 1989, No. 22
79. B.N. Sastry, *op. cit.*, 1989, Nos. 16 & 18.; *I.A.P.* Wg. No. 54.
80. B.N. Sastry, *op. cit.*, 1989, No. 15.
81. *I.A.P.,* Ng., II, No. 30, 32; B.N. Sastry, *op. cit.*, 1989, Nos. 1,3, & 6.
82. *Ibid.*, No. 35.
83. *Ibid.,* No. 45
84. *Ibid.*, No. 49.
85. *Ibid.,* No. 66
86. B.N. Sastry, *op. cit.*, 1989, No. 10.
87. *Ibid.,* No. 20
88. *I.A.P.* Wg. No. 50
89. *Ibid.*, No. 51.

90. *I.A.P.* Ng. II. No. 31.
91. *Ibid.; Corpus*, No. 41.
92. *Corpus,* No. 41
93. B.N. Sastry, *op. cit.*, 1989, p. 11.
94. *I.A.P.* Ng. I, No. 31.; *Corpus,* No. 41.
95. *Corpus,* No. 42.
96. *Ibid.*, No. 41.
97. *Ibid.*, No. 42.
98. *Ibid.*,
99. *Ibid.*, No. 41.
100. *I.A.P.* Wg. No. 36.
101. *I.A.P.* Wg. No. 50.
102. B.N. Sastry, op. cit., 1989, p. 17.
103. *I.A.P.* Wg. No. 52.
104. B.N. Sastry, op. cit., 1989, p. 18.
105. Corpus, No. 42.
106. *Ibid.*
107. *Ibid.*, No. 43.
108. B.N. Sastry, op. cit., 1989, p. 23.
109. Corpus, No. 38.
110. *I.A.P.* Wg. No. 73.
111. *J.A.H.R.S.* V, p.3 and pp. 143-144.
112. *I.A.P.* Wg. No. 50.
113. *I.A.P.* Wg. No. 69.
114. *A.P.R.E.* 1966, p. 97.; S.I.I. IV, No. 1117.
115. P.V.P. Sastry, op. cit., pp. 107-111.
116. B.N. Sastry, op. cit., 1989, p. 31.
117. *I.A.P.* Wg No. 73.; S.I.I. IV, No. 1277.
118. *I.A.P.* Wg. No. 51.
119. P.V.P. Sastry, op. cit., p. 109.
120. *I.A.P.* Wg. No. 55.
121. *I.A.P.* Wg. No.56.
122. *I.A.P.* Wg. No. 54.
123. *I.A.P.* Wg. No. 73.
124. *I.A.P.* Wg. No. 69.
125. *Ibid.*
126. *Corpus,* No. 42.
127. *A.P.A.* [illegible].3, No. 26.
128. *Corpus,* No. 27.
129. *S.I.I.* X. No. 375.

130. *Corpus*, No. 17
131. *Ibid.*, No. 28.
132. B.N. Sastry, *op. cit.*, 1989, p. 40.
133. *Corpus,* No. 31.
134. *Ibid.*
135. P.V.P. Sastry, *op. cit.*, p. 145.
136. B.N. Sastry, *Cherukuvamsha Charitra Śāśanamulu,* Hyderabad, 1989, p. 11.
137. *Ibid.*, p. 28.
138. *Corpus,* No. 22.; *A.P.R.E.*, 1966, No. 133; *I.A.P.* Ng. I, No. 62 & 72.
139. *I.A.P.* Ng., I, p. 349.
140. B.N. Sastry, *op. cit.*, 1989, No. 12.
141. *Ibid.*, Nos. 4,7 & 9.
142. *Ibid.*, No. 6.
143. *Ibid.*, No. 14.
144. *Ibid.*, No. 10.
145. B.N. Sastry, *Nallagonda Mandala Sarvaswamu,* p. 713.
146. *I.A.P.* Ng., I, Nos. 62 & 72.
147. *A.P.R.E.*, 1966, No. 133.
148. *I.A.P.* Ng., I, No. 62.
149. *Ibid.*, No. 72.
150. *A.P.R.E.*, 1966, No. 147.; *I.A.P.* Ng., I, No. 62
151. P.V.P. Sastry, *op. cit.*, p. 91.
152. B.N. Sastry , *op. cit.*, p. 13.
153. B.N. Sastry, *Nallagonda Maṇḍala Sarvaswàmu,* p. 713 (Jalalpur Inscription).
154. B.N. Sastry, *op. cit,* 1989, No. 2.
155. *Ibid.*
156. *Corpus,* p. XVIII; *I.A.P.* Ng., I, No. 72.
157. *Ibid.*
158. B.N. Sastry, *op. cit.*, 1989, p. 19.
159. *Ibid.*, No. 6.
160. *Ibid.*, No. 9.
161. *Ibid.*,
162. M. Rama Rao *(ed) op. cit.*, Hyderabad, 1991, p. 420.
163. N. Ramesan, *op. cit.*, pp. 98ff.
164. *I.A.P.* Ng., I , No. 91.; B.N. Sastry, *op. cit.*, 1989, No. 11
165. B.N. Sastry, *op. cit.*, 1984, p. 72.
166. *I.A.P.* Ng., II, No. 59.

167. N. Ramesan, *op. cit.*, I, pp. 98ff.
168. B.N. Sastry, *op. cit.*, 1989, No. II.
169. *Ibid.*, p. 30.
170. *Ibid.*, p. 31.
171. *Ibid.*, No. 5.; *I.A.P.* Ng., I, No. 80.
172. *Ibid.*, No. 12
173. *Ibid.*, No. 13.
174. *Ibid.*, No. 16.
175. *S.I.I.*, X, No. 508.
176. B.N. Sastry, *op. cit.*, 1989, No. 16.
177. *Ibid.*, No. 14.
178. *Ibid.*, No. 15; *I.A.P.* Ng., I, No. 98.
179. P.V.P. Sastry, *op. cit.*, pp. 153-154.
180. K. Ishvaradattu, *Prācheenāndhra Chāritraka Bhūgōlamu, Hyderabad*, 1962, pp. 112-114.
181. M. Rama Rao, (ed) *op. cit.*, *Avatārika of Śivayōgasāram* are given in the Appendix.
182. *Ibid.*, p. 52.
183. *I.A.P.* Kn., No. 30.
184. *S.I.I IV*, No. 1117.
185. P.V.P. Sastry, *op. cit.* pp. 111-112.
186. B.N. Sastry, *op. cit.*, 1984, No. 51.
187. *Ibid* No. 55.
188. P.V.P. Sastry, *op. cit.*, pp. 162-163.
189. *Ibid.*, p. 163.
190. *A.R.E.*, 308 of 1915.
191. P.V.P. Sastry, *op. cit.*, p. 130.
192. *A.R.E.*, 238 of 1905.
193. *S.I.I.*, VI, No. 1807.
194. *E.A.* IV, pp. 103ff.

Chapter-III

POLITICAL HISTORY OF THE SUBORDINATE RULERS OF THE KĀKATĪYAS (LATER PHASE)

Another line of subordinate chiefs viz., the Malyāla, Kōṭa, Kāyastha, Chālukyas of Niḍadavole, Gona and the Velamas had also served the Kākatīyas from the times of Rudradēva and continued to be their subordinates till the downfall of the kingdom. Some of the above families had matrimonial relations with the Kākatīyas. Gaṇapatideva offered his daughter Rudrama to a prince of his subordinate chief namely Virabhadra of the Chālukyas of Niḍadavole. Gaṇpatideva's another daughter Gaṇapāmba was married to Kōṭa Beta Rāja of Yanamadala branch. Thus the imperial family maintained good relations with their subordinates, and consolidated their political power without facing any problem from their powerful feudatories. Some of the prominent chiefs were given the high ranking positions such as Military Generals and Commanders befitting their talents. For instance Malyāla Chaunḍa senāni, Gona Buddha Reḍḍi, Prasāditya, the Velama chief was instrumental in introducing the *nāyankara* system in the Kākatīya polity and also protected the queen Kākatīya Rudramadevi was murdered in a war at Chandupatla waged by Ambadeva. However, most of the subordinates remained faithful and rendered sincere and loyal service to their overlords.

THE MALYĀLA CHIEFS

The Malyāla chiefs that they had been born in the line of Durjaya, like the Kākatiya and their subordinate Viriyāla chiefs. The Malyāla chiefs maintained matrimonial relations with the Viriyāla chiefs. They served the Kākatīyas as Commanders, and ministers and participated in their administration.

Gunḍa danḍādhiśa of this family is said to be the ruler of Budapur and Vardhamānapura areas.[1] Budapur is the present Bothpur of Mahabubnagar taluq and Vardamānpura is the present Vaddamānu village in Nagarkurnool taluq of Mahabubnagar district. The following table shows the areas under the control of the chiefs as seen from their inscriptions.

Inscriptional toponyms	*Identifications*
Nurukurki Chaunḍapura, Konḍaparti	Konḍaparti, Wardhannapet Tq., Warangal Dist.[2]
Budapur	Bothpur, Jadcherla Tq., Mahabubnagar Dist.[3]
Kaṭukūru	Kaṭukūru, Huzurabad Tq., Karimnagar Distt.[4]
Vardhamānapura	Vaddamānu, Nagarkurnool Tq., Mahabubnagar Dist.[5]

Mahabubnagar and Nagarkurnool taluqs of Mahabubnagar district appear to be the areas that were ruled by the chiefs of Malyāla family. The Konḍaparti inscrption of Kāṭa and his son Chaunḍa state that they made Konḍaparti in Wardhannapet taluq their temporary seat as they wanted to be close to Warangal in view of their active participation in the imperial affairs.

Dannaya Mantri, the earliest member of the family was the lord of the town of Malyāla. Chaunḍa senāni's Konḍaparti inscription[6] dated A.D. 1203 refers to him as *Malyālanātha*, *Sēnanātha* and *Pedamuttaganḍa* which suggest that he was a general of great prowess. The following are the inscriptions which refer to Dannaya. Kaṭukūr inscription of Mailama dated A.D. 1202,[7] Konḍaparti inscriptions of Chaunḍa senāni dated A.D. 1203 and of Kāṭa sensāni dated A.D. 1241[8] and Bothpur inscription of Gunḍa senāpati dated A.D. 1259 and A.D. 1272.[9] He appears to hve been appointed as the feudatory chief of *Sankisapura* by Kakati Rudradeva. His son Sabbasenāpati continued to rule *Sankisapura* and assumed the title *Sankisādhiśvara*.[10] Even the Bothpur branch of Malyāla chiefs described themselves as Sankisa*puraadhinatha*.[11] The title which Dannaya held was also assumed by his grandsons

Kāṭa Senāni[12] and Gunḍa Senāni[13] respectively. Dannaya must have secured Bothpur for his second son Bācha.

THE SANKISAPURA FAMILY

Sabba Senāni

Sabha senāni known as *Sankisaadhiśvara* was the eldest son of Dannaya. He had a wife by name Achama. The name of his son was Kāṭa Senāni.

Kāṭa

He was a worthy son of his father Sabha Senāni. He was described as a great warrior with the title *Rāya garuḍah peda muttu ganḍah* and *Kōṭageluvāta* in the Kaṭukūru inscription[14] of his daughter-in-law Mailama. His Konḍaparti epigraph[15] records that king Rudradēva appointment him as his minister and accompanied by Kāṭa senāni and other subordinate defeated the Kōṭa chief Doḍḍa Bhima and captured his town Dharanikōṭa or Dannalakōṭa in about A.D. 1181.[16] In recognition of the services of Kāta, the king Rudradeva conferred on him the title *Kōṭagelpata* (the conqueror of Kōṭa). Kāṭa Senāni, must be the son of Bollama for the name of Bollama is explicity mentioned in his inscriptions.

Prola

Kāṭasenāni's eldest son was *Prola Pradhane sutah potabhi-dharmah*[17] which his more illustrious brother Chaunḍa was the commander-in-chief of the forces of Kākatīya ruler Gaṇpatideva. Prola must have lived at *Sankisapura* i.e. Konḍaparti ruling over his fief.

Chaunḍa Senāni

Kāta's second son was Chaunḍa Senāni. He married Mailama the daughter of Viriyala Annaya. Thus the two families of Malyāla and Viriyāla chiefs of the Kākatīya rulers came to be united strengthening the hands of Kakati Gaṇapatideva. He was described as *Gaṇapati mahipāla senabhibhartuh* (commander in-chief) of king Gaṇpatideva.[18] Kaṭukūru inscription describes the conquests of coastal Andhra and the participation of Chaunḍa-senāpati at the behest of Gaṇapatideva. When the Velanāṭi king

Prithviśvara changed his capital from Chandanavōlu to Pithapuram and began to reassert his power in the Krishṇa region, there upon Gaṇapatideva entrusted the important task of leading the army against the Velanāṭi king to Chaunḍasenāni in A.D. 1201. The Bezawāda epigraph of Natavāḍi Rudra, brother-in-law of Kākatiya rulers under took the conquest of the Krishṇa region from that date.[19] According to Konḍaparti record Chaunḍasenāpati conquerred the Divi Island in the Krishṇa region and took possession of the invaluable dimons belonging to treasury of the Velanāṭi king. No wonder Gaṇapatideva who was immensely pleased with the military victory of Chaunḍa conferred the title *dvipi-luṁṭāka* on him.[20] P.V. Parabrahma Sastry describes the military achievements of Chaunḍa, the commander-in-chief of the Kākatiya armies thus: "The credit of subjugating the coastal Andhra, particularly the defeat of Prithviśvara, the Velanāṭi Chief who was holding sway over the the entire coastal districts at that time, according to the Konḍaparti record goes by all means to the famous general Chaunḍa. No doubt several other generals and subordinate chiefs of that period claim for themselves the title *Prithviśvara-sirah Kandukakrīḍa-vinōda*, the player with the ball of Prithviśvara's head. But Malyāla Chaunḍa was described inthe record to be holding the post of commander-in-chief of the Kākatīya armies,where as all other chiefs were mere participants in that engagement which took place sometime between A.D. 1203-1206. Prithviśvara was not a small king. During the last part of the 12th century when the imperial Chōḷas had almost retired from Vēngi politics, the Velanāṭi chief Rajendra Chōḍa II rose to power among all the *mānḍalikas* of the coastal Andhra and held sway over the region from Simhachalam in the north to Nellore in the South. Prithviśvara who came to power in A.D. 1185 inherited the vast region of his grand-father and stood as the main obstacle in the way of the Kākatīyas in the east. Rudra in the last years of his reign could succeed in paving the way to some extent by subjugating the Kōṭa chiefs. But the major task of reducing the Velanāṭi chief Prithviśvara remained for Gaṇapatideva. Soon after his accession he despatched an army with Malyāla Chaunḍa. Who proceeded to *dvipa,* i.e., Divi the Island province of the Velanāṭi kingdom. The Island was captured and Pridhviśvara was driven out. The treasures of th enemy was plundered and presented to the king Gaṇapati, who being pleased with the valorous deed of Chaunḍa conferred on him the titles *divichūrakāra* and *dvipa-luṁṭāka* (the plunderer of *dvīpa* or Island). To commemorate his great victory Chaunḍa built a temple to the god Chunḍeśvara at Konḍaparti in A.D. 1203".[23]

THE BOTHPUR FAMILY

Bothpur is a mandal situated in the present day Mahabubnagar district. It was secured by Dannaya mantri for his second son Bācha. It is not known how this branch came to Bothpur leaving their ancestral home at Konḍaparti near Warangal.

Bācha

This Bācha Varudhinisa was not as famous as that of his son Gunḍa. The name of his wife was Bāchāmba. Perhaps he was content to rule over his principality Bothpur like his brother Sabba.

Gunḍa Danḍādhīśa

The Vardhamanupura inscrption describes Gunḍa as *Peda muttuganda*[22] who served Kākati Gaṇapatideva and also Rudrama devi. Gunḍa seems to have died some time before A.D. 1277 as suggested by an inscription of his wife Kuppāmbika recording some lands for his merit.[23] Incidentally it may be mentioned that Kuppāmbika was the daughter of Buddhaya of Gona family, the renowed author of *Ranganātha Rāmāyana*. A note worthy feature of Gunḍa and his wife Kuppāmbika was their patronage to men of letters, some of whom being qualified as *ghaṭa śāsins* i.e professors in a *ghaṭika* or an institution for higher education on various *śāstras*. Kuppambika constructed a temple at Bothpur, and consecreated a *linga* in memory of her husband and gifted some lands to the temple in A.D. 1276. At the time of consecretion she was accompanied by her sons Bāchaya, Boppa and Gaṇapatideva.[24] It seems Gunḍaya's sons Bāchaya, Boppa and Gaṇapatideva did not attain prominence as general like their illustrious father.

In this connection, the observation of N. Venkāṭaramanayya

and M. Soma Sekhara Sarma are worth producing: "The Malyāla, the Gona and Recherla, the great feudatory families who played such an important part in the early history of the Kākatīya, appear at this time (during the reign of Kākati Rudrama devi) to have ceased to take much active interest with affairs of kingdom. Malyāla Gunḍa, a general of Rudradeva (Rudramamba), was alive until A.D. 1274 and he seemed to have been living in retirement, taking no part in stirring events which shook the kingdom to its foundations during the first decade of the queen's reign. His sons and other members of his family were now interested more in the construction of temples and the excavation of irrigation tanks than they were in political matters.[25] The Malyāla chiefs entered the service of Kākatīyas during the rule of Beta II (A.D. 1076-1108) and served upto A.D. 1276, for a period of nearly two hundred years. The greatest among them was Chaunḍa, the commander-in-chief of the Kākatīya forces who strove hard to strengthen the Kākatīya power.

Though both the writers are not very complimentary about the contribution of Malyāla chiefs during the first decade of Rudramāmba's reign, neverthless the service of Chaunḍa senāpati in the conquest of Coastal Andhra cannot be ignored. The constrution of temples and excavation of irrigation tanks were considered as pious deeds or *saptasantānas*. As a matter of fact these were the items on which the elite in all ages used to spend their hoards of money and other resoruces.

Genealogy of the Malyāla chiefs

Durjaya
↓
Dannaya
↓

Sankisapura family	Bothpur family
Sabba *senāni* m. Achama	Bācha *Varudhinisa* m. Bāchama
↓	↓
Kāṭa *senāni* m. Bollama & Kāchama	Gunḍa *Danḍādhisa* m. Gona Kuppāmbika
↓	↓
Prola *senāni*; Chaunḍasenāni m. Viriyāla Mailama	Bāchaya; Boppa; Gaṇapatideva

THE KŌTA CHIEFS

The Kōṭa chiefs who were also relatives of the Kākatīyas ruled over the area called *Shaṭsahasrānāḍu* i.e. the Velanāḍu six thousand country situated towards the southern bank of river Krishṇa for over a century and half from the beginning of the 12th century to the last quarter of the 13th century. They obtained the region by the favour of Trinayana Pallava. They were the political successors of the Konḍapaḍumatis who served as wardens of the Western marches of the Velanāṭi kingdom and their kingdom was largest in extent.

The following is a brief description of the geographical area that the Kōṭas ruled over i.e., the Velanāḍu- 6000 country situated on the southern bank of the river Krishṇa which is also known as Kōṭabhūmi and *Āruvēlanāḍu*. The main branch of the Kōṭas ruled with capital at Dhānyakāṭaka and as many as four collateral branches exercised their sway with capitals at Yanamadala, Tripurantakam, Tadikonda and Drāksharāmam. All the Kōṭa chiefs bore the common *praśasti*, claiming to be rulers of *Shaṭsahasrā*, lords of Dhānyavati and devotees of Amarēśvara at Amarāvati. At the height of power, the boundaries of the Kōṭa principality touched Tripurantakam on the west, Drāksharāmam on the east and Nallore district on the South.[26]

The inscriptions of Kōṭa chiefs mention the names of villages that were in the Konḍapaḍumati, Konḍanatavāḍi and Kanḍravāḍi regions. So the assumption that these regions were included in the kingdom of Kōṭa chiefs is not far fetched.[27] During the period of Kōṭa Bhima II, Konḍapaḍumati region was merged with the fief of the Kōta chiefs. It appears that were 73 villages in Konḍapaḍumati region. Some of the villages shown in inscriptions are as follows.[28]

Inscriptional Toponyms	*Identification*
Jeedipundi	Jupudi, Narsaraopet Tq., Guntur Dist.[29]
Getepalli	Kētavaram, Sattenapalli Tq., Guntur Dist.[30]
Durupāḍu	Dondapāḍu, Sattenapalli Tq., Guntur Dist.[31]
Erraguntala	Erraguntalapāḍu, Sattenapalli Tq., Guntur Dist.[32]
Chenuchuluru	Satulūru, Narsaraopet Tq., Guntur Dist.[33]

The Konḍanatavāḍiseema must be the Western region of Sattenapalli taluq in Guntur district as is evidenced by the inscriptions of the chiefs.[34]

Inscriptional Toponyms	*Identification*
Challagara	Challagariga, Sattenapalli Tq., Guntur Dist.[35]
Kuntamaddi	Kuntamaddi, Sattenapalli Tq., Guntur Dist.[36]
Uppalapāḍu, Ammalapudi	Uppalapāḍu, Sattenapalli Tq., Guntur Dist.[37]

Kandravāḍi is another region mentioned in the inscriptions of the Kōṭa chiefs. It is also called Kanderuvāḍi *vishaya*. Some of the villages of Kandravadi that found mention in inscriptions are as follows :

Inscriptional Toponyms	*Identification*
Kranteru	Kranteru, Guntur Tq., & Dist.[38]
Guḍlapūḍi	Guḍipūḍi, Sattenapalli Tq., Guntur Distt.[39]
Andukuru	Andukuru, Guntur Tq., & Dist.[40]
Kunchulapalli	Kunchulapalli, Guntur Tq., & Dist.[41]
Gundimeda	Gundimeda, Guntur Tq., & Dist. [42]
Duggiala punḍi	Duggirala, Tenali Tq., Guntur Dist.[43]
Davuluru	Davuluru, Tenali Tq., Guntur Dist.[44]
Mandaḍam	Mandaḍam, Guntur Tq., & Dist.[45]
Velanagapundi	Velagapūnḍi, Guntur Tq. & Dist.[46]
Ravipundi	Rāyapūḍi, Guntur Tq., & Dist.[47]
Penumbaka	Penumaka, Guntur Tq., & Dist.[48]
Uppalapāḍu	Uppalapāḍu, Guntur Tq., & Dist.[49]

Obviously the Kanḍravāḍi region consisted of Guntur and Sattenapalli taluqs and northern portion of the Tenali taluq in Guntur district.[50] The Amaravati inscription of Kōta Keta II mention Doddi Kanḍravāti region also in connection with the gift of a village called Onkadona or the present Uyyanadona of Sattenapalli taluq.[51]

Enumanḍala Stala

The Yanmadala pillar inscription of Ganapāmba, the queen of Kōta chief Beta III, refers to *Enumanḍalastala*. Having been the headquarter of a large division of 6000 *grāmas,* Emmaḍala or Eṇumanḍala was a town of considered importance which might have inspired Ganapāmba to construct a temple there in memory of her deceased husbanbd.[52] The Kōṭa chiefs appears to have ruled an extensive land lying south of river Krishṇa from Dhānya-kāṭaka to Tripurantakam and the area comprised of the present Guntur district. At its height of power it touched Drāksharāmam on the north and Nellore on the south.

They owed allegiance to the Chālukya Chōḷas in the beginning but later to the Kākatīyas. The Kākatīyas, the Chāgis, the Konakanḍravāḍis, the Konḍapadumaṭis and the Haihayas of Palanāḍu sought matrimonial alliances with them. The prefix Kōṭa, borne by all the members of the family is derived from Dharanikōṭa near Amarāvati also known as Dhānyakāṭaka, popularly known as Kōṭa. The seal of the Kōṭa chiefs bore the crest *Ganḍabhērunda*.[53] The Mogalutla grant of Kōṭa Gānapāmba contains a seal with the symbol of *ganḍa-bhērunḍa*, the royal insignia.

The earliest known Kōṭa chief was Beta I of Dhanunjaya *gōtra*. He was followed by Ganḍa who was succeeded by Bhima I alias Mummaḍi Bhima, owed allegiance to the Chola emperor Kulothunga and loyally served his master and distinguished himself in the Kalingan war along with many other local rulers of Vengi. Betarāja or Beta II succeeded Bihma I on the Kōṭa throne, but his relationship to either Bhima or his father Ganḍa is not known. Beta II was succeeded by Keta I whose relationship with the former is not known. Keta I seems to have had a peaceful and eventless reign, for by this time the Chōḷa suzerainty was completely restored in Vengi and the local kingdom had no trouble from the Chālukyas. Keta I was succeeded by his son Bhima II who established close relations with the Kākatiyas. The following is the geneology of the Kōṭa chiefs.

Beta I (A.D. 1050-1081)
↓
Ganḍa Bhūpati (A.D. 1081-1108)
↓
Bhima I (A.D. 1108 -1127)
↓
Beta II (A.D. 1127 -1148)
↓
Keta I (A.D. 1148 -1156)
↓
Bhima II (A.D. 1156 -1182)

Bhima II

He is also known as Kōṭa Doḍḍa Bhimarāja. Bhima's earliest record is from Velpur[54] dated A.D. 1156 mentioing Bhima and Rajendra Choḷa, the Velanāṭi chief. His reign must have lasted till A.D. 1182 the earliest record of his son Keṭa II. The *praśasti* of Bhima II has the following titles *Kommanadanda nāyaka śirahchchedana; chidpulivadhu mangaḷasūtra harana; Chaunḍarāya chanura murantaka; yuriyabetamatta-mātanga simḥa, chōḍa ataka sāmanta venkolva siddhi chōḍa mṛiga śardula; mallaya chōḍa mastaka sula; buddhakuru kunddala*; pregnant with political significance, besides others refering to his capacities as a distinguished warrior.[55] The Kōṭa chiefs were originally allied to the Chālukya Choḷa soverigns and later changed their allegiance to the Kākatīyas.

From the time of Prola II, the Kākatīyas were interested in leading expeditions on Veṅgi region. Prola II invaded Veṅgi towards the close of his reign, when he appears to have met his fatal death in a battle. The Drāksharāmam inscription of Kōta Sūramahādevi, dated A.D. 1169 mention *Kākati prola nirdahana* as one of the titles of her husband Kōṭachōḍayarāja of the Kōṭa family which indicates that Ḳākati prola was slain by him[56] This Kōṭa Chōḍayarāja appears to be a scion of the Kōṭa family who joined hands with the Haiheya chiefs of the Kōṇa country and killed Prola II. This is confirmed by the Piṭhapuram inscription dated A.D. 1195.[57] However, the death of Prola II was avenged by his son Rudradēva who defeated the Kōṭa chief Doḍḍa Bhima, who in alliances with the Velanāṭi chiefs prevented the extension of Kākatīya authority in the coastal Andhradeśa.

When Nalagāma of the Haiheyas sought the help of Kākati Rudra in the fratricidal war, Rudradeva readily responded to it since it gave him an excellent opportunity to extent his power over the part of the coastal track lying along the valley of the Krishṇa. He set out with a large army accompained by the *Nāyakas* of Malyāla, Kumaravalli, Vipparla, the Natavāḍis of Maḍapalli and other feudatories, and passed through the bank of the river Krishṇa. Though, he does not appear to have taken much interest in Palnāti war, Rudra defeated the Kōṭa chief Doḍḍabhima or Bhima II and captured his town Dharanikōṭa. The family *praśastis* of Recherla, the Vipparla, the Desatla and the Komaravalli families who participated in the battle bore title *Donnāla kōṭa parivesttita kodana:*, *Doḍḍa bhīmuni garvapahāra*, *Dannāla Kōṭarāya vesya bhujanga* and *Doḍḍavibhuni śirahchchedana* respectively signifying their victory over Bhima. Though Rudra killed Bhima as a concilatory measure Rudra installed Keta II, son of Bhima throne and gave him back his ancestral territories. With the help of Keta II Rudra proceeded against the Velanāḍu chief Rajendrachōḍa and subjugated the Konḍapadamaṭi chiefs who served as the wardens of the western marches of the Velanāṭi kingdom.

Keta II

Bhima II had two sons Chōḍarāja and Keta II. Keta's succession suggested that his elder brother died before his father. For the first time in Kōṭa history, the actual days of the enthronement of a king is given Kōṭa Keta II ascended the throne at Dhānyavati in A.D. 1182 and ruled the entire Kōṭa kingdom, consisting of *Śatasahāsra*, *Konḍanatavāḍi*, *Kanḍravāḍi*, *Doḍḍi Kanḍravāḍi and Konḍapaḍumati* regions from A.D. 1182. He was assisted by governors of the royal family under him, namely Mummaḍi Rudra and Bhima for the rest of his reign.[58]

The Kōṭas of Danyavati or Dharani Kōṭa

Bhima III

Bhima, the eldest son of Keta II, succeeded his father and ruled with his capital at Dharanikōṭa. He reign lasted only for three years. His earliest inscription is from Kolluru dated A.D. 1233,[59] which describe him as *Mahāmanḍalēśvara Erabhimarāya*. The record mentions the names of his sons as Ketarāja, Provrāja, Tripurāja and Rāmarāja. His grandson Gaṇapati (son of Mannaketa or Keta III) was stated to be ruling at Prattipāḍu in A.D. 1234.[60] Therefore Bhima's rule might have ended in A.D. 1234 and it is likely that he maintained good relations with his brother Rudra who was ruling a part of the Kōṭa principality with capital at Yanamaḍala.

Keta III

Keta III was the eldest son and successor of Bhima III. Keta is mentioned as *Mahāmaṇḍaleśvara* Manma Ketarāja in his Amarāvati inscription dated A.D. 1235.[61] The copper plate grant dated A.D. 1240[62] described king Keta or Manma Keta, as lord of the city of Dhānyakāṭaka Bayyaladevi the queen of Keta III was the daughter of Natavāḍi Pakkidi Rudra by his wife Mailāmba, the sister of Gaṇapatideva. Though the records of Keta III and Gaṇapati do not mention any allegiance to the Kākatīyas, yet it may be assumed that they maintained cordial relations with the Kākatīyas.

Gaṇapatideva

The records of Keta III are not available after A.D. 1240. After that date Gaṇapatideva ruled the Kōṭa kingdom for 22 years. His record from Taḍikonḍa dated A.D. 1247[63] mentions him as Kōṭa Irmaḍi Gaṇapatirāya. In A.D. 1254, the queen mother Bayyaladevi and king Gaṇapati acknowledged the suzerainty of the Kākatiya rulers Gaṇapatideva as is evident from the Velpuru record dated A.D. 1254.[64] In the Madala record dated A.D. 1256[65] the Kōṭa king Gaṇapati was mentioned as *Mahāmandaleśvara Jaga Mecchuganḍa*. It appears that Gaṇapati's kingdom extended as far as Tripurantakam in the west and he acknowledged the overlordship of the Kākatīyas as testified by the Velpuru record which is significant.

Bhima IV

Bhima, son of Keta III and brother of Gaṇapati had a brief reign of six years. His Velpuru inscription datd A.D. 1264[66] refers to him as Mahāmanḍaleśvara and as having acknowledged the suzerainty of the Kākatīya ruler Rudradeva mahārāja. Bhima IV must have ruled upto A.D. 1268, the earliest date of his successors.

Devarāja and Mummadi Rāja

Devarāja and Mummaḍirāja succeeded Bhima IV on the Kōṭa throne and seemed to have ruled in partnership. Their only record is from Kollur dated A.D. 1268 mentioning grants by

Mahamandaleśvara Devarāju and Mummaḍirāja were the last rulers of the main branch, of the Kōṭa chiefs and it is likely that their territories subsequently passed under the Kākatīya rule.[67]

The Kōṭas of Yanamadala

Rudradeva Rāja

Rudradeva, the second son of Keta II and younger brother of Bhima III was the first ruler of the Yanamadala branch. The kingdom originated in the partition of the *Kōṭadeśa* in A.D. 1218 between Bhima and Rudra. With their capital at Yanamadala Rudradeva and his successors ruled the Kōṭa kingdom. They owed allegiance to the Kākatīya rulers from the beginning of their rule.[68]

The Yanamadala inscription of Gaṇapāmba, daughter of Kākatiya Gaṇapatideva married to Beta of the Yanamadala family dated A.D. 1241[69] explicitly refers to Rudra as the son of Keta II. The Velpuru inscription states that Rudra became the ruler of Yanamadala.[70] His son Betarāja husband of Gaṇapāmba seems to have died very young and so the records of his rule are not available.

Gaṇapāmba

Gaṇapāmba was the daughter of Kākati Gaṇapatideva and the sister of well known Rudramadevi. Several inscriptions give information about Gaṇapāmba. The Moguluṭla Copper plate inscription dated A.D. 1219 registers the grant of village Moguluṭa by Gaṇapāmba in the presence of Kākati Gaṇapatideva to Rudra Peddimgaru for the spiritual merit of her husband Betarāju. The villages Mogaluṭla and Pellutla mentioned in the inscriptions are identified with the villages of the same name in Sattenapalli taluq of Gunturu district. The grant was made immediately after the death of Betarāju for performing *gaya śraddha*. Therefore, the death of Betarāju can be placed before the date of Moguluṭla copper plate grants i.e., A.D. 1218. The inscription states that the *suṁkas* to be paid to the Kākatīya king on the granted villages were given to Rudra Peddimgaru by Gaṇapatideva, in whose presence the grant was made by Gaṇapāmba. From this it is clear that the Kōṭa kingdom was governed by Gaṇapāmba. The widow queen of Betarāja after his death as the principality of Kākatīyas.[71] The Ipuru inscription dated A.D. 1257 [72] refer to queen Gaṇapāmba as *Mahāmaṇḍaleśvara Gaṇapamadeva yammangāru*.

On the death of her husband in about A.D. 1219 Gaṇapāmba took the responsibility of governing the southern part of the Kōṭa mandala as *mahāmaṇḍalēśvara* with Yanamadala as her capital.[73] She maintained cordial and friendly relations with the Kōṭa chiefs of Dhānyavati and Natavāḍi. Like the other Kōṭa kings Gaṇapamadevi also assumed the usual *praśasti* as, *śrīmat trinayana pallava prasadadi to krishṇa vennanadi dakshiṇa shaṭsaharāvani vallabha bhaya lōbha durlabha, pratāpalaṅkēśvara, gaṇḍabhēruṇḍa, nandi martāṇḍa, śrīman mahāmaṇḍalēśvara* etc., she ruled like any other male member of the line, and it appears that she was at no time impeded because she was a woman.

Devarāju

The Velpuru inscription[74] of A.D. 1264 speaks of Kōṭa Devarājulu remitting some taxes during the reign of Kākati Rudradeva *maharāja*. No details of his relationship to Gaṇapāmba and the duration of the rule are available.

Besides, these two branches, there were also Kōṭa chiefs ruling from Taḍikonḍa, Drāksharāmam and other places as well. It is difficult to establish the relationship of these familes with the Kōṭas of Dhānyakāṭaka and Yanamadala. But as they bear the usual Kōṭa *praśastis*, they undoubtedly belonged to the same stock as the other Kōṭas. Of the several titles assumed by the Kōṭa chiefs, two deserve particular mention. Keta II acquired the title *jagamecḷuganḍa* and perpectuated the same by naming a village *Jagamecḷuganḍapura* after that title. The title *gaṇḍabhēruṇḍa*, fabulous bind of two heads was adopted by the Kōṭa chiefs as their royal crest which is found on the seals of the Eḍavalli plates and the Moguluṭla grant.

The Genealogy of the Kōṭa chiefs

Beta I
↓
Gunḍa Bhūpati
↓
Bhima I
↓
Beta Rāja II
↓
Keta I
↓
Bhima II or Doḍḍa Bhima Rāja
m. Sabbāmbika
↓

Chōḍarāja — Keta II

Dhānyavati Branch — Yanamadala Branch

Dhānyavati Branch:
Bhima III
↓
Keta III, Prov Rāja, Tripura Rāja, Rama Rāja

Keta III
↓
Gaṇapatideva, Bhima IV

Gaṇapatideva
↓
Deva Rāja, Mummadi Rāja

Yanamadala Branch:
Rudra
↓
Beta Rāja
m. Gaṇapamadevi
↓
Deva Rāja

THE KĀYASTHA CHIEFS

The Kāyastha chiefs, the most powerful rulers though nominally subordinate to the Kākatīyas held sway over a vast tract of land in Andhra from Panugal to Mārjavadi with capitals at Vallur and Ganḍikōṭa during the 13th century A.D. The Kāyastha armies, along with the Kākatīyas, marched into the territories, comprising some parts of present day Guntur, Kurnool, Cuddapah districts of Andhra Pradesh and North Arcot of Tamilanāḍu.[75]

The kingdom of Gangaya sāhiṇi extended from Pānugal identical with Pānugal of Nalgonda district to Mārjavāḍi which comprised within it Vallur and Mindigal (Kolar District). Thus the country which included in one of the important viceroyalities of the Kākatīya dominions ruled by the Kāyastha chiefs appears to have been a very large area extending over the modern Telugu districts of Cuddapah, Kurnool, Ananthapur, Nellore, Guntur and Ballary district in Karṇaṭaka.[76] The Karempuḍi inscription[77] dated A.D. 1264 shows that Jannigadeva, the successor of Gangaya ruled Mulikināḍu , Pottapināḍu and Ganḍikōṭa. Kammanāḍu was later added during the time of Tripurāri, who had his capital, first at Nellore and then shifted to Vallur.[78]

Ambadeva, the greatest of the Kāyasthas issued the largest number of records. The Attirala inscription dated A.D. 1287 of Ambadeva mentions his capital Vallūrupattaṇa, and the divisions of the kingdom *Ēruva, Pottapināḍu, Mulikanāḍu, Ganḍikōṭa Renāḍu, Pendekallu and Sakili*.[79] The following table give a list of components of the region.

Inscriptional Toponyms	*Identification*
Turumidlapāḍu	Pushpagiri, Cuddapah Tq., & Dist.[80]
Kongapuram	Pushpagiri, Cuddapah Tq., & Dist.[81]
Mottaikatta Alias Manumapuram	Moṭakatta Rāyachoti Tq., Cuddapah Dist.[82]
Recherla	Turumella, Giddalur Tq., Kurnool Dist.[83]
Rovulakolanu Botteru, Śivapuram	Brahmanapalli, Siddavattam Tq., Cuddapah Dist[84]
Boyalapalli, Redlapalli (K) Enukulakunta, Pulacheruvu GandraKōṭa, Anungurajupalli, Gangavaram.	Tripurantakam, Markapuram Tq., Prakasham Dist.[85]
Nandapura, Duggiyapattana Neypura, Marepalli	Durgi, Palnadu Tq., Guntur Dist.[86]
Ambāpuram, Lembaka	Attirala, Rājampet Tq.,

Uṭukūru, Śivapuram	Cuddapah Dist.[87]
Mudumala	Itigullapāḍu, Budevel Tq., Cuddapah Dist.[88]
Purundaluru,	Ponduluru, Rājampet Tq., Cuddapah Dist.[89]
Gangāpuram (Mulkinātiseema)	Gangavaram, Kamalapuram Tq., Cuddapah Dist.[90]
Penavāḍi, Renāḍu, Sirivolu, Pottapi Ēruva, Mulikināḍu, Julapalli, Gunjanageśvaram, Kulukunta.	Rājampet, Siddavattam Tq., Cuddapah Dist.[91]
Gundluru Marepakkināḍu	Gundluru, Rājampet Tq., Cuddapah Dist.[92]

All of the foregoing suggest that the Kāyastha kingdom included *Ēruva, Ganḍikōṭa, Kaivaram Kōṭa, Kammanāḍu, Mārjavāḍi-7000, Mottavāḍi, Mulikināḍu, Pānugal, Penḍekal, Pottapinaḍu, Renāḍu, and Sakali* regions.

Ēruvanāḍu: It consisted of some parts of the present Podili and Darsi taluqs in Nellore district, Badvel and Siddavattam taluqs in Cuddapah district and the Mārkapur taluq in Prakasham district.[93]

Ganḍikōṭa: It is the famous hill fort in Jammalamadugu taluq of Cuddapah district. It is situated to the right of Pinakini gandi and 1670 feet above the sea level. River Pinakini forms a natural trench with deep water around the fort. The Ganḍikōṭa seema consisted of the present Badvel, Jammalamaḍugu, Proddutūru and Kamalapuram taluqs of Cuddapah district.[94]

Kaivaram Kōṭa: The Karempudi inscription dated A.D. 1264 mentions that Jannigadeva ruled from Panugal to Kaivaram Kōṭa. Pānugal is in Nalgonda district and Kaivaram fort is situated in Chintamani taluq or Kōlar district in Karṇāṭaka state. This suggest that the region extended to Karnataka.[95]

Kammanāḍu: This region should have acquired its name from the river Gunḍlakamma. The Kammanāḍu comprised of the area around Narasaraopet taluq of Guntur district of the east of Srikakulam in Krishṇa district. Bapala taluq to the south of Velanāḍu. Gunḍlakamma on the west and the Mārkapur taluq in Prakasam district.[96]

Mārjavāḍi: When Gaṇapatideva was ruling, his minister *Ganḍapenḍara Gangaya sāhini* was the governor of the region extending from Pānugallu to Mārjavāḍi. It was a large division comprising of 7,000 *grāmas*, entire Cuddapah district and some parts of Chittoor and Nallore districts.[97]

Mottavāḍināḍu: It was one of the administrative division of the Kāyastha chiefs. The village of Pulacheruvu is stated to have been granted to the temple of Tripurantakeśvara at Tripurantakam by Gangaya *sāhini* for the merit of his master, king Gaṇapatideva. The division is also recorded in the Mallikārjuna Temple inscription at Śriśailam. From the identification of the place names mentioned in the Tripurantakam inscription referred to above, the division under the Kākatīyas can be identified with Mārkapur taluq of Prakasam district.[98]

Mulikināḍu: Lebaka inscription[99] of the time of Kākatīya king Pratāparudra refers to Mulikināḍu and the villages of Rājavōlu, Malayavemula and Perakapāḍu. On the basis of identification of the place names, and find spots of the inscriptions, this division may be identified with Kamalapuram taluq and parts of Cuddapah and Pulivendula taluqs of Cuddapah district of the present day.

Pedakallu: The Attirala inscription[100] dated A.D. 1287 mentions Pedekallu as a part of Ambadeva's kingdom. It was the headquarters of the administrative division called Pedakal *vishaya*. Pedakallu is in Dhone taluq of Kurnool district. from the proximity of *Ayije* 300, *Kanne* 300 and *Naravāḍi* 500 the division can be identified with a large portion of Kurnool district, comprising Koilakuntla, Nandyala and Banaganapalli taluqs.

Renāḍu: In an inscription[101] of A.D. 1313 belonging to the time of Kākatiya king Pratāparudra, Renāḍu is refered to alongwith its villages of Aruluru and Koilakuntla. The division appear to be a large one embracing parts of Cuddapah and Chittoor districts.

The Kāyastha chiefs were the most powerful among all the subordinates of the Kākatīyas. It is believed that the Kāyastha chiefs originally belonging to a class of warriors of Western India and migrated to Andhra in search of better opportunities. According to an inscription[102] discovered at Chityal in Nalgonda district different families like *Āre, Perika, Patkāri, Kāyast*ha etc., migrated from Mahārāśtra to Andhra and Kalinga countries during the period between 10th and 13th centuries A.D. The same inscription mentions that the early known member of Kāyastha family was Dhamsa. They were originally stationed at Pānugallu as governors of king Gaṇapatideva. Horsemanship and commanding of the cavalry were their specialized branches of war craft (as is denoted by their title *sāhini*) and most likely Gaṇapatideva brought them for the particular purpose of training his horses and to build the cavalry forces.[103] Gangaya sahini held the post of *turaga sadhanika* or the commander of the cavalry as mentioned in his Tripurantakam inscription.[104] The Kāyasthas claim themselves to be *kshatrīyas*. On the other hand, B.N. Sastri, opines that they were brāhmins. Some of the *danḍanāyakas* who were in the service of Gangas of Kalinga were Kāyasthas and they were brāhmans. Gangaya *Sāhini's* minister Nāmadeva, and his father Vāyi Panḍita were Brahmins.[105] It is possible that the Kāyasthas were *Kshatrīyas* since they were professional fighters and soldiers.

Gangaya Sāhini

Gangaya's several records attest to the extent of his kingdom and his ability in war-craft. His Gundluru inscription dated A.D. 1239[106] mentions his as *Ganḍapenḍara* Gangaya Sāhini who might have taken advantage of the chaotic political atmosphere prevailing in Palnāḍu and carved out a principality for himself with headquarters at Gundluru. His another record dated A.D. 1242 states him to be ruling over *Ēruva*-73 region with Krocherla as capital as a subordinate under Gaṇpatideva. It credits him with the title *Ariveera Brahmarākshasa*.[107] It suggests that by A.D. 1242 Kākati Gaṇapatideva vanquished Haiheyas of Palnāḍu, and merged the region under their control with his kingdom. After this Gaṇapatideva took the services of Gangayasāhini and made him his subordinate chief of Ēruva-73. Satrasala inscription[108] dated A.D. 1244 describes Gangayasāhini as *Padmaradaka* of Kākati Gaṇapatideva, *māṇḍalika brahmarākśasa, ganḍapenḍera, ativishamahāyarudha prouḍa rēka rēvanta and paśchimarāya dāmōdarasainya diśapaṭṭa.* It is significant that Gangaya described himself as devoted to the lotus feet of Gaṇpatideva.

The unique title *Paśchimarāya Dāmōdara Śainya diśapaṭṭa* borne first by this chief and later by his successors is quite significant in the sense that Gangaya Sāhini led a military expedition to the west on the command of his master Gaṇapatideva and forced Damōdara, the king of the region to run away from the battle field. The identify of king Dāmōdara of the west (*Paśchimarāya*) is different to ascertain. To the west of the Kākatīya kingdom lies the Seuṇa territory and the mutual enmity between the rulers of the two regions was an esatblished fact. The Seuṇa king Dāmōdara might be the same as Kannara mentioned in the Tripurantakam inscription dated A.D. 1250, and who ruled from A.D. 1247 to 1261.[108A] Judging from the title and date of the expedition led by Gangaya *sāhini* against the Seuṇa kingdom, it is not far fatched to identify Dāmōdara with Kannara. Gangaya sāhini's brother-in-law Ambadeva I and his three sons Jannigadeva, Tripurāri I and Ambadeva II who also bear this title might have taken part in this military compaign. It is likely that the Seuṇa king Kannara encroached on the Kākatīya territory and was repelled by the Kākatīya general as suggested by the word diśapatta. (i.e., who made the enemy flee). In recognition of his great military achievement, Gaṇapatideva elevated Gangaya Sāhini to the position of Mahāmanḍaleśvara and conferred on him several titles including his famous titles *chalamartigaṇḍa* as noticed in the Durgi inscription of A.D. 1251.[109]

Gangaya Sāhini expressed his gratitude to Gaṇapatideva by granting the village of Dupali to the temple of Śiva seeking the blessing of Lord Siva for the prosperity of Gaṇapatideva mahārāja. Among other titles mentioned in the *praśasti,* the title *Bāhattaraniyōgādhipati* and *Nāyakanarāyana* i.e., the chief of 72 branches of administration in the Kākatīya Kingdom is significant. It is evident that Gangaya held the highest position of *bāhattaraniyōgādhipati*, that is the president of the seventy two branches of administration in which the *Sēnādhyaksha, Mahāpradhāna, Pradhānas* were included. By virtue of this position he attained the status of *Mahāmaṇḍalēśvara* and became the ruler of a large region. An inscription from Durgi dated A.D. 1251[110] states that Gangaya's principality extended from Panugal to Mārjavāḍi. Not only that Gangaya appointed several ministers to assist him in the administration. For instance Sāranganāyaka was mentioned as one of the ministers of Gangaya. Gangaya not only enjoyed great prominance and influence in the council of Gaṇapatideva, but also influenced his policies towards the chiefs like Recherla Reḍḍi and other *māṇḍalikas, mahāsāmantas* and *sāmantas*.

Gangaya sāhini participated in several battles on behalf of his overlord whose ambition was to expand his empire. Tripurantakam inscription[111] dated A.D. 1254 describes Gangaya with the title *Rakkasa ganga·rasa diśapaṭṭa* denoting that he defeated the Vaidumba chief Rakkasa Ganga, ruler of Mārjavāḍi and Pottapināḍu regions.[112]

Manumasiddhi who was deprived of the territory in the Cuddapah district by Tikkarasa Ganga alias Rakkasa Ganga, a Vaidumba chief, appealed to Gaṇapatideva for help. Gaṇapatideva there upon sent armies against Tikkarasa Ganga under the territory Pottapinadu seized by him was taken back and restored to Manumasiddhi II. Tikkana's *Nirvachanōtthara Rāmāyana* provides valuable information in this regard.[113] Thus on account of this military achievement of Gangaya the Kāyastha chief became the ruler *Mārjavāḍi, Ēruva, Pallināḍu* and other regions with their capital at Valluru in the Cuddapah district. Thus Gangaya sāhini succeeded in wiping out the Telugu Chola rule in Pottapināḍu and brought the area under the control of the Kākatīyas. After subduing Rakkasa Ganga, Gangaya sahini made Somideva *Mahārāja* as his subordinate and installed him at Kalukada. Gangaya acquired the village Musampalli which was under the rule of his subordinate and gifted it to a Brāhmin.[114] In A.D. 1257 Gangaya and his wife granted Gangavaram in Mulikināḍu to the Śiva temple at Pushpagiri in the reign of Kākati Gaṇapatideva.[115] That was the last record of Gangaya's reign and he must have ruled upto A.D. 1258.

Gangaya Sāhini, his Relatives and Ministers

Among his relatives mention must be made of Ambakshmapati, brother-in-law of Gangaya. The titles held Ambakshmapati similar to those of Gangaya sāhini give the impression that Gangaya sahini and Ambakshmapati amicably ruled the kingdom together. This is the only inscrption of Ambakshmapati, and leads us to believe that he did not live after A.D. 1244 and might have been killed in some expedition.[116]

Ambakshmapati's three sons, Janniga deva, Tripurāri I, Ambadeva and daughter Padmabāi were brought up by Gangaya sāhini. Jannigadeva and Tripurāri I were right and left hands of Gangaya sāhini.[117] The title *mavankara*, held by Jannigadeva denote that he was very intimate to Gangaya sāhini. His ministers Sāranganāyaka, Vāyideva and Nāmadeva are mentioned in Nandalur inscription dated A.D. 1250.[118] The Tripurantakam inscription of Nāmadeva dated A.D. 1250.[119] records he was described as *suraguru samāna, sakala śāstra para varaka, mantrimānikya, niti chāṇakya, patikārya duranḍhara.* This suggest that he was a great teacher, well versed in *śāstras* and a Chāṇakya in polity.

The boundaries of Gangaya's principality included Pānugal in Nalgonda district and Mārjavāḍirājya of 7000 villages, which comprised of Vallur and Mindigal Kaivaramkōṭa. Thus the country which was included in one of the royalties of the Kākatīya dominions appears to have been a very large area comprising the modern Telugu districts of Cuddapah, Kurnool, Anantapur, Nellore and Guntur.[120] He had two capital cities one at Vallur and another at GandiKōṭa known as Manoradhapura.

Jannigadeva

Jannigadeva was the eldest son of Ambakshmapati and Chandubāi and nephew of Gangaya sāhini. He was well experienced in administration as he had already received the necessary training by Gangaya. He associated his brother Tripurāri I in carrying on the government as he inherited a large Kingdom from Gangaya. There are as many as 15 records of Jannigadeva available.[121] Janniga is mentioned as *mahāmaṇḍalēśvara, gaṇḍapeṇḍara jannigadēva mahārāja, brahmarākshasa gaṇḍapeṇḍara* etc. Some titles in his *praśasti* were *murarinārāyana, oddarāya abhimāna chūrakāra chalamarti-gaṇḍa*, besides *brahmarākshasa, gaṇḍapeṇḍara* etc. He served as the subordiante chief of Kākati Gaṇpatideva during the last days of his reign and Kākati Rudrama during the early days of her reign. He seems to have exercised great authority and enjoyed a privileged position in the court of Gaṇpatideva. He was described as *dakshina bhuja daṇḍa* to Gaṇpatideva in an inscription dated A.D. 1259.[122] He was a great warrior and took part in the war with the Pāṇḍyas at Muthukuru in the Nellore region. He also gave battle to the Pallava chief Siddayadeva *mahārāja* of Kanchi at Somasila on the bank of the river Pinākini. Thus Jannigadeva over powered the chiefs who probably showed signs of disobedience and helped the Kākatīya rulers in consolidating their authority. He ruled Pottapināḍu. Mulikināḍu and Gandikōṭa upto A.D. 1268 and was succeeded by his younger brother Tripurāri.

Tripurāri I

Tripurāri I, brother of Jannigadeva ruled only for a short period of three years from A.D. 1270-1272. During this period the Kāyastha kingdom remained intact and Tripurari owed allegiance to the Kākatīyas. His earliest record is from Potlapāḍu of Darsi taluq in Nellore district.[123] There are two inscriptions of the same period and they describe Tripurāri as *kākati kula tilaka rudradēva mahārāja charana nalina yugal samārādhaka,* which suggest his loyalty to Rudramadevi. The next inscription[124] from Alavulapāḍu dated A.D. 1272 recording Tripurāri's gifts for the increase of his life, health, wealth etc., incidentally mentions Kammanāḍu, Mulikināḍu, Pottapināḍu and Gandikōṭa which were governed by him. Tripurāri had his capital, first at Nellore and later at Vallur, Besides the usual titles of Kāyastha family *mahāmaṇḍalēśvara, brahmarākshasa, gaṇḍapeṇḍara*, he bore th epithets *samādhigata sakala rājyadhipatya mahā vibhava* i.e. who has acquired the lordship of the whole kingdom, and Mururāya *Jagadala* and *chalamartuganḍa*. Tripurāri I seems to have lost his life in one of the wars waged against his enemies, the Senagapūḍi family and Vipparla family. The titles *tripurāri dēvuni talagonḍu ganḍa* and the epithest Allu Tripurāri *mānamardana*, assumed by the members of the Senagapūḍi family and Vipparla family suggest that Tripurari was killed by them.[125] The Akkalareḍḍipalli inscription[126] dated A.D. 1283 records that one Goureśvarabāi built a temple for Lord Śiva and made gifts for the merit of Tripurāri I. Though it is difficult to identify this lady it may by assumed that she dedicated the temple to lord Śiva and made provision for worship in the temple to cherish the memory of Tripurāntaka.

Ambadeva

Tripurāri I was succeeded by his younger brother Ambadeva, the third nephew of Gangaya sāhini. He was the greatest of the Kāyasthas and issued a number of recrods. He was also the first Kāyastha ruler who setup the standard of revolt against the Kākatiyas and declared independence unlike the earlier Kāyastha chiefs.

Ambadeva's reign and his Political Relations

Ambadeva's records are found in continuous series from A.D. 1272 to 1305.[127] His capitals were Vallur and Gandikōṭa or Manorathapura. He was described as *mahāmanḍalēśvara*, *ganḍa-penḍara ambadeva mahārāja* and *ambadevarāju* in records of his son Tripurāri II. Ambadeva served the Kākatīya rulers Rudrama-devi and Pratāparudra but while his brother Janniga and Tripurāri-I were loyal to the Kākatīya rulers, he rebelled against them, made friends with their enemies and tried to carveout an independant principality for himself. Only the Śivapuram record[128] dated A.D. 1290 mentions him as the subordinate of Kākatīyas rulers. Through out his career, as observed from his other records he maintained an independent stance, being ambitious to carve-out his own kingdom. His constant engagements in warfare with his neighbours and the failure to mention the overlord in his records, indicate his defiant attitude towards the queen Rudramadevi.[129]

An analysis of his lengthy Tripurantakam inscription[130] dated A.D. 1290 gives us a list of his exploits. The first enemy whom he vanquished according to the Tripurantakam epigrapy was a chief named Śripati Gaṇapati who bore the title *Rāyasahasra malla*. The chief was identical with Gurindala Gaṇapati mentioned in the Nila Gangavaram inscription[131] dated A.D. 1268 of Ambadeva. Śripati Gaṇapati was then ruling at Gurindala or Gurijala in Guntur district, obviously as vassel of Rudrama. The circumstances under which he came into conflict with Ambadeva are not known. It may be assumed that Ambadeva, an ambitious chief desired to extent his territory by way of penetrating into other regions like Guntur. Whatever the reason for the conflict it seems certain that Śripati was worsted in the battle in A.D. 1273 and his possessions along with the title *Rāyasahasra malla* were taken away by Ambadeva. In this conflict Ambadeva seems to have fought with many of the Seventy five *nāyakas* of the Kākatīyas whose heads he claims to have cut off in battle. These *nāyakas* might have been sent by Kākati Rudrama to punish Ambadeva who killed them and worshipped with their lotus like heads the goddess of anger that came out of his eyes. He killed several chiefs who attacked him at a time.

Then Ambadeva proceeded against Manu Mallideva of the Ēruva region who was faithful to Rudramadevi. Earlier a branch of the main Chōḍa kings of Orayuru ruled over the *Ēruva* region. It is not known whether the *Ēruva* region extended on both sides of the river Krishna. It is possible that the region is called after the *Ēru* in Telugu. As Ambadeva could not tolerate it, he marched against him and killed him in the battle field. As a mark of his victory Ambadeva assumed the title Ēruva *mallidēvuni tala goṇḍu gaṇḍa* i.e., the destroyer of the head of the Ēruva Mallideva, as testified to by his Tripurantakam inscrption[132] dated A.D. 1287 mentions the epithet *ēruva bhudeva parasainya kodandagaṇḍa*, which also indicates his victory over Mallideva. Judging from epigraphical evidence it may be assumed that the conflict between Ambadeva and Ēruva Chōḷas was over by A.D. 1287. The legend on the coins of Ambadeva *Ēruvadisapaṭṭa* signified that he scattered in several directions the army of Ēruva rāja.[134] This was an important victory for Ambadeva and so is recorded in his inscriptions and coins.

Next, he is credited with the defeat of Kōṭa chief bearing the titles *uttama gaṇḍa, gaṇḍaragaṇḍa* and *gaṇḍabhērunḍa,* and appropriated his titles. This Kōṭa chief is stated to be ruling the eastern part of Tripurantakam and Palnāḍu.[135] He may be identified with Bhima IV who was the ruler of Dharanikōṭa in A.D. 1265. He was obviously a contemporary of Ambadeva. As the kōta chiefs reaffirmed their allegiance to the Kākatīyas, Ambadeva wanted to supress them. The Tripurantakam epigraph[136] states that Ambadeva vanquished Kesavadeva, Somideva and Allugangu. Kesevadeva and Somideva were Vaidumba chiefs with their capital at Kalukada. Allu Ganga was the father of the Telugu Choḷa king Gangayadeva, who ruled over Jagadapi Gutti in Ananthapur district around A.D. 1322. Kesavadeva and Somideva tried to break away from the Kāyasthas and extend their rule as the inscriptional eveidence indicate. The YellaReḍḍipalli epigraph[137] dated A.D. 1267 records that Somideva extended his principality by adding *Honnavādi*-90 of *Mulikināḍu* and *Peda Kallentu*-800 with his capital at Vallur. The Gundlur inscription[138] dated A.D. 1284 records the extension of his rule upto Pottapinadu. By the time of Ambadeva, Somideva must have occupied Honnavāḍi and Pottapināḍu and ruled with his capital at Vallur. This posed a series threat to the political ambitions of Ambadeva, who consequently lead an expedition against Somideva and other Kalukada chiefs. Somideva and Kesavadeva appealed to Alluganga, the Telugu Choḷa ruler of Gutti for help. In the battle ensued all these three chiefs were vanquished by Ambadeva. Ambadeva's Attirala recorded[139] dated A.D. 1287 confirms this event, and refers to the extent of his kingdom which includes Pottipināḍu, Mulikināḍu, Pedakallu. The capital is stated to be Valluru paṭṭṇa. This suggests that Ambadeva after defeating his enemies extended his kingdom. Ambadeva strengthened Gandikōṭa, a strong hill fort on the bank of the river Pennar. Next, Ambadeva gave battle to Mallikārjunapati who was considered an enemy of Brahmins and gods[140] Some identify this Mallikārjuna, as an Ēruva Chola chief, for the inscription of Peddadandalur[141] dated A.D. 1294 of Ambadeva described him as *Vairivira Ēruva Mallikārjuna,* instead of the usual Vairīvira Mallikārjuna. Some scholars identify him as Mallikārjunapati, the Kākatīya general of Pānugallu region[142]

What ever may be the identity of this Mallikārjuna, Ambadeva instead of killing him in the battle field because he did not deserve it deprived him of his seven limbs or *Saptāngas* which mean the seven constituent parts of a kingdom namely, *Avani, Amātya, Suhṛit, Kōsa, Rāśtra, Durga and Bala* (King, Minister, friend, treasury, territory, fort and force). The Attirala inscription dated A.D. 1287 refers to Ambadeva's victory and the assumption of the title Mallikārjuna *māna madamardana* which means the humilition of Mallikārjuna. At any rate Ambadeva must have subdued this Mallikārjuna by A.D. 1287.

The boastful praise of Ambadeva in Chandupaṭla inscription[143] dated A.D. 1289 *Sarvam Āndhramahipattin rana mukhe jeta yeso labdhavan* is significant. For it indicates that he conquered all the kings of Andhra including the queen Rudramadevi. That Ambadeva got the support of all the chiefs of the Kākatīya enemies, the Seuṇas and Pāṇḍyas in his enterprise is clear. Ambadeva next availed the opportunity to extent his sway in the East as far as Nellore when Vijayagaṇḍa Gōpāla of the Telugu of Nellore died in about A.D. 1279.[144] The Telugu Choḷa chief Manumagaṇḍa Gōpāla who was driven out of his kingdom by Vijayagaṇḍa Gōpala appealed to Ambadeva to restore him to his throne. So Ambadeva responding to his appeal marched against the Pāndya general Kopperunjinga who was guarding the Nellore Kingdom, killed him in a battle and rainstead Manumagaṇḍa Gōpāla on the throne of Nellore some time before A.D. 1282. Kopperunjinga it may be noted was a ally of Vijayagaṇda Gōpāla. The Pāṇḍaya made fresh attempts to regain the lost fortunes in the Southern Andhra under the leadership of Jatavarman Pāṇḍya,

Mārvarman Sundar Pāṇḍya and Māravarma Kulasekhara Pāṇḍya marched into Pottapināḍu in A.D. 1282-3 probably accompanied by Somideva and Kesevadeva, the Vaidumba chiefs of Kalukaḍa., who had earlier been driven away by Ambadeva. Ambedeva collecting all his forces attacked the Pāṇḍayas and defeated them finally in about A.D. 1286[145] But inscriptional evidence indicate that Ambadeva was not completely successful in Suppressing the Pāṇḍyas. We find the inscriptions of the Pāṇḍya kings in Pottapināḍu between A.D. 1285 and A.D. 1292. In Ranganāyaka temple at Nellore and Nandaluru, inscriptions[146] (undated) of Sundara Pāṇḍya II. Jatavarma Sundara Pāndya were found belonging to his 10th regnal year.[147] In Vepaka of Rājampet Taluq, there is a record of Māravarma Sundara Pāṇḍya raised in his 13th regnal year. So, it is certain that some Pāndaya kings ruled Pottapināḍu during the period between A.D. 1285 and 1292. If Ambadeva had completely vanquished the Pāṇḍyas there is no possibility of their inscriptions being discovered in Pottapināḍu belonging to the period referred to above. Hence it is pertinent to conclude that Ambadeva did not completely wipe out the Pāṇḍyas from Pottapināḍu. The other rulers who thought that prudence is better than valour like the Yādavas sought his friendship because of their enimity with the Kākatīya rulers. They made gifts of horses and money to express their friendship and admiration of his prowess.[148] Thus Ambadeva achieved astounding success and established himself as a powerful chief. By A.D. 1290 he proclaimed indepence and as a mark of gratitude to his favourite diety Tripurantakadeva he made lavish gifts. He even got the inscriptions inscribed in his own name without making any reference to the Kākatīya queen Rudramadevi. The Attirla inscription explicitly states that he was the ruler of a vast area consisting of the regions of Gandikōṭa, Mulikināḍu, Renāḍu, Pendakallu, Sakili, Ēruva and Pottapi. Pratāparudra, the successor of Rudramadevi realised that of Ambadeva was not overpowered and suppressed, the Kākatīya kingdom would lose a major chunk of territory and the prestige of the kingdom also would suffer. Pratāparudra came to the conclusion that it was not wise to tolerate a rebellious and powerful chief like Ambadeva. So he made preparations to reconquer all the regions seized by Ambadeva.

Fall of Ambadeva

Dr. P.V. Parabrahma sastry gives a graphic account of the fall of Ambadeva thus: "Pratāparudra's immediate responsibility was to wipe off the disgrace caused to the family and kingdom by rebellion of the Kāyastha chief Ambadeva. He therefore lost no time in consolidating the military of the kingdom which lost it vigour during the previous years. The *Nāyaṅkara* units were reorganised and set on march agaisnt the traitor. Being fully award of this treat to the security of his newly acquired kingdom Ambadeva took necessary steps on its defence. No withstanding the series of victories on several fields of battle he felt that his army was decidedly no match to fight with the Kākatīya forces. As hinted in his Tripurantakam record he entered into alliance with the Seunas in the North and the Pāṇḍyas in the South".[149] The Nilagangavaram inscrption[150] states that the Pāṇḍyas came to the rescue of Ambadeva by sending elephants and horses. Kumāra Rudradeva sensing that a war with Ambadeva would result in a war with his powerful allies organized a three pronged attack simultaniously on the territories of Ambadeva and his allies. In the A.D. 1291 an army was despatched to Tripurantakam under the command of Manuma Gannaya, son of Kolani Soma mantri and his cousin Annayadeva, son of Induluri Peda Gannaya mantri. Though unfortunately no details of the conflict in this region are available, it is certain that Ambadeva was defeated and forced to retreat southwards to Mulikināḍu. The latest record of Ambadeva at Tripurantakam dated A.D. 1291 and the earliest Kākatīya record of Indulūri Annayadeva at the same place is dated A.D. 1291[151] There is gap of two months between these records. Thus the rule of Ambadeva over Tripurantakam and its neighbourhood disappeared within a short period of two months. Though some records of his son Tripurāri are available in the Cuddapah region, they do not bear any testimony to the revival of Kāyastha authority.

Ambadeva's Ministers

We hear of Gangadeva, son of Immaḍideva and *Sarvādhikāri* of Ambadeva from the epigraph of Lebaka.[152] The Attirala inscription[153] dated A.D. 1287 speaks of his Prime Minister

Ghoderāya Gangadeva. The Brahmanapalli inscription[154] dated A.D. 1290 also mentions him. It is said that Gangadeva made many administrative refroms in the kingdom of Ambadeva, got the tanks and canals dug and improved irrgational facilities. He was involved not only in secular affairs, but also in religious matters. He was known as a great Śaiva preceptor, who established *Ghoderāya gurupīṭha*. He was the guru of Kondavīti Prōlaya Vēmareḍḍi who was the founder of Addanki kingdom with the help and advice of Ghoderāya Gangadeva. According to M.Somasekhera Sarma Gangadeva took the forefathers of Vēma into the service of Ambadeva and appointed them to responsible positions in the region of Tripurantakam.[155] The Attirala inscription dated A.D. 1287 refers to Nideva Mahārāju, a minister of Ambadeva. One of the important subordinate of Ambadeva was Khadeva who is mentioned in the Tripurantakam inscrption dated A.D. 1291. Savadara Ambaya Reḍḍi was also one of his subordinates mentioned in Tripurantakam inscription dated A.D. 1288.[156]

Tripurāri II

Tripurāri, the son and successor of Ambadeva came to power after his father in A.D. 1302. Ambadeva had two sons and a daughter. The Pattapurāya village inscrption[157] records a grant for the prosperity of Ambadeva and Jannigadeva Mahārāja. This Janniga must have been Ambadeva's eldest son. He must have named his sons after the names of his brothers Jannigadeva and Tripurāri for whom he had great resepct. When Janniga was killed in some battle, Tripurāri II must have succeeded his father, Ambadeva.[158] Three records from Lebaka,[159] Kadapayapalli and Varikunta all dated A.D. 1304 mention Tripurarideva II. The Lebaka inscription mentions his titles *mahāmanḍalēśvara*, *mānḍalika brahmarākshasa*, *ganḍa penḍara*, suggesting that he exercised considerable authority. Tripurārideva *Mahārāju* ruled Mulikināḍu with Vallur as his capital. The Varikunta inscrption[160] records the grant of Tripurarideva, son of *mahāmanḍalēśvara mānḍalika brahmarākshasa* and *ganḍapenḍara* Ambadeva. It seems Tripurāri II did not rule the Kāyastha kingdom for long.

For the Kākatīya general Mahārāya Patta *Sāhini* Somaya Nāyaka led an expedition on Kāyastha kingdom and after defeating Tripurari II merged it with the Kākatīya kingdom. This supposition is based on inscriptional evidence. The Devigudi inscription[161] dated A.D. 1309 records the reign of Mahārāja Pattasāhini Somanāyaka. The Kanarla inscription[162] dated A.D. 1308 records the grant of Rāyapatta Sāhini Somaya Nāyaka who ruled Gandikōṭa, Mulikināḍu, Penampadi, Pottapināḍu, Pedakallu, Natavāḍi *vishaya* as the viceroy of Kākati Pratāparudra. Obviously the Kāyastha rule ended by A.D. 1308 and the Kāyastha territories were annexed to the Kākatīya kingdom.

Accoding to one opinion Tripurari II became a vassal of Pratāparudra after Ambadeva's defeat, but later on tried to assert his independence, when Pratāparudra was totally involved in repulsing the Muslim invasions. Pratāparudra was also engaged in the suppression of the revolts in the Southern part of his kingdom. After suing for peace with Mālik Naib, the deputy of Sultan Alla-ud-din in A.D. 1310, Pratāparudra took concerted measures to suppress the rebels and bring back the southern districts under his control. He sent an army with Juttaya leṅka at its head against the Kāyastha chief, whom the Kākatīya general defeated and captured Gandikōṭa. Pratāparudra appointed Gonkayareḍḍi as the governor of Mulkināḍu and other adjoining place with its headquarters at Gandikōṭa.[163]

In the annals of the Kākatīya history, the Kāyastha chiefs had played a prominent role both as loyal subordinates and traitors. Of these five rulers, *Gangayasāhini* and Ambadeva were enterprising warriors. The Kāyastha family ruled for a period of 69 years from A.D. 1239-1308. Their rise was as fast as was their fall. Within this short period, they achieved greatness unequalled of any other subordinates of the Kākatīya rulers. Their reign of 69 years was really eventful.

The Genealogy of the Kāyastha chiefs

Dhamsa
↓
- Gangaya sāhini m. Kamala Bai
- Chandala Devi or Chandu Bai m. Ambakshmapati
  ↓
  - Jannigadeva m. Goureswarabai
  - Tripurari I
  - Ambadeva
    ↓
    Tripurari II

THE CHĀLUKYAS OF NIḌADAVOLE

The Chālukyas of Niḍadavole held sway over portions of the Krishṇa, West Godavari, Nalgonda and Warangal districts from the last quater of the 11th century to the first quater of the 14th century. The marriage of Kākatīya queen Rudramdevi, with prince Virabhadra, son of Induśekara of this family elevated its status among other contemporary local chiefs. Throught their rule they were under the suzerainty of the Chālukyas of Jananatha-pura, then the Velanāṭi chiefs and lastly the Kākatīyas depending on the political fortunes of the rulers.

Gaṇapatideva after the subjugation of the Kolanu region proceeded against the Chālukyas of Niḍadavole where the *Mandalika* named Indusekhara was ruling. The inscriptions from Juttiga dated A.D. 1257 and Palakol dated A.D. 1264 of the period of Virabhadra, husband of Rudrama indicate the location of the seat of these chiefs in West Godavari.[164] Gaṇapatideva offered his daughter Rudrama in marriage to Indusekara's son Virabhadra in order to make the Chālukyas of Niḍadavole, that is the family of Induśekhara, political allies of the Kākatīya rulers.

The Chālukya chiefs of Niḍadavole were the descendants of Yuddhmalla II, Chālukya chief of Veṅgi who ruled over the coastal Andhra for more than four centuries and a half.[165] It was during the reign of Mahadeva, that the Kākatīya forces invaded the coastal country. Kakati Gaṇapatideva's commanders Recherla Rudra

Reddi and Rājanāyaka took in active part in this compaign. It is not unreasonable to think that the petty chiefs in these areas who were disturbed by this campaign, might have transferred their allegiance to the Kākatiya conquerors and Mahadeva also accepted the suzerainty of the Kākatīyas.[166] So we persue the genealogy and political history of the Chālukyas of Niḍadavole since the times of Mahadeva who accepted the overlordship of the Kākatiyas.

Mahadeva I

Mahadeva I is the first prominent ruler of the Chālukyas of Niḍadavole. There are three inscriptions of his period, one from Taḍikalapūḍi of the West Godavari district and two from Bezawāda. One of his inscriptions from Bezawada[167] describes him as *mahāmanḍaleśvara siddhipura-varādhiśvara*. The later epithet suggest his conquest over Siddhipura and it is likely that he extended his conquests to *shaṭsahasravāni*. This Siḍḍhipura, evidently the place where he vanquished some of his enemies, is identified with Siddhapuram in Taḍepalligudem taluq of West Godavari district. Like the kings of the earlier period, he must have been loyal to the Chālukyas of Jananathapura and after the incursion of Kākatīya forces into the Eastern coastal belt he might have shifted his loyalty to the Kākatīyas.[168]

Vengiśvara II and Induśekhara I

Mahadeva I had two sons Vengiśvara II and Induśekhra I Vengiśvara II succeeded his father Mahadeva I in A.D. 1233. He issued only two records. One is from Denduluru[169] dated A.D. 1238 and the other is from Kumaradevam dated A.D. 1250[170] both in west Godavari district. So he appear to have ruled from A.D. 1233 to A.D. 1250 and in the later period of his rule, his brother Indusekhara I joined him as co-regent, between A.D. 1238 and A.D. 1255.[171]

The Kākatīyas had tried several times to penetrate into the Kalinga*seema* and were once even forced to retreat to the south of the Godavari by Ganga king Ananaga Bhima III.[172] Bhima even extended his influence in the Veṅgi country also. The Veṅgi region was ruled by Kolanu chiefs who had their head quarters at Kolanu or Sarasipuri in the West Godavari district. *Mahāmanḍalēśvara* Kolani Kesavadeva ruled this region from A.D. 1192 to 1228. It appears that Kolani chief Kesavadeva with the active support of Aniyanka Bhima, the Eastern Ganga king repelled the Kākatīyas incursion. There is no positive evidence in Vengi before A.D. 1240. The references to Gaṇapati's conquest of Kaliga, noticed in the Gaṇapeśvaram, Upparalli and Moṭupalli inscriptions no doubt indicate his attempt to subjugate Kalinga and Veṅgi countries right from A.D. 1212, but they did not fetch him any material benefit. Conquest of Kolanu might have taken place before A.D. 1240 that is after the death of Kolanu Kesavadeva. Whose inscriptions are noticeable upto A.D. 1231. The provenance of the inscriptions of Kākatīya general Mallala Hemadri Reḍḍi dated A.D. 1237 in the Drāksharāmam temple supports this view.[173] So, in order to lay his hold over the Eastern coastal belt firm, Gaṇapatideva sought to secure the political allegiance of the Chālukyas of Niḍadavole by offering his daughter Rudrama to the Chālukya Prince Virabhadra, younger son of Induśekhara I. Even for the Chālukyan chiefs Veṅgiśvara II and Induśekhara I this matrimonial alliance with the powerful Kākatīyas seemed profitable.

As a matter of fact they had been trying to strengthen their political power and in view of this, Induśekhara I offered his daughter Anyamamba in marriage to Kōna Bhima of the Haiheya family. At the same time the Chālukyan kingdom of Jananāthapura to whom the Niḍadavōle family owed allegiance and under whom it gained political power came to an end. Hence it became necessary for Veṅgiśvara I and Induśekhara II to strengthen their position by foregoing direct links with powers like the Haiheyas and the Kākatīyas. This wise step, enabled them to continue rule for one more century and created opportunities for them to enter the tracts of Teleṅgāna.[174] It seems Veṇgiśvara II was issueless and Induśekara had two sons Mahadeva II and Virabhadra and a daughter Anyamadevi by his wife Udayambika.

Mahadeva II

There is only one inscription from Juttiga dated A.D. 1255

which records a grant for the merit of Mahadeva. So it seems Mahadeva might have ruled for a short period after the death of his father, either cojointly with Virabhadra or independently. The former assumption is more probable as there are evidences for the rule of Virabhadra from A.D. 1250 onwards.[175] He had four sonsViriyāladeva, Induśekhara II (by queen Lakkāmba), Induśekhara III (by queen Bhimimdevi) and Pṛithvivallabha and a daughter Odaya Mahadevi who was given in marriage to *Mahāmanḍalēśvara* Kōna Gaṇapatideva of Haiheya family. Thus matrimonial alliances with the Haiheya family were continued.

Virabhadra II

The illustrious prince of the Chālukyas of Niḍadavole, Virabhadra seems to have been active even during his father's reign. There are three inscriptions of his period from Juttiga,[176] Pālakollu[177] and Narsapur.[178] The Juttiga inscription dated A.D. 1259 records the marriage of Virabhadra to Rudramadevi. We do not know what happened to Virabhadra in his last years. The Pālakollu inscription dated A.D. 1275 of his sister Anyamadevi does not refer to him. But in A.D. 1266[179] his mother Udayāmbika offered gifts in the temple of Kshiīrārāma at Pālakollu for the *puṇya samprāpti* of Virabhadra. Virabhadra and Rudrama had only three daughters Mummadāmma, Ruyyama and Rudrama and had no sons. Mummadāmba was married to prince Mahadeva, Ruyyama to Indulūri Annayadeva, and Rudrama to Yādava prince Ellanadeva. Because Virabhadra had no male issue his nephews became successors to his political fortune.

Vīrāyadeva

As the Chālukyas of Niḍadavole proved their loyalty to the Kākatīya rulers they seemed to have refrained from intervening in the affairs of succession. Vīrāyadeva succeeded his uncle Virabhadra to the Chālukyan throne probably in A.D. 1266. According to Kolanupalli[180] record dated A.D. 1311 of his son Rudradeva. It records the gift of taxes levied on certain communities of the village for the worship and offering to god Mallanāthadeva by Rudradeva, son of Vīrāyadeva. His rule might have continued upto A.D. 1279, the earliest date for Induśekhara II.

Induśekhara II

Induśekhara II succeeded his brother Virāyadeva around A.D. 1279 the date of his younger brother Prithvi vallabha. The Kolanupāka inscription dated A.D. 1279[181] suggests that Indusekhara accepted the overlordship of Kākatīya rulers and served as the governor of Niḍadavote. The Uttareśvara[182] copper plate grant dated A.D. 1290 and Onapalli[183] grant dated A.D. 1292 reflect the strong political affinities between this family and the Kākatīyas. The power of the Chālukyas of Jananathapura under whose umbrella Niḍadavole family flourished until then, came to an end during the reign of Induśekhara I. In this period the Kākatīya king Gaṇapatideva made efforts to bring the entire Andhra under his banner. The Chalukya chiefs probably realised that they could not survive individually in contemporary politics without the support of a big power, and as a Virabhada's marriage brought them nearer to the Kākatīyas they readily accepted the supremacy of Gaṇapatideva. Owing to his close contacts with the rulers of the Kākatīya family, it is possible that Indusekhara II was entrusted with some important political position.[184] It seems he was placed in-charge of Kollipāka region for some time.[185] Induśekhara II's rule was probably limited to the areas around Taṇuku in West Godavari district, and almost all the villages mentioned in his grants are identified in the same vicinity.

After Induśekhara II, his brother Prithvi Vallabha entitled *sarvalōkāsrāya vishṇu vardhana* seems to have ruled the kingdom for a short period, as per the evidence of Mullapūḍi[186] record dated A.D. 1297. An inscription at Pālakollu dated A.D. 1300[187] refers to one Toleti Induśekhara, whom Kolluru Suryanarāyana[188] identifies as Induśekhara III, sone of Mahadeva II. The prefix Toleru is the name of his capital, situated in the present Bhimavaram taluq of the West Godavari district.

During this period a grave danger shook all the Hindu kingdoms, which made its appearance on the frontiers of Teleṅgāṇa. The Seuna capital Devagiri was seized in A.D. 1295 by Alla-ud-din. The Kākatīya ruler, the farsighted Pratāparudra anticipated such danger from the Muslims and hence reorganised the defences of his kingdom, and as a part of it he might have invited Chālukya chiefs of Niḍadavole to attend to that work. Being faithful subordinates and relatives, these chiefs moved to Teleṅgāṇa to save the situation. Their migration must have been the cause for the absence of their records in their native home in West Godavari district. The records of the Kolanu chiefs who served as loyal supporters to the Kākatīyas are also not found from this period. From that it is evident that all the trusted generals and loyal subordinates went to Orugallu to strengthen the defence of the Kākatīya kingdom. The Kolanupalli record[189] dated A.D. 1311 of Rudradeva, the elder son of Vīrāyadeva, and grand son of Mahadeva II, who was in the service of Kākati Prataparudra testify to this. It is possible that the support of these chiefs continued till the downfall of Kākatīya power.

In the absence of any clear evidence it can be assumed that the Chālukya chiefs of Niḍadavole also were destroyed along with their overlord Pratāparudra in the battle with Muslims in A.D. 1323. It appears, they seemed to have established small principalities in the region of Teleṅgāṇa with capitals at places like Tallapalli.[190] It was their last attempt to revive their political power, but they were vanquished by the sons of Singa I, the Velama chief and massacred in A.D. 1361.[191] That was the end of the Chalukya chiefs of Niḍadavole.

The Chālukya chiefs of Niḍadavole

- Vengīśvara I
  - Malla
    - Veṅgi Gonka I
      - Ayyapa II
        - Gaṇapati
        - Manuma Gonka
      - Mahadeva I
        - Vengisvara II
        - Induśekara I
          - Mahadeva II
            - Vīrāya deva
            - Induśekara II
          - Virabhadra m. Kakati Rudrama
            - Mummadamma m. Mahadeva
            - Ruyyama m. Indulūri Annaya
            - Rudrama m. Ellanadeva (Yadava prince)
          - Anyamadevi
  - Veṅgi Ayyapa I
  - Daughter ?

THE GONA CHIEFS

The Gonas or Konās, of Haiheya descent, ruled over tracts around Raichur, with capital at Vardhamanupura (i.e. Vaddemani of Nagarkurnool Taluq in Mahabubnagar district) and they owed fealty to the Kākatīyas during 12th -13th centuries A.D.M. Rama Rao states that Gannaya Reḍḍi ruled Vardhamanupura, where as Vithalanātha ruled over the Raichur and Ballary district.[192]

The Raichur inscription dated A.D. 1294 states that during the reign of Gona Ganna Reḍḍi, Vittalanātha conqured Adavāni, Tumbalam, Manuva and Haluva forts and entered the city of Raichur.[193] He erected a strong fort at Raichur to protect the inhabitant of Raichur. It is obvious that Gona Vīthala must have wrested the Krishṇa-Tungabhadra doab from the Yādavas of Devagiri. The fiefdom of Gona chiefs consisted of Nagarkurnool, Mahabubnagar, Gadwal, Aiza taluqs of Mahabubnagar district, some part of Raichur in Karṇātaka state, and Adoni taluq of Kurnool district. They owed loyalty to the Kākatīyas. In accordance with the traditions of the Haiheyas of Kona manḍala, Panchadharala and Palnadu, the Haiheyas of Vardhamanupura claimed descent from Kārtaviryārjuna and as in the case of the first two dynasties, had the prefix Gona or Kona prefixed to their names. The fact that they claimed descent from *Kārtaviryā* suggest that they were Kshatriyas. Consequently Gona or Kona became the family name of the Haiheyas as in the case of the Panchadharala Haiheyas, and interestingly their names ended with Reḍḍi and *Nayani*. The relationship of these Haiheyas to other Haiheyas dynasties is not known. The Gona had some political achievements to their credit and had marriage alliances with the Malyāla family, another powrful feudatory family in the Kākatīya dominions.[194]

The *Ranganātha Rāmāyana (Dvīpada)* composed by Gona Buddha Rāja, furnishes the genealory[195] in its prologue. The earliest known historical member of the family was Gona Kāṭa bhupati. The genealogy is as follow :

Gona Kāṭa Bhupati
↓
Budha I
↓
Vithala or Ganna
↓
Buddha II
↓
Kācha | Vithala

Gona Kāṭa, one of the ministers of Gaṇapatideva who is mentioned in an epigraph from Kāñchi dated A.D. 1255 of Allu Tikka Mahārāja Ganḍagōpala deva is identical with Gona Kāṭa.[196] According to Bothpur inscriptions[197] of Kakati Gaṇapatideva dated A.D. 1259 and A.D. 1263 respectively, Gona Buddha had a daughter Kuppāmbika alias Kuppasānamma and her husband Malyāla Gunḍa was a general of Gaṇapatideva. According to the Bothpur inscription dated A.D. 1277,[198] Kuppāmbika constructed Śiva temple in her husband's name after the death of her husband, which also suggest that Malyāla Gunḍa was a devotee of Śiva. She is also said to be the daughter of Buddhaya of Gona family, the renowed author of *Ranganātha Rāmāyana*. Interestingly, when she made gifts to the temple, her three sons and her brothers Mallya, Budhaya, Vithalaya were present. In the *Uttarākānḍa* of the *Ranganātha Rāmāyana*, Buddhaya mentioned that Kācha and Vithala were the sons of Buddha, and their grand father was Ganna Reḍḍi or Ganna Kshitindra. The Raichur inscription dated A.D. 1294[199] credits Vithalanatha, son of Buddha with the capture of the forts of Advani, Tumbalam, Manuva, Haluva and the city of Raichur while Gona Ganna Reḍḍi was ruling from Vardhamanupura. M. Ram Rao's[200] observation is valuable in this regard "when Kākati Rudrāmba and Pratāparuda ruled around A.D. 1290, the Raichur doab and Kurnool district were dense with thick forest which was cleared and reclaimed for cultivation by the feudatories of the Kākatīyas kingdom. Gannayareḍḍi ruled Vardhamanupura, Vithalanatha, Raichur and Bellary districts and Kāṭa Reḍḍi and his son Immaḍi Kāṭa Reḍḍi, the Raichur doab. All of them were the feudatories of the Kākatīyas. In this work of clearing and reclaiming forest lands Immaḍi Kāṭa Reḍḍi was helped by Buddha Reḍḍi or Polavi Reḍḍi, a resident of Aija village. The Kākatīya general Immadi Kāṭa Reḍḍi was very much pleased with Buddha Reḍḍi's services and used his influence to obṭain Mānuva, Beludoni, Raichur, Mosalakallu, Ālampur, Aḍoni, *simas* from his king, Pratāparudra in A.D. 1290. From then Buddha Reḍḍi and his descendents were called the Aija nāḍa Gouḍs.

M. Somasekhara Sarma arrived at the following genealogical table, based on the prologue of the *Ranganātha Rāmāyana*.[201]

Gona Kāṭa Bhupati (A.D. 1250)

↓

Rudra Narendra (A.D. 1275)

↓

? (A.D. 1300)
↓
Buddha I (A.D. 1325)
↓
Vithalanatha (A.D. 1350)
↓
Buddha II (A.D. 1375)

Ārudra in his eminent work on Telugu literature *Samagrāndhra Sāhityam*[202] Provided the following genealogical table of the Gona family thus

Gona Kāṭa I
↓
Rudra
↓
(Name not known)
↓
- Buddha I
  - ↓ Gannaya
    - ↓ Buddhaya III
      - ↓ Kāchaya
      - ↓ Pina Vittaya II (The author of *Uttara Rāmāyana*)
  - ↓ Kuppama
  - ↓ Mallaya
  - ↓ Buddhaya II
  - ↓ Vitthala I
    - ↓ Buddhaya IV (The author of *Pūrva Rāmāyana*)
- Kāṭa II (1250-58)
  - ↓ Gunḍaya

Thus different accounts were presented to determine the genealogy of the Gona family, but the attempt of Ārudra (as given above) appears to be sound in the light of the knowledge available now. Ārudra gave a more detailed account of the genealogy of the family based on the inscriptions referring to Kāṭa, Gannaya,

Kuppama, Vithala are available. M.Somasekhara Sarma based his account of the family on an inscription from the Tiruppakkui, Kāñchi taluq dated A.D. 1250-58 and suggested that Gona Kāta was the founder of the family. Kuppama's Bothpur inscription states that she was the daughter of Buddha and her brothers were Mallaya, Buddhaya, Vithala, Kāṭaya's son Gunḍaya (perhaps he was adopted by Kāṭaya). Vithala who was the brother of Kuppama was described as *Rājya rakshāmaṇi* and credited with the capture of several forts. Buddha, the author of *Ranganātha Rāmāyana*.

Gannaya

Ganna or Ganna Reḍḍi eldest son of Buddha I was an illustrious member of the family. His many titles speak of his valour and political victories. The fact that he was one of the important Kākatīya feudatories and generals is attested by the epithets he bore *Kākatīya Kāṭaka sannaha* and *Rudradeva dakshiṇa bhuja danḍa* etc.[203] Obviously, Ganna's political victories were achieved during the closing years of Rudrama's reign. His title *Ladapi Kuvarakunpedara* is significant as it indicates that he led a successful expedition against Lata country. Ganna seems to have come into conflict with the Telugu Chōḷas, won a victory and assumed the title *Choḷajagajalavira*. Ganna claims to have cutoff the heads of the rulers of Kosagi, Moili, Uppula Manni, Akkināyaka and the *nāyakas* like Madipalli Kachayanāyaka, Kanduri Kesināyaka. He vanquished Rapaka Bhima, Terala Kāṭa, Ēruva Tonda, and Chōḍa Chelukināyaka also. He further claims to have stolen the necklace of Kōṭa Permadirāya and the horses of Odaya pata of Bodda and over powered the lord of Kuduputuripura. Of these Kanduri Kesināyaka probably belonged to the Telugu Chōḷas of Kanduru and Ēruva Tanda of the Ēruva branch of the Telugu Chōḷas. Kōṭa Permadirāya was member of the later Kōṭa chiefs and Bodda was probably a Telugu Pallava. Ganna must have achieved all these victories when he helped the Kākatīya rulers Rudramadevi and Pratāparudra in the expansion of their kingdom.[204]

Vithala I

Vithala I, father of Buddha IV, the author of *Ranganātha*

Rāmāyana is said to have been bright like the sun, a moon to the ocean i.e., the Gona family and a lion in destroying the elephants (i.e., enemies). His wife was Anyamāmba. He bore the epithts *Misaragaṇḍa* and *Arigaṇḍabhairava.*[205] The Raichur inscription states that Vithala conqured the forts of Adavani, Tumbalaṁ, Mānuva, Haluva, occupied Raichur and built a fort for the protection of the people. All these forts taken by Vithala were situated in Kuntaladesa under the rul of Seunas or Yādavas of Devagiri. Obviously Vithala, the younger brother of Ganna seized these forts from Yādavas of Devagiri.

Buddha IV

We do not have much information about Buddha IV. He may be identified with Buddha *nayinimgāru* of the Kunkalagunta inscription unfinished and undated. Some of his titles show that Buddha was valiant, destroyer of his enemies and was like a fight arm to Velumu Bhupala which must be Telugu Bhupala referring to Prataparudra.[206] He bore the epithets *Samasta lakshana lakshmi sampura, Prata laṅkēśvar, Vairi sandōha gaja panchānana and Samara-Shadanana.*[207]

There is no information regarding the achievements of other chiefs. It appears that as long as the Kākatīya Kingdom prospered, The Gonas also prospered and ruled at Raichur till the end of Pratāparudra's rule. With the decline and fall of the Kākatīya kingdom, the Gona Haiheyas also declined and are not known after Pratāparudra's time.

THE VELAMA CHIEFS

Among the subordinate families of the Kākatiyas the Velama chiefs of *Padmanāyaka* community also distinguished themselves as great generals and the loyal subordinates to the Kākatīyas. They survived the Muslims onslaught on Kākatīya kingdom and flourished as *Padmanāyakas* in post Kākatīya period. Rāchakoṇḍa and Devarakoṇḍa in the Nalgonda district were the strong holds of these Velama chiefs. Their place of origin is Āmanagallu of Miryalaguḍa taluq in Nalgonda district. It was for a time capital of the feudatories of Kanduru Chōḍas as well as Rechelra Reḍḍi chiefs. It also emerged as a prominant town in medieval Andhradesa.

They early history of these Velama chiefs is shrouded in mystery. The sources of the early history of the *Padamanāyaka* chiefs are the dynastic histories of Pitapuram, Bobbili, Jataprole and Venkāṭagiri *samsthānas.*[208] An old palm leaf manuscripts called *Surabhi Vamśāvali* and *Velugōṭivāri Vamśāvali* are also important sources.[209] Of these *Velugōṭi Vāri Vamsavali* seems to be a trust worthy work. According to the literary works the anscestor of the *Velama* chiefs was born from the *Pāda Padma* (feet) of *Maha Vishṇu* and hence his successors were called Padmanāyakas.[210] According to another version these chiefs were originally *Kshatriyas* and were for a long time in the service of Mahāpadmananda on account of which they lost their status of *kshatriyas* and lived like *śudras* and henceforth called themselves as *Padmanāyakas.*[211] The *Padmanāyaka charitra* however stated that sum of the chiefs were Reḍḍis and fought with them. Thus the traditional history of the Padmanāyakas furnishes evidence of intermingling of several communities.[212] They were also stated to be the descendants of Padmanna, brother of Palṅāṭi Brahmanāyaka.[213]

What ever may be the origin of these *Padmanāyakas,* it can not be denied that they were great warriors and belonged to the *chatrthakula* or the forth caste, later on recognised as Velamas. Tradition unanimously associates the rise of *Padmanāyakas* with the Kākatīya kings. They were closely associated with the Kākatīya rulers from the time of Gaṇapatideva though they rose to power towards the close of the reign of Kakati Rudramadevi. The Gārla inscription dated A.D. 1287[214] refers to certain Boppa of Recharla family of the fourth caste, as subordinate chief of Rudramadevi. This Boppa was the son of Gaṇanātha and grandson of Beta. Calculating at the rate of thirty years for a generation we may place Beta in the last quarter of twelfth century and identify him with the Beta, Betināyaka or Betalanāyaka of the traditional accounts. According to the *Velugōṭi Vāri Vamśāvali* the sons of Beta of Betalanāyaka were Dama, Prasāditya and Rudra. Prasāditya is said to have restored the Kākatīya throne to Rudramadevi in supressing the rebels who strongly opposed the accession of

Rudramadevi. It is possible that some of the nobles did not approve the rule of a woman and rose the revolt. Prasāditya held the cause of Rudramadevi. An other member of the family was *mahāmaṇḍaleśvara* Mummadi Nāyuḍu, son of Kontala Nāgināyuḍu, who held the office of *Sakala Senādhipati,* supreme commander of all forces, during the last year of Rudramadevi's reign.[215]

Bhetalanāyaka or Chevvi Reḍḍi

According to the *Velugōṭivāri Vamśāvali,* the earliest member of the *Padmanāyaka* dynasty was Betāla Nāyaka or Chevvireḍḍi. He was perhaps a native of Āmanagallu of Miryalgūḍa in Nalgonda district. It was during the reign of Kākati Gaṇapatideva that he was appointed as the ruler of Pillalamarri and Āmanagallu, perhaps after the Recherla Reḍḍis had lost their prominence at the imperial court. The *Velugōṭivāri vamśāvali* speaks of his valour, courage and statecraft and it is possible that Kakati Gaṇapatideva who had heard of this great warrior invited him and made him the ruler of Āmanagallu.[216] He ruled from A.D. 1210-1265.[217] He might have been born in an ordinary peasant family and attracted the attention of Gaṇapatideva who perhaps initially took him into his services later to be elavated as the ruler of Āmanagallu principality. He had three sons Dāmanāyaka, Prasādityanāyaka and Rudranāyaka.

Dāmanāyaka

Dāmānāyaka was the eldest son of Beṭala Nāyaka. It appears that he served Kākati Gaṇapatideva as general when his father was alive. He was faithful to Rudrama and took active part in her expeditions. Dāmānāyaka ruled Āmanagallu from A.D. 1265 to 1285,[218] as a loyal and subordinate chief of Rudrama.

Prasādityanāyaka

Prasādityanāyaka was a great and loyal general in the service of the Kākatīya rulers. The nomination of Rudrama by Gaṇapaideva as his heir and successor and her appointment as his co-regent did not meet with the general approval. Some of the nobles of the country who were unwilling to acknowledge a woman as ruler and submit to her authority took up arms against her and attempted to throw off her yoke. Certain other member of the royal house, according to the *Pratāpacharitra,* also made a bid for the throne. It is stated that Hariharadeva and Murārideva, sons of Gaṇapatideva by another queen who was not the mother of Rudrāmba gathered their forces captured Orugallu, and ousted Rudrāmba from the capital city. But she had powerful supporters who rallied round her and helped her to put down the rebels with a stern hand. Most of the feudatories, generals and officials remained firmly loyal to the queen, The Kāyastha cheifs, Jannigadeva and his younger brother Tripurari and Āmbadeva, Prasāditya of the Recherla family, and some of the Reḍḍi chiefs like Gona Gannaya Reḍḍi espoused her cause and helped her to defeat the rebels. According to *Velugōṭ ivārivamśāvali*. Rudrama's victory over her rebels was entirely due to the unswerving loyalty and military prowess of Recherla Prasāditya. After canquishing the queen's enemies, he was said to have installed her on the throne and assumed the proud titles *Kākatīya Rājya Sthāpanāchārya* and *Rāyapiṭamahānka.*[219]

Another achievement which is attributed to Prasāditya was the introduction of the *Nāyaṅkara* system in the Kākatīya administration. Accordingly the defence of the kingdom was entrusted to seventy two *nāyakas.* We notice this system of military administration only from the period of Rudramadevi.[220] However, the system was in vogue under the Eastern Gangas a little bit earlier. Prasāditya was made the *Bāhattara niyōgādhipati.* It is likely that many vassal chiefs were killed when they opposed Rudramadevi. And some of them who proved disloyal were removed by her. In their place new *sāmantas* and *danḍanāyakas* ruled over the principality of Āmanagallu, it appears, Prasāditya became a key figure in the imperial affairs and stayed at Orugallu. He was a contemporary of Rudramadevi and no definite date can be assigned to him in the present state of knowledge. It is likely that Prasāditya was in imperial services berween A.D. 1265 to 1285 synchronising with the period of Rudramadevi.

Rudranāyaka

We do not have much information about Rudranāyaka, younger brother of Prasāditya except to assume that he was also active in the political affairs of the kingdom assisting his brother Prasāditya. Dr. P.V.P. Sastry states, "The unpublished Visunuru epigraph datable A.D. 1280 refers to certain Bichināyaka son of Rudranāyaka who held the *nāyaṁkara* of the place bearing the title *Kākatīrāja sthāpanāchārya*. On the basis of predominance of Velama community in the village even today it is quite likely that Rudranāyaka of the record was identical with his name sake, the younger brother of Prasāditya."[221]

Vennama I

Vennama I or Vennamanāyaka was the eldest son of Dāma. He seems to have entered the service of Kākati Rudrāmba during the last years of he reign and also served Pratāparudra during the early years of his reign. The Ayyanavōlu inscription[222] dated A.D. 1369 simply refers to him and does not speak of his exploits. Even in tracing the history of Vennama I we have no other source except the tradition. The Chroncles of Velama chiefs embodied in the *Velugōṭivāri vaṁśāvali* allude to the Kākatīya victory over Muslims of Delhi, prior to the advent of Mālik Naib Kafur. The earliest of Alla-Ud-Din's expeditions against Teleṅgāṇa took place in A.D. 1303 and it was worsted in an encounter with the Kākatīya forces. Venna and Potuganti Maili, a commander of Pratāparudra claims to have destroyed the pride of *turushkas* of Delhi in a battle near Upparapalli in the Karimnagar district. The Muslim army was led by Malik-Fakhr-ud-din Juna.[223] Zia-ud-din Barani informed that the army returned to Delhi in the beginning of winter greatly reduced in number.

Sabbināyaka

Sabbināyaka was the second son of Dāma and it seems that he was not as enterprising as his illustrious brother. It is likely that he was contended wih the rule of his fief Āmanagallu, while his brother Vennama I was involved in imperial affairs and was station at Orugallu. However, it is possible that he also took part in the expeditions of the Kākatīya ruler against their opponents.[224]

Eṟṟa Dācha and Nalla Dācha

Vennama and Sabbi had each a son bearing the names Eṟṟa

Dācha and Nalla Dācha respectively. But Nalla Dacha was not as enterprising as his cousin Eṛṛa Dācha. We have several records of Eṛṛa Dācha which suggest his valour and popularity. The undated Domalapalli inscription[225] mentions Dachaya Singa Bhupala, son of Eṛṛa Dācha. The Rāchakoṇḍa inscription[226] dated A.D. 1365 found in Rāchakoṇḍa fort at Bhairavagoṇḍi belonging to Eṛṛa Dācha's grandson Anapōta gives valuable information about his titles like *Mahāmandaleśvara, Andhradēśadhiśvara, Gajadala viphala, Rāyagaya gōpala, Pañchapāṇḍya vibhal, Pratigoṇḍa bhujabala, Bhima khadga Nārāyana, Kākati Rājya Stāpanāchārya, Astadikku Rāya* and *Manōbhayankara*. The Rāchakoṇḍa Rāma temple inscription[227] dated A.D. 1365 also refers to Anapōta, the grandson of Eṛṛa Dācha. The Ayyanavōlu inscription[228] dated A.D. 1369 described Eṛṛa Dācha as *Pāṇḍyarāya Gaja Kēsari Pāṇḍyan Vijetan Abhishekayatah Pratāpa Śri Rudra Deva nripateḥ*. The Kandikoṇḍa inscription[229] dated A.D. 1375 interestingly speaks of Dācha and his wife Pochāmbika. The exploits of Eṛṛa Dācha and Nalla Dācha are dealt with at some length in the chronicle, *Velugōṭiavari Vamśāvali*. It is stated that they killed the chief called Kuntluri Immaḍi in a fierce engagement near the village Gollapalli. They also encountered the Pāṇḍyas in a battle near Kāñchi.[230] The Ayyanavolu inscription[231] dated A.D. 1369 states that Eṛṛa Dāchaya, at the command pf Pratāparudra, proceeded against the Pāṇḍyas, defeated them and obtained the title *Pāṇḍya rāya gaja kēsari*. The *Velugōṭivāri vamśāvaḷi*[232] furnishes more information about the Pāṇḍyan expedition. Dācha overpowered the Pāṇḍyas who put the 90,000 Telugu forces to flight on a former occassion, captured the famous Pāṇḍyan elephant squadron, attacked the Five Pāṇḍyas, viz, Virapāṇḍya, Vikramapāṇḍya, Parakramapāṇḍya, Sundarapāṇḍya and Kulashekharapāṇḍya and inflicted and irrevocable defeat on them. In appreciation of Dācha's valour, Pratāparudra conferred on him the titles of *Pāṇḍya dala Vibhala and Pāṇḍyarāya gaja kesari*.

The Umamaheśvaram inscription[233] throws more welcome light on the exploits of Eṛṛa Dācha. He subjugated the Bhilla army, in a battle fought near Nellore and established the Telugu

Chōḍa king Tirukalatideva on the throne, Although these victories are attributed to the Velama chiefs in Vamśāvali, as a matter of fact, several other chiefs like Induluri chiefs, Muppiḍināyaka and others also participated in this compaign and won the victory for the king as evidenced by the titles borne by them.[234]

However, the subjugation of the hilly track of the Nārāyana-vanam region by the Kākatīya generals precipiated a conflict with the Hoyasala king Vira Ballala III. His subordinate Tiruvenga-lanatha Yādavarāya was holding at the time the fort of Chandragiri in the vicinity. A battle was fought in which Indulūri Pedda Rudra and the Velama chief Eṛṛa Dācha inflicted a defeat in the Hoyasala armies and took possession of territory belonging to Ballala III[235] Eṛṛa Dācha might have been killed in A.D. 1323, fighting the forces of Ulugh Khān. It is well known that Orugallu fell into the hands of Muslims in A.D. 1323.

Nalla Dācha always accompanied his cousin Eṛṛa Dācha in all expeditions and also distinguished himself in the Pānḍyan invasion.[236] Singama I, with Venna II and Echa, sons Eṛṛa Dācha, took a prominent part in the defence of the kingdom at the time of Tughluq invasions in A.D.1323. His cousins Madanēni and Rāmānēni sons of Nalla Dācha must also have participated along with him in his expeditions. Singama I according to the *Paradanasodara Rāmanāthanakathe,* also led the Kākatīya expedition against Kampili where he suffered defeat at the hands of Kumāra Rāmanātha.[237] Singama I was the distinguished member of the family who, after survival in the invasion of A.D. 1323, came to prominence and established an independent Padmanāyaka kingdom.

The Recherla Velama chiefs after the downfall of the Kākatīyas, established an independent kingdom and ruled from Rāchakonḍa and Devarakonḍa which were their strong holds. The later *rājas* of Venkāṭagiri, Pithapuram, Bobbili and Jataprole claim their descent from this Velama family of the Kākatīya period.

The Geneology of Velama chiefs :

- Chevvi Reḍḍi (Bhetāla Nāyaka)
  - Dāmanāyaka
    - Vennama I
      - Eṟṟa Dācha
        - Singama
        - Vennama II
        - Echa
    - Sabbināyaka
      - Nalla Dācha
        - Madānēni
        - Rāmānēni
  - Prasāditya
  - Rudranāyaka

REFERENCES

1. S.J. Mangalam, *Historical Geography and Toponomy of Andhra Pradesh,* New Delhi, 1986, pp. 1-2.
2. *Corpus* Nos. 8 & 9.
3. *Ibid.*, Nos. 51 & 52.
4. *I.A.P.* Kn., No. 29.
5. *Telaṅgāṇa Inscriptions,* I, No. 13. (Vardhamanapura Inscription).
6. *Corpus,* No. 8.
7. *I.A.P.* Kn., No. 29.
8. *I.A.P.* Wg., Nos. 48 & 64
9. *Corpus*, Nos. 51 & 52.
10. *Ibid.*
11. *Ibid.*
12. *I.A.P.* Kn., No. 29.
13. *Teleṅgāṇa Inscriptions*, 1, No.13. (Vardhamanapura Inscription).
14. *I.A.P.* Kn., No. 29
15. *Corpus*, No. 8.
16. P.V.P. Sastry, *The Kākatīyas,* Hyderabad, 1978, p. 98.
17. *I.A.P.* Kn., No. 29.
18. *Corpus*, No. 8.
19. *E.I.*, VI, p. 159.
20. *I.A.P.* Kn., 29.
21. P.V.P. Sastry, *op. cit.*, p. 150.

22. *Telengāṇa Inscriptions,* I, No. 13. (Vardhamanapura Inscription).
23. *Corpus*, No. 50.
24. *Ibid.*
25. *E.H.D.* p. 638.
26. *J.A.H.R.S.*, XIX, p.60.
27. K.Iśvaradath, *Prācheenāndhra Chāritraka Bhūgōlamu,* Hyderabad, 1962, p.116; J.A.H. R.S., XIX, p. 70.
28. *Ibid.* pp. 105-106.
29. *S.I.I.*, VI, No. 229
30. *Ibid.*
31. *Ibid.*
32. *Ibid.*
33. *S.I.I.*, p. 97.
34. K. Iśvaradath, op.cit., p. 104.
35. *Epigraphia Indica*, VI. No. 15.
36. *S.I.I.*, VI, No. 229..
37. *Ibid.*, No. 236 & 102.
38. *Epigraphia Indica*, VI, pp. 147-160.
39. *S.I.I.*, VI, No. 229.
40. *Ibid.*
41. *Ibid.*42.
42. *Ibid.*
43. *S.I.I,* X, No. 96.
44. *Ibid.*, No. 109.
45. *Ibid.*, No. 395.
46. *Ibid.*
47. *Ibid.*
48. *Ibid.*
49. *Ibid.*
50. K. Iśvaradath, *op. cit.*, pp. 51-51.
51. *Ibid.*, p. 53.
52. S.J. Mangalam, *op. cit.*, pp. 27-28.
53. *J.A.H.R.S.*, XIX, pp. 60-61.
54. *A.R.E.*, 571 of 1925.
55. *J.A.H.R.S.*, XIX, p. 65.
56. *S.I.I.*, IV, No. 1242.
57. E.I., IV, p. 91.
58. *J.A.H.R.S.*, XIX, p. 71.
59. *A.R.E.,* 299 of 1934-35.
60. *A.R.E.,* 141 of 1917.

61. *A.R.E.*, 484 of 1913.
62. *A.R.E.*, 65 of 1911.
63. *A.R.E.*, 175 of 1917.
64. *A.R.E.*, 564 of 1925.
65. *A.R.E.*, 302 of 1932-33.
66. *A.R.E.*, 565 of 1915.
67. *J.A.H.R.S.*, XIX, p. 78.
68. *Ibid.*, p. 79.
69. *Epigraphia Indica*, III, No. 16.
70. *A.R.E.*, 585 of 1925.
71. M. Krishṇa Kumari, *Social and Cultuure Life in Medieval Āndhra,* Delhi, 1989, pp. 32-33.
72. *A.R.E.*, 535 of 1913.
73. *E.I.*, IV, pp. 100ff.
74. *A.R.E.* 565 of 1925.
75. *J.A.H.R.S.*, XXIII, p. 34.
76. *Ibid.*, pp. 34-35.
77. *Ibid.*, pp. 39-40.
78. *Ibid.*, pp. 40-41.
79. *Ibid.*, pp. 41-42.
80. *A.P.R.E.*, 1965, No. 75; *I.A.P.*, Cd., II, No. 139.
81. B.N. Sastry, *Kāyatha Rajulu*, Hyderabad, 1991. No.4.
82. *A.P.R.E.*, 1965, No. 88.
83. *A.P.R.E.*, 1965, No. 209.
84. *I.A.P.*, Cd., I No. 145.
85. *S.I.I.*, X, No. 332, 343, 346, 370 and 465.
86. *S.I.I.*, X, No. 334.
87. *S.I.I.*, X, No. 446.
88. *I.A.P.*, Cd., I, No. 140.
89. *I.A.P.*, Cd., I, No. 42.
90. *A.R.E.*, 1967, No. 212.
91. *A.R.E.*, 1967, NO. 367; *I.A.P.* Cd.,1, No. 146.
92. *S.I.I.*, XXIII, No. 618.
93. K. Iśvaradath, *Op.cit.*, pp. 39-40.
94. *Ibid.*, 124-126.
95. *Ibid.*, 215.
96. *Ibid.*, p. 68.
97. S.J. Mangalam, *op.cit.*, p. 57.
98. *Ibid.*, p. 57.
99. *A.R.E.*, 68, 367 of 1967.

100. S.J. Mangalam, *op.cit.*, p. 71.
101. *Ibid.*, pp. 79-80.
102. *I.A.P.*, Ng., I, No. 71.
103. *Ibid.*; P.V.P. Sastry, *op.cit.*, p. 157.
104. *S.I.I.*, X, p. 334.
105. B.N. Sastry, *op.cit.*, 1991, p. 157.
106. *A.R.E.*, 69, of 1929-30.
107. *A.R.E.*, 267 of 1959-50.
108A. K.R. Basavarāja, *History and culture of Karnataka,* Dharwad, 1984, p. 116.
109. P.V.P. Sastry, *op.cit.*, pp. 157-158.
110. *A.R.E.*, 505 of 1907.
111. B.N. Sastry, *op.cit.*, 1991, No. 2.
112. *Ibid* , No. 3.
113. P.V.P. Sastry, *op.cit.*, pp. 157-158.
114. *Epigraphia Indica,* XXVI, p. 120.
115. B.N. Sastry, *op.cit.*, 1991, No. 6.
116. *A.R.E.*, 314 of 1930-31.
117. *S.I.I*, VI, No. 599.
118. *A.R.E.*, 595 of 1907.
119. B.N. Sastry. *op.cit.*, 1991, No. 1.
120. *J.A.H.R.S.*, XXIII, p.35.
121. B.N. Sastry, *op.cit.*, No. 7,8,9,10 and 11.
122. B.N. Sastry, *Tripurānthaka Dēvālaya Śaśanamulu*, Hyderabad, 1984, No. 52.
123. *N.D.I.*, No.57.
124. *A.R.E.*, 248 of 1905.
125. *J.A.H.R.S.*, XXIII, pp. 40-41.
126. B.N. Sastry, *op.cit.*, 1991, No. 16.
127. *Ibid.*, No. 15, 16, 17, 18, 19, 20, 21, 22, 23, 26 and 27; *A.R.E.*, 406 of 1912; *A.R.E.*, 261 of 1905.
128. Mack. Ms. 15-3-32.
129. P.V.P. Sastry, *op.cit.*, p. 122.
130. B.N. Sastry, *op.cit.*, 1984, No.
131. Epigraphia Indica, XXV, p. 227.
132. B.N. Sastry, *op.cit.*, 1991, No. 22.
133. *A.R.E.*, 406 of 1912.
134. *I.A.*, LVI, pp. 191-192.
135. P.V.P. Sastry, *op.cit.*, p. 160.
136. B.N. Sastry, *op.cit.*, 1991, No. 22.

137. *A.R.E.*, 226 of 1937-38.
138. *A.R.E.*, 622 of 1907.
139. *A.R.E.*, 406 of 1912.
140. *J.A.H.R.S.*, XXIII, p. 44.
141. *A.R.E.*, 304 of 1935-36.
142. P.V.P. Sastry, *op.cit.*, p. 160.
143. Studies in Indian Epigraphy, I, No.9; *I.A.P.*, Ng., I, No. 59.
144. M. Rama Rao (ed), Kākatīya Saṇchika, p. 66.
145. P.V.P. Sastry, *op.cit.*, p. 124.
146. *N.D.I,* II, p. 830-832.
147. *A.R.E.,* 588, 590, 591, 592 of 1907; *A.R.E.*, 594 of 1905.
148. B.N. Sastry, *op.cit.*, 1984, No. 72.
149. P.V.P. Sastry, *op.cit.*, pp. 129.
150. *Epigraphia Indica*, XXV, pp. 270ff.
151. *S.I.I.*, X, 466, 467.
152. *A.R.E.*, 423 of 1911.
153. *A.R.E.,* 406 of 1912.
154. *I.A.P.*, Cd., I, No. 145.
155. M. Somasekhar Sarma, *History of Reḍḍi Kingdom,* Srisilam, 1993, p. 66.
156. B.N. Sastry, *op.cit.*, 1984, No. 70.
157. *A.R.E.*, 98 of 1939-40.
158. B.N. Sastry, *op.cit.,* 1991, p. 39.
159. *I.A.P.,* Cd., I, No. 152.
160. *I.A.P.,* Cd., I, No. 153/
161. Ch. Veerabhadra Rao, Āndhrula Charita, I, p.548-549.
162. *A.R.E.*, 260 of 1935-36.
163. *A.P.R.E.,* 1966, No. 54.
164. S.J. Mangalam, *op.cit.*, p. 45
165. *J.A.H.R.S.,* XXXV, p. 421.
166. K.Suryanarāyana, *History of the Minor Chālukya Families in Medieval Āndhradeśa,* Delhi, 1986. p. 159.
167. *S.I.I,* IV, No. 735.
168. K. Suryanarāyana *op.cit.*, p. 158.
169. *S.I.I.*, VIII, No. 737.
170. *A.R.E.*, 250 of 1935-36.
171. K. Suryanarāyana, *op.cit.*, p. 160.
172. P.V.P. Sastry, *op.cit.*, p. 111.
173. *Ibid.,* p. 112.
174. K. Suryanarāyana, *op.cit.*, pp. 160-161.

175. *Ibid.*, p. 161.
176. *S.I.I.*, X, No. 360.
177. *Ibid.*, V, No. 122.
178. *A.R.E.*, 8 of 1956-57.
179. *S.I.I.*, V, No. 122.
180. *I.A.P.* Wg., No. 87.
181. M. Rama Rao (ed). *op.cit.*, Ins. No. 30, pp. 400-403.
182. Bhārathi, June, 1976, p. 20.
183. Epigraphia Andhrica, IV, p. 110.
184. K. Suryanarāyana, *op.cit.*, pp. 165-166.
185. P.V.P. Sastry, *op.cit.*, p. 166.
186. *S.I.I.*, X, No. 481.
187. *S.I.I.*, V, No. 147.
188. K. Suryanarāyana, *op.cit.*, pp. 167.
189. *Ibid.*, pp. 167-168.
190. *I.A.P.* Wg., Introduction, p. XXV.
191. N. Venkāṭaramanayya, (ed), velugōṭivāri Vamshāvali, Madras, 1939, Introduction, p. 11.
192. M. Rama Rao (ed), op, cit., p. 261.
193. *Ibid.*, Appendix, pp. 416-417. No. 33.
194. *J.A.H.R.S.*, XIX, pp. 23-24.
195. M. Somasekhara Sarma, Introduction to Ranganātha Rāmāyana, Rāyala publications, p. 7.
196. *A.R.E.*, 608 of 1919 cited in E.H.D., p. 695.
197. Teleṅgāṇa Inscriptions, I, Nos. 20 & 21.
198. *Corpus,* No.50.
199. M. Rama Rao (ed) *op.cit.*, Ins. No. 33.
200. *Ibid.*, p. 261.
201. M. Somasekara Sarma, *op.cit.*, p. 7.
202. Arudra, Samagra *Āndhra Sāhityamu,* III, Secunderabad, pp. 252-253.
203. *J.A.H.R.S.*, XIX, p. 26.
204. *Ibid.*, p. 27.
205. M. Somasekara sarma, *op.cit.*, p. 9.
206. *J.A.H.R.S.*, XIX, p. 25.
207. *A.R.E.,* 151 A of 1899; *S.I.I.*, VI, No. 590. cited in *J.A.H.R.S.*, XIX, p. 25.
208. M.Rama Rao (ed), *on cit.*, p. 31.
209. *Ibid.*, p. 50.
210. *Ibid.*, p. 31.

211. *Ibid.*, p. 31.
212. *Ibid.*, p. 31-32.
213. *Ibid.*, p. 32.
214. *J.A.H.R.S.*, VI, Pt. I, p. 31.
215. *E.H.D.*, p. 638.
216. B.N. Sastry, *Recherala Padmanāyakulu*, Hyderabad, 1991, p. 5.
217. *Ibid.*, p. 12.
218. *Ibid.*,
219. *E.H.D.*, pp. 621-622.
220. P.V.P. Sastry, *op. cit.*, p. 164.
221. *Ibid.*, pp. 164-165.
222. *I.A.P.* Wg., No. 103.
223. *E.H.D.*, pp. 164-165.
224. M. Somasekara Sarma, *A forgotten chapter of Āndhra History*, Madras, 1945, p. 6.
225. *I.A.P.* Ng., I. No. 111.
226. *Ibid.*, No. 108.
227. *Ibid.*, No. 107.
228. *I.A.P.*, Wg., No. 103.
229. B.N. Sastry, *op.cit.*, 1991, Ins. No. 7.
230. *A.P.R.E.*, 1965, pp. 100-101.
231. *I.A.P.* Wg., No. 103.
232. N. Venkāṭaramanayya, *op.cit.*, p. 5.
233. P.V.P. Sastry, *op.cit.*, p. 165.
234. *Ibid.*,
235. *Ibid.*, pp. 165-166.
236. *E.H.D.*, p. 661. 244.
237. *Ibid.*, pp. 661-662.

Chapter-IV

MILITARY ADMINISTRATION : NĀYANKARA SYSTEM

The Kākatīya kings like othr Hindu kings understood that the first and primary duty of the king was to afford protection to all his subjects and redress their grievances. The king was not only expected to protect the country from external aggression but also to ensure the preservation of peace and order in the country. Thus to discharge both these responsibilities, the king had to maintain sufficeint number of elephants, horses and soldiers. In the middle ages a strong army was a necessary feature of a stable empire. When the kings declared war against enemies and before the starting of the expedition, the feudal vassals were summoned to the court and honored by rich presents and a lavish banquest at the capital.[1]

Forts played a prominent part in the wars of the middle ages. In all most all the provinces of the Kākatīya kingdom, there were forts containing military contingents to guard the country. The Kākatīya kings realised the necessity and the usefulness of forts. They constructed many forts as testified by inscriptions. For example in the kingdom of Pratāparudra there were forts such as Chebrolu, Padminipura, Devapura, Enamadala, Podili, Polacherla, Ādoni, Nujella, Suravaram, Rājamahendravaram, Samalakōṭa, Piṭhapuram, Bodasakuru, Bendapūḍi etc.[2] King Rudradeva laid the foundation for the fort near Orugallu or Omtikonda or *Ēkaśilanagara*. The fortification was raised around the Svayambhu Śiva temple which became the family deity of the Kākatīyas. Gaṇapatideva continued the construction of the fort and built two forts one within the other, in stone and mud respectively. According to tradition the new fort was provided with 75 bastions and 72 *nāyakas* were apointed to protect the bastions. After the construction of the fort was completed, Gaṇapatideva changed his capital from Anumakoṇḍa to Orugallu.[3]

Thus the military organisation and defence of the Kingdom were given top priority by the Kākatīya rulers. In order to provide the state with sufficient number of military contingents to fight loyally on behalf of the king. The Kākatīya rulers evolved a military system known as the *Nāyaṅkara* system. This was a novel experiement undertaken by the Kākatīyas which was adopted later by the Vijaynagara rulers. It should be noted that this system was not to be found in the administration of the Western Chalukyas, the Eastern Chālukyas and the Rāshṭrakūṭas, under whom the Kākatīyas served as subordinate chiefs. S. Pushpalatha has rightly appreciated the introuduction of the *Nāyaṅkara* system by Rudramadevi and her feudatory Prasāditya as a bold experiment in the military organisation of the Kākatīyas.[4] For a better understanding and appreciation of the role of the feudatories in the introduction and maintenance of the *Nāyaṅkara* system, the administrative system of the Chālukyas of Bādami, Kalyāṇi and Rāshṭrakūṭas may briefly be mentioned. The feudatory chiefs of the Chālukyas paid tribute to the emperor and also rendered military service required by the king. The Vishayapatis or the provincial heads equivalent to *deśādhigarigas* of the Kannade language lookd after the interests of the kings. But their powers and responsibilities are not clearly stated.[5] Under the Rāshṭrakūṭas the provincial heads were appointed by the king in recognition of their military services. Some provinces were ruled by a hereditary *mahāsāmanta* or feudatory chief and they contributed military and other services required by the king. The *Vishayapatis* or the provincial heads were assisted by afew subordinates. The military contingents under the control of the provincial chiefs and feudatories were requisitioned by the king in times of emergency. The Rāshṭrakūṭas recruited soldiers from all classes of society including Brahmins. But heredity was an important factor in recruitment. The hereditary force (maula-bala) was stated to be most efficient and trust worthy.[6] The feudatories of the Eastern Chālukyas provided military assistance to their rulers. They received from the Chalukya kings the insignia of feudal chieftainship namely the *Śridvaru, Chatra*, Chāmara, peacocks tail, water jars, horses and musical instrucments like *Kahala* and others.[7] B.N. Puri observed that "the practice of supplying forces to the overlord by the feudatories for fighting against his enemy was fairly common by the feudatories for fighting against his enemy was fairly common in Northern India at the time".[8] It is also to be noted that the provincial governors under the Rāshṭrakūṭas were appointed on the basis of military service thus giving importance to military service as criteria for appointment as provincial governors. Thus it appears that taking military service as the foundation for a new administrative structure, the Kākatīya kings evolved the *Nāyaṅkara* system which became famous in Kākatīya history. No doubt it was so significant that it was adopted by the great Vijayanagara rulers later.

It was the great and innovative ruler Rudramadevi who founded the *Nāyaṅkara* system. It this comendable endeavour, the enterprising Velama chief Prasāditya played an imporant role in giving a shape to the system conceived by Rudramadevi.[9] An inscription dated A.D. 1279 refers to the *Nāyaṅkara* system.[10] It is worthwhile investigating the causes for the introduction of the *Nāyaṅkara* system by Rudramadevi. Firstly there was opposition to her rule in the initial stages. Some feudatories and officials felt it infradig to serve a woman and opposed her rule. Nextly the Yādavas of Devagiri the sworn enemies of the Kākatīya territory and laid siege to the fort of Warangal. Thirdly Rudramāmba found that the Kākatīya control over Vēngi was weakended. Bhānudeva, the Gajapati ruler of Orissa invaded Vēngi. Though the outcome of the conflict is not clear, it can be presumed that the Kākatīya forces failed to repulse the attack of the Gajapatis. Firstly the Kākatīya authority was greatly impaired after the defeat of Gaṇapatideva at the hands of the Pāṇḍyas in the battle of Muthukuru.[11] Their control over Nellore and Kāñchi was nominal. Rudramāmba considering all the problems the Kākatīyas had to face, though of a mechanism which would elicit the loyalty and military service of the feudatories and the generals. Though the exact date of the introduction of the system (with the help of Prasāditya) is not known it is possible to arrive at a period on the basis of inscriptions. According to an inscription dated A.D. 1279, Rudramadevai granted some place (name effaced) as *Nāyaṅkara* to Bolli *Nāyaka* who was acting as her bodyguard.[12] The unpublished Visnuru epigraph datable to A.D. 1280 refers to certain Bichināyaka, son of Rudranāyaka who was the *amaranāyaka* of Visnuru. Bichināyaka incidentally assumed the title *Kākati-rājya- Sthāpanachārya*, suggesting his support to the Kākatīya rulers.[13] Thus the two epigraph referring to the *Nāyaṅkara* system were dated A.D. 1279 and A.D. 1280. It may be inferred that Rudrama held consultations with her feudatories particularly the Velama chiefs and evolved the system to promote the best interests of the state and also the defence of the kingdom, prior to A.D. 1279 the date of Bolli *Nāyaka*'s epigraph cited earlier.

Kolanu Rudradeva, grandson of Soma mantri and junior contemporary of Annayadeva, son of Peda Gannaya, brother of Soma mantri was the superintendent of the 72 *durgas* in the kingdom of Pratāparudra. He is said to have ruled *durgas* or forts such as Chebrolu, Padminipura, Devapura, Enamadala, Podili, Polacherla, Ādoni, Nujella, Suravaram, Rājamahendravaram, Samalakōṭa, Piṭhapuram, Bodasakuru, Bendapūḍi etc.[14]

Mayideva- *leṅka* was the *Nāyaṅkara* of *Konduri Sthala* consisting of 18 villages. A hamlet in the present Tenali taluk called Virulapalem still exists and the residents of the village belong to Reḍḍi caste. Māyideva- *leṅka* remitted the taxes called *Bantila Āayanu* on the temple lands of the *Konduri Sthala* in A.D. 1317. *Bantala* was a levy probably collectd from the people for the maintenance of *bantus* or warriors. As Māyideva-*leṅka* was expected to maintain a fixed number of warriors to serve the king in times of war, he naturally collectd the levy from his subjects in order to raise the extra funds within his fief. It is interesting to note that near the village Pedakonduru in the Guntur district where the inscription giving the above information is available, some Virakals or Hero stones are found suggesting its being a cantonment of warriors in the past. The entire village of Virulapalem even now consists exclusively of people belonging to different castes.

According to Yedlapalli epigraph of Rudradeva, son of Mayideva-*leṁka*, Konduru was a Nāyaṅkara village.[15]

The *leṁkas* appear to be *Nāyaṅkaras* during the time of Rudramadevi *Leṅkas* or *leṁkas* were the enbodiments of devotion and loyalty towards their lords. They represented *Prabhu bhakti* and dedicated their lives for the service of their lord with the same religious favour of a *bhakta* or a spiritual aspirant towards his God. Mayideva *leṁka* was *Nāyaṅkara* of Konduri Sthala consisting of 18 villages in the present Tenali taluk.[16] In some cases some *leṁkas* were appointed to supervise a cantonment situated in *Nāyaṅkara Sthala*. Tikkaya Rudra-leṁka, Maraya-*leṁka*, Pichaya-leṁka and Rudraya-leṁka were in-charge of the cantonment of Kopparam in the Guntur district.[17] Juttaya leṁka Gomkaya Reḍḍi was the governor of Gandikōṭa *Sima*.[18] His brother Rudraya leṁka was also a *Nāyaka*.[19] Maharaya Sakala Sēnādhipati Somaya-leṁka and his son Pochu-*leṁka* also figure as *Nāyakas* in the Kākatīya records.[20] Pratāparudra granted some place as his *Nāyaṅkara* to Mahāpradhāni Gangideva.[21] He also granted the *Nāyaṅkara* of Mellachembu to a certain Chami Yeṛṛa Preggeḍa.[22] An inscrpiton dated A.D. 1311 from Damagallu mentions two villages which Pratāparudra granted to Videmu Kommarāju as his *Nāyaṅkara*.[23] Prolaya Nāyaḍu and Kali Nāyaḍu, the bodyguards of Pratāparudra were granted the Velanāṭi *Nāyaka-Sthala Vritti* in A.D. 1313.[24] An epigraph dated A.D. 1314 from Penumalli registers the grant of 22 villages to Eneya, the gate keeper of the royal palace for his *Nāyaṅkara*.

Pratāpacharitra credits Pratāparudra with the introduction of the *Nāyaṅkara* system. it states that Pratāparudra entrusted the defence of his capital to 77 Velama *Nāyakas*. He is said to have divided his kingdom into 77 districts and entrusted them to 77 Velama *Nāyakas*.[25] But inscriptional evidence testify to the existence of the system during the reign of Rudramadevi. So Pratāparudra shoud not be considered as the founder of the *Nāyaṅkara* system. It is possible that he strengthened the framework and put it on a solid base.

Dr. N. Venkataramanayya stated that the real author of the

reform was probably the queen Rudramba herself. Tradition might have wrongly attributed its origin to her grandson under whom the *Nāyaṅkara* system came into force. Whatever might be the manner in which the *Nāyaṅkara* system had arisen, there is no doubt that it came into practice for the first time during the regions of the last two Kākatīya monarchs. Since the system was unknown in every part of South India and Deccan except in Teleṅgāṇa, the Rāyas of Vijayanagar, must have inherited it from the rulers of that country.[26]

According to Dr. P. Raghunatha Rao, Pratāparudra made some changes in the *Nāyaṅkara* system keeping in view the revolt of Ambadeva and the death of Rudramadevi. Hence forth, only Velamas belonging to the Padmanāyaka section were chosen as *Nāyakas.*[27]

Regarding the number of *Nāyakas* there is no uniformity. As stated earlier for instance Pratāpacharitra mentions 77 *nāyakas*. Velugōṭvāri Vamśāvaḷi mention 77 *nāyakas.*[28] The Kaluvacheru grant of Avitalli mention 75 *Nāyakas.*[29] Siddheśvara Charitra of Kāse Sarvappa *Nāyaka* give the number of *nāyakas* as 77. It further states that each feudatory had 15,000 soldiers under his command and the total number of feudal forces worked out to 11,55,000.[30] Thus it appears that the number of *Nāyaṅkaraships* varied from time to time depending on the requirement of the rule. However it was never less than 72 mentioned in Śivayogasaramu.[31]

Some of the names of the *Nāyakas* who were in the service of the Kākatīya rulers are as follows:[32]

1. Recherla Prasāditya.
2. Maldeva Pratruḍu.
3. Anachi Maldevuḍu.
4. Mallu Rudra Deva.
5. Murāri MalDevuḍu.
6. Sangarāju.
7. Modukuri Rāma.
8. Ammanaboli Rudra Devuḍu.
9. Somarāju Rudraiah.
10. Nachi Rāju Beemaiah.

11. Sandhaya Devuḍu.
12. Pōthughanṭi Mailu.
13. Indhu Mouli.
14. Kondaparthi Gaṇapati Deva.
15. Mahadeva Nayani Soma Devuḍu.
16. Dadhi Naga Deva Soma Devuḍu.
17. Mallikārjunuḍu.
18. Kolipaka Nāgi Reḍḍy.
19. Taḍiparthi Ganna Reḍḍy.
20. Chanda Malla Reḍḍy.
21. Bachi Malla Reḍḍy.
22. Gaddi Manna Reḍḍy.
23. Bachi Penchala Malla Reḍḍy.
24. Bedadha Kōṭa Bairava Devuḍu.
25. Kovuvi Nachi Devuḍu.
26. Kalgaya Muggunḍu.
27. Koravi Nrishuḍu.
28. Gundaya Nāiḍu.
29. Cheruvu Thona Chennu.
30. Natlarani Balaya.
31. Gona Kōṭa Reḍḍy.
32. Malaḍi Potha Reḍḍy.
33. Kumara Gaṇapathi.
34. Yathadi Balayya.
35. Maraya Nashemi.
36. Rudra Deva.
37. Machi Rudra Deva.
38. Yeṛṛa Nashemi.
39. Veera Baluḍu.
40. Kantuḍu.
41. Pedha Manchi Rudra Deva.
42. China Koori Rudra Deva.
43. Hinḍutari Annaya Deva.
44. Appaka Maddavunḍu.
45. Chanda Deva.
46. Kari Deva.
47. Nevarāju.

48. Veeranna.
49. Vessanna.
50. Vishalakshuḍu.
51. Veena Kommayya.
52. Venkateshwarunḍu.
53. Mallu.
54. Govula Pocheneḍu.
55. Naganadhunḍu.
56. Karuna Kumarunḍu.
57. Ranikia Deva.
58. SomiRāju Yaluḍu.
59. Abonga Rahathu Rayanala.
60. Annaya Deva Venka.
61. Gundayam Gunḍu.
62. Ganta Venka.
63. Goole Venka.
64. Kolani Rudra Deva.
65. Muppiḍi Nayakuḍu.
66. Machavla Nāgu Venka.
67. Kōṭa Mallu Venka.
68. Manku Ganna Venka.
69. Paruvara Bharama Venka
70. Vundavellu Venka.
71. Dhiltakamu Venka.

It is quite evident from the list of the *Nāyakas* given, that the office of the *Nāyaṅkara* was open to talent irrespective of caste or community to which a person belonged. A scrutiny of the above list makes it clear that not only Velamas and Reḍḍis but also men of other castes also were given command of armies. The feudatories were given top priority in the appointment of *Nāyaṅkaras*.

The terms one comes acrose in the study of *Nāyaṅkara* system should be given due consideration for appopriate interpretation. The term *amara Nāyaka* means one who held land known as *amaram* (military chief) from the king.[33] *Sūryarāyandhra Nighanṭvu* explains that *Amaram* was a piece of land given to tributary princes on condition of supplying military forces when required.[34] According to another opinion *amara* means a grant of a revenue by the prince on condition of service military of police. *Kara* means an office. The word *amara nāyankara* is a piece of land yielding some revenue granted to a military chief.[35] All of the foregoing suggest that the *amara nāyakas* were those who received grants of land yielding a certain amount of revnue on condition of performing military service to the king. By virtue of this grant the *amara Nāyaka* did not become the proprietor of land but was allowed to enjoy the revenue from that land. With the revenue raised from the land in his possession he had to maintain a fixed number of elephants, horses and foot soldiers and supply to the king whenever needed. The *Nāyaṅkara* system is military in nature. K.R. Basavaraja and N. Venkata Ramanayya interpreted the word *amaram* as military tenure. So the interpretation of *amaram* as a military tenure in the Vijayanagara rulers followed the main framework of the system adopted by the Kākatīya rulers. The only different was that the Vijayanagara model was more comprehensive inview of the size and resources of the kingdom.

As in *Nāyaṅkara* system is military in nature many feudatories who were bound to the central authroity by ties of military service were appointed as *Nāyaṅkaras*. As stated earlier the Velama chiefs were prominent among the *Nāyaṅkaras*.

The *Amarams* of the grants of land were given by the king to an individual, yielding a certain amount of revenue on the condition that he rendered military service or more precisely supply contingents of elephants, horses, foot soldiers etc. The *Nāyaka* paid the share of revenue accrued from the land, already assigned to other agencies. However, the *Nāyaka* never enjoyed any absolute right over these lands as the king was supposed to hold the proprietory rights on the entire land in the kingdom. It is well known that the Hindu law givers like Manu, Narada and Kautilya reiterate that the king was the owner of the land.[36] It is pertinent to say that while the basic proprietorship rests with the king the second ownership of the land rests with the individual.[37]

This is evident from the fact that Devari *Nāyaka*, the *Nāyaka* of Pratāparudra inspite of many political and military achievements to his credit had to obtain the consent of the king to grant the revenue of the village Salakalavīdu situated in his *Nāyaṅkara* to Lord Sriranganātha of Kāveri. Thus all the *Amara Nāyakas* were expected to take prior permission from the king and then only donate village to individuals or religious institutions.[38] The Vijayanagara inscriptions also testify to this practice.[39]

The *Nāyaka*'s authority was restricted in administrative matters. For instance the local assemblies sometimes exercised more power than the *Nāyakas* and took to task an unjust *Nāyaka*. For instance, Doddapotipeddi of Pinapādu village protested against the imposition of some undue taxes by the *Nāyaka* Era-*leṁka* on *devavritti* lands in the Konduri-*Sthala* consisting of 22 villages. Doddapotipeddi the village elders headed by Potireḍḍi also recorded the case so that the *Nāyakas* would not commit similar mistakes in future. Ultimately Era-leṁka had to grant remission of those taxes.[40]

The *nāyakas* did not possess any right village or villages to individuals or institutions. They were also not permitted to grant remissions on lands under their jurisdiction. But they enjoyed the privilege of not only collecting taxes but also remitting those taxes in favour of individuals and institutions. For example Mayidea-lenka, a *Nāyaka* collected a tax called *baṁṭala-āyamu* in A.D. 1317.[41] *Banṭu* means soldier and *Āyamu* menas tax. Obviously it was a levy collected from the people by the *nāyaka* in order to raise funds for the maintenance of horses and soldiers. As the main duty of the *nāyaka* was to maintain horses and soldiers and any lapse was viewed seriously by the king and punishment meted out, the *nāyaka* generally collected as much fund as possible from the people.

The nāyaka collected other taxes also like the grazing tax. For instance a tax called *Pullari* (pull=gross; ari=tax) a levy imposed on the cattle breeders for grazing the sheep, goats, oxen, cows, buffalow and other domestic animals in the forest lands and pastures was collected from the people.[42] It appears that the *nāyakas* collected different taxes from the people in order to raise as much fund as possible. They were eager to keep their financial position sound and stable.

The Industrial taxes were also collected by the *Nāyaṁkapuvāru*. For example oil mongers and the weavers have to pay taxes for running the industry, for selling their products in the market etc. The *Nāyaṅkara* had the right to grant remissions on the oil mills as means or privileges of *Sarvamānya* nature. An inscription dated A.D. 1269 informs that the *Nāyaṅkara* Mallikārjuna who was entitled to collect taxes such as *ari, sunkamu, pannu and kaṇika* on the oil mills remitted the taxes in favour of the temple on the occasion of the donation of a *ganuva* or oil-mill to the temple. Thus the *Nāyaṅkara* enjoyed the privileges of granting remissions on taxes due to him.[43]

There were other responsibilities the *Nāyaṅkara* had to fulfil. In addition to tribute on the lands the *amaranāyaka* offered presents to the sovereign when he has blessed with a son or when he performed the marriages of his children. The New Years Day was also the occasion for making presents to the king.[44]

The foregoing account reveals that the *Nāyaṅkara* system introduced by Rudramadevi under the guidance of the Velama chiefs had great significance in the history of the Kākatīyas. The entire credit should be given to the Velama chiefs particularly Prasāditya for evolving a system which had great politico-administrative significance. If it became a model to the Rāyas of Vijayanagara later, it was because of the merit and strength of the institution. The term *Amara Nāyaka* means an office (kara), possessed by a military chief. (*Nāyaka*) in comman of a body of troops according to which land was held by the *Nāyaka* for military service. Thus the intent and content of the institution appear to be military service as the *Nāyaka's* main function was to supply contingents of elephants, horses and foot soldiers in time of war. The high office of *bāhattara-niyōgādhipati* or the president of the 72 *niyogās* or 72 branches of administration in which the *Senādhyaksha, Mahāpradhānas, Pradhānas* etc., were included was generally bestowed on the subordinate chiefs who were *Nāyakas*. Gangaya Sahini was described as *Nāyaka*s under the

Kākatīyas were bound to the king by military service and the defence of the kingdom. Nevertheless it may be inferred that the *nāyakas* combined in themselves not only the military functions but also administrative responsibilities. This is understandable that collection of revenue, maintenance of military contingents demand civil, military and administrative duties.

Most of the *nāyakas* were described as *bāhattara niyōigādhipatis*. The term *bāhattara niyōgādhipati* is interpreted as an officer in charge of 72 *niyōgas* or 72 branches of administration. K. Satyanarayana in his Telugu version of *Andhra History and Culture* has given it as *Bhattara*.[45] The meaning of the term *Bhattara* however is not known.

We do not come across this term *bāhattara niyōgādhipati* in the Vijaynagara inscriptions. This suggests that the Kākatīya *nāyakas* were given charge of 72 departments in addition to military service of the Kākatīya rulers.[46] Kolani Rudradeva is stated to be the superintendent of the 72 *durgas* in the Kingdom of Pratāparudra.[47] If this is interpreted that *Nāyaka* was the superintendent of the 72 forts it may be inferred that the *Nāyaṅkaras* protected the forts in their *Nāyaṅkaras* and rendered military service. This is not to say that the *Nāyaṅkaras* ignored the welfare and prosperity of the people in their fiefs. According to K. Satyanarayana, the *Nāyakas* brought under cultivation uncultivated and deserted lands by employing the serfs. In such cases they were allowed to enjoy the temporary ownership of the land along with the fruits.[48]

The *Nāyaṅkaras* were obedient to the central authority as long as the king was powerful and strong enough control the constitutents of the kingdom and keep them in tact. But once they found that the power of the king was weakened, they took advantage of it and revolted. Though it was not universal, instances of revolt like that of the Kāyastha *Nāyaka* Ambadeva are not wanting. Speaking of Vijayanagara *Nāyakas*, Robert Sewell observed that the nobles proclaimed their independence during the period of anarchy.[49] Similarly like their Vijayanagara counterparts, the Kākatīya *Nāyakas* tried to transform the temporary occupation of their *Amarams* into permanent hereditary estates. However some *Nāyaka* families like the Viriyāla, Malyāla and the Cheraku were loyal and rendered great service to the Kākatīya rulers in establishing their authority.

The *Nāyaṅkaraship* under the Kākatīyas was not a permanent possession and it depended on the will and pleasure of the king. When the king was displeased with the performance of the *Nāyaka*, he was deprived of his estate. In some cases he was transfered to another fief. Obviously the *Nāyaka* could never claim to be a permanent owner of the fief. Not with standing their sense of insecurity, the *Nāyakas* played an effective role in the economic sphere. They constructed tanks, dug canals, reclaimed land, and improved agriculture. In the sphere of religion their contribution was significant. They constructed temples dedicated to Lord Śiva and Lord Vishṇu and named them after their names, their brothers, fathers and grand fathers. Thus the *Nāyaka* expressed his devotion to a particular god individually and collectively. In the process of the construction of temples, they made significant contribution to the cause of architecture and sculpture. Thus many subordinate rulers rendered valuable service to the Kākatīya rulers as *Nāyaṅkaras* and strengthened the kingdom in its administrative and military organization.

REFERENCES

1. A. Rangaswamy Saraswathi & S.K. Aiyanagar, *Sources of Vijayanagar History*, Madras, 1919, p. 91.
2. Subhasi, October, 1927, pp. 33-35.
3. P.V. Parabrahma Sastry, *The Kākatīyas*, Hyderabad, 1978, pp. 101-116.
4. S. Pushpalatha, *The Nāyankara System in Vijayanagara Empire*, unpublished M. Phil Thesis, Osmania University, Hyderabad, 1986, p. 70.
5. B.N. Puri, *History of Indian Administration,* Bombay, 1968, p. 211.
6. *I.A.* XI, p. 126; *E.I.* II, p. 96; *E.I.* XIII, p. 334.
7. *E.I.* XXIV, pp. 271-272.
8. B.N. Puri, *op. cit,* p. 276 fn 27.

9. N. Venkata Ramanayya, *Velugōṭivāri Vamśāvaḷi*, Madras, 1939, p. 9, verse 18.
10. *S.I.I.*, IV, 705.
11. P. Raghuntha Rao, *Ancient and Medieval History of Andhra Pradesh*, New Delhi, 1995, p. 69.
12. *S.I.I.* IV, 705.
13. *Bharati*, May 1977, pp. 56 ff
14. M.S. Sarma, *Forgotten Chapter of Andhra History*, Waltair, 1945.
15. *S.I.I.* X, 521.
16. *J.I.H.* XIV, p. 109.
17. *S.I.I.* X. 533
18. *S.I.I.* X. 536
19. *A.R.E.* 1939-40, No.5
20. *S.I.I.* X, 523.
21. *Teliṅgāṇa Inscriptions* : Kākatīya 43.
22. *Ibid*, 50
23. *Local Records*, XV, p. 287.
24. *S.I.I.* IV, 952.
25. Pratapacharitra, *A.S.P.P.* VII, p. 298-288.
26. N. Venkata Ramanayya, *Vijayanagar : Origin of the city and the Empire*, New Delhi, 1990, pp. 110-111.
27. P. Raghunatha Rao. *History and Culture of Āndhra Pradesh*, Delhi, 1995, pp. 77-78.
28. *Āndhrula Charitra*, Part- II, p. 288.
29. *A.S.P.P.* IV, pp. 93-112.
30. *Siddheśvara Charitra*, p. 120.
31. *Śivayogasaramu*, p. I-43.
32. *Reḍḍi Sanchika* Editors by V. Appa Rao, 1991, Hyderabad, pp. 6-7.
33. K.R. Basavaraja, *History and Culture of Karnataka*, Dharwad, 1984. p. 397.
34. *Sūrya Rāyāndhra Nighanthuvu*. Kakinada Vol. I, p. 248.
35. N. Venkata Ramanayya, *Studies in the Third Dynasty of* Vijayanagara, Madras 1935. p. 180.
36. Manu, VII-39.
37. P.V. Parabrahma Sastry, *op. cit.* p. 200.
38. *Ibid.* p. 201.
39. *S.I.I.* XIV, No. 150.
40. *S.I.I.* X, 509.
41. *S.I.I.* X, 521.

42. *E.A.* IV, p. 123.
43. *S.I.I.* X, 422.
44. N. Venkata Ramayayya, *op cit*. 1935, p. 171.
45. K. Sathyanarayana, *A study of the history and culture of Andhras*-II New Delhi 1983. P. 15.
46. S. Pushpalatha, *op. cit.* p. 70.
47. M.S. Sarma, *op. cit.* p. 37.
48. K. Satyanarayana, *Andhra History and Culture,* part II, Hyderabad, 1986, p. 12.
49. Robert Sewell, *A Forgotten Empire*, New Delhi, 1970, pp.201-202

Chapter-V

SOCIO-ECONOMIC AND RELIGIOUS CONDITIONS UNDER THE SUBORDINATE RULERS

SOCIAL CONDITIONS

During the period under study, the society was organized into the four fold Hindu Varṇa institution, despite occasional attacks on it by Viraśaiviam. Dr. Y. Gopala Reddy says that a close study of the Varṇāśramadharama in all ages existed in all its essentials in India as distinct from Hinduism irrespective of the dominant religion.[1] The Varaṇāśramadharma may be explained as unique classification of society into various castes or Varṇas viz., Brāhmaṇa, Kshatriya, Vaisya and Śūdra. According to A.L. Basham there is indeed a common *dharma*, a general code of conduct which all must follow equally, but there is also a *dharma* appropriate to each class and to each stage in the life of the individual.[2]

The *Dharma Śāstras* emphasize that the primary duty of a king was to maintain social order based on the *varṇas* Manu states that the kingdom can prosper only as long as the purity of castes was maintained. The *Nārada-smriti* enjoins that if the king does not dictate punishments to any caste, when they violated the *dharma* of the caste, the created beings of the world would perish. The responsibility of the king to uphold the varṇa system is echoed in the literary and epigraphical records of the period.[3] The *Siddhēśvara Charitra* styles Gaṇpatideva *mahārāja* as *nanavarṇa vara māṇḍalika karaganda*.[4] The subordinate chiefs like their masters also upheld the Varṇa system enjoined in the scriptures. The Tripuranatakam inscription dated A.D. 1290. refers to the Kāyastha chief Ambadeva as *Chaturvarṇa Samuddharna*.[5] Not only the kings, *Sāmantas, mahasmantas* but even merchant guilds, *rājagurus* and private individuals protected atleast in principle, the varṇa system in medieval Andhradesa.[6]

Brahmins

The subordinate chiefs of the Kākatīyas, the brahmins retained their earlier status in the fields of education and religious affairs. They held the power to accord religious sanction and recognition to the rulers. The brahmins lived mostly on the patronage of kings and the charity of the public. The brahmins were described as men with *vēdas* emanating from their mouths, lords of the goddess of learning, praised by learned men and performers of numerous sacrifices.[7] The subordinate chiefs donated *agrahāra* to the brahmins to accrue religious merit, as the donation of *agrahāra* was one of the constituents of the *Saptasantānas* or seven deeds of ever lasting virtue. *Agrahāras* were Brahmin settlements formed out of land reclamation or by rehabilitation of people in deserted villages. The *agrahāra* were given to scholars well versed in *vēdas, purāṇas* and philosophy. Kōta Keta II donated to brahmins Erukogallu in Konḍanatavāḍi area renamed Subhambikapuram after the name of his mother and Tadivada Challageru Gangipāḍu renamed Bhimapuram after the name of his father, Ammalapūḍi region with new appellations after his own name.[8] He also rehabilitated the brahmins in the area lying between the seven *agrahāras* of Gunturu, Polasamirru, Kochchera, Vangipuram, Inumgallu, Uppuluru and Karamchēḍu.[9] Kundāmba, the daughter of Kākati Mahadeva and wife of Natavāḍi Rudra I gifted the village Vemulatonṭa renaming it as Kundavaram to the brahmins, as *agrahāras.*[10] Immaḍi Viśvanātha granted Lenjita and Sarepalli as *agrahāras* to the brahmins.[11] These land grants are generally followed by the expressions like *Sarvakāra Pariharuvu* (exemption from all texes and immunities.), *bhara pariharuvu* (exemption from all texes and immunities) etc.[12] *Sarva Vastubhōgamu* (the enjoyment of property and all other kinds of essential things), *Sarva Krantamu* (entire possession of rent free ināme) etc.[13] This suggest that brahman donees were not expected to render any kind of service to their benefactors, and the fiefs held by them were exempted from confiscation. This aspect is clearly indicated by the imprecatory verses appended at the end of the grants. They were also exempted from taxation and empowered to enjoy criminal and administrative powers in the areas under their jurisdiction. P.V. Parabrahma Sastry observed that brahmans *agrahāras* which come under *Sarvamānya* tenure or tax free villages were subjected to a concessional rate of tax.[14]

We often get references to *mahājanas* in connection with the administration of *agrahāra* villages. According Prof. R. Narasimha Rao, *mahājanas* or *mahājanulu* means 'greate people' who looked after the village administration. The *mahājanas* were incharge of the administration of an *agrahāra* village also known as *brahmadēya* and *Chaturvēdimangaḷam*. They are described as the excellent brahmins proficient in *Śāstras, Vēdas, Vedangas, Upāngas* and eighteen *purānas* and other branches of learning.[14A] The Nutakki inscrpiton dated A.D. 1128 describes the 500 *mahājans* of Malavana as a set of Brahmins who migrated from Masapuri on the west bank of Godavarto Nutakki. The Durgi epigraph of A.D. 1319 records that the *mahājanas* of Dharavemula granted certain portion of their income to the temple of Rudreśvara and Bolleśvara of Dharavemula. The Kaṭakūru inscription dated A.D. 1303 records certain gifts by the *mahājans* fostered education, offered food to the *Sanyāsis*, acted also showed very keen interest in the cultivation of the lands assigned to the temple.[15] Thus, the *mahājanas* played a vital role in the administration of *agrahāras*.

The Brahmins guided the villages in religious life. They after consultating the *panchānga* (calender), selected auspicious days for commencing various agricultural operations like tilling, planting, irrigating, harvesting etc. During the times of draught or famine, they also performed *yajnas* as well to propitiate the rain gods. They performed *sraddhas* for the departed souls for which they were granted vrittis. For instance the Moguluṭla copper plate inscription dated A.D. 1219 registers the grant of village

Moguluṭla by Kōṭa Gaṇapāmba, in the presence of Kākati Gaṇapatideva, to Rudri Pedimgaru for the spiritual merit of Betarāja for performing *Gaya Sraddha.*[16] Similarly, Rāja Rudra, son of Cheraku Veluri Bolla, as per the Goruvankapalli copper plate inscription dated A.D. 1292, sent four brahmins to Gaya to perform *sraddha* of his father and granted Goruvanakapalli village to them for the services rendered.[17]

Brahmins also were appointed as *Karanams* in villages to keep the land records, collect taxes and resolve the disputes that arose in the villages. The Duggirala inscrption dated A.D. 1214 records the resolving of boundary dispute by the village *Karanam* Suraparāju.[18] It is relevant to note in this connection that at the present time the word *Karanam* is held as a synonym for *Niyōgi* a member of that section of Brahmins who accepted administrative posts in the state. The other section of the brahmins, now known as *Vaidikas* were during the period under review generally referred to as the *mahājanulu.*

Brahmins also occupied important posts in the kingdom. The Indulūri family of subordinate chiefs were brahmins, though the case of Kāyastha chiefs is a disputed one. Normally the brahmins is expected to be a teacher, a *purohita* or a priest. The *Varṇaśrama dharma* was some times violated and brahmins also took to sword. According to *Śivayōgasāra,* Kākati Rudradeva appointed, Pedamalla as the *nāyaka* or commander of the armies and Pinamalla, the chief Accoount (*Peda Samprati*). They were the sons of Induluri Nana Goura.[19] Somamantri was another member of the family who distinguished himself as a general. The *Śivayōgasāra* describes his exploits. Somamantri led an expendition with a large army on the regions west of Warangal, annexed the lands and vanquished the *māṇḍalikas* of Gogulanāḍu, Kolanividu, and beyonds the river Godavari, the two *Madiyas,* the twelve *Manniyas* and the territory included in the Kalinga seema.[20] Maṇuma Gaṇna of Indulūri family under the overlordship of Rudrāmadevi could disperse the armies of the enemy and capture 72 (*bahattara*) forts.[21] Two Tripurantakam inscriptions dated A.D. 1259[22] and A.D. 1261[23] refer to one Gannaya, son of Indulūri

Ganapaya. The inscription dated A.D. 1259 refers to him as *Mahāpradhāni* and *Bāhattariniyōgādhipati*. Indulūri Rudra also known as Kolani Rudra served the king Pratāparudra as *mudrāpaka*, officer incharge of royal seal. He was also the governor of the region between Orugallu and Simhachalam in the east. The *Śivayōgasāra* states that he was made the *bāhattari durga nāyaka* by Pratāparudra. He is also credited with the victory over the *Pancha* Pāṇḍyas or the five Pāṇḍya kings.[24]

Mahāpradhāna Pomkala Mallaya *Preggaḍa* held the post of *bahattaraniyōgādhipati* under Rudrāmadevi.[25] Rājanāyaka, a brahmin, served Recherla Rudra as *Pradhāni* as well as military commander.[26] Pradakshinamu Mahadevamanchi was the minister of Vennapareddi of Kanta Madhuka family, a *sāmanta* of Recherla Kata IV. [27] *Somamantri* served as minister of Recherla Virapasayita *Chamupati*.[28] Vāyideva pandita and his son Namadeva pandita served as ministers of Gangaya *Sāhini*. Namadeva's Tripurantakam inscription dated A.D. 1250 described Namadeva as *Suragaru samāna, sakala śastra parā varaka mantri-mānikya, nīti-chāṇakya, pati-kārya durandhara* etc.[29] Ambedeva had a brahmin minister Ghodarāya Gangadeva.[30] Thus brahmins not only acted as religious leaders but also rendered meritorious services as chiefs, governors, ministers and head of departments. This trend continued later during the Vijayanagra period also.

Kshatriyas

The *Kshtriyas* who basically belonged to the fighting class were reṇowed warriors and served the kings as soldiers, commanders and governors of forts. They claim to belong to the solar and lunar dynasties or *sūryavamśa* and *Chandravamśa* dynasties. The Chāgi chiefs who ruled Natavāḍi and who claimed to belong to the Durjaya family like the Kākatiya rulers were *Kshtriyas*. Though the Chāgis were *Kshatriyas* like their overlords, the Kākatiya rulers, they however did not mention either their political relationship or caste affiliation. Not withstanding this they were kshatriyas. According to a Telugu Kāvya *Rāma Vilāsamu,* the name Chāgi was changed into Vatsavaya in course of time. It seems Chāgi Eṛṛa Potaraja shifted his headquaters to a place called Vatsavāya in the early post Kākatiya period on account of which the family of Eṛṛa Pōtarāja came to be called Vatsavāya instead of Chāgi.[31] The members of the family assumed the title of Pesani *Hanumantha*.[32] There were other *Kshatriya* families like the Chōḍas, the Chālukyas of Elamanchi land Veṅgi etc. That flourished in the Coastal region. It appears that some *Kshatriya* families, descendants of the Kākatīyas, the Kōṭas, the Parichedi and Varṇataka migrated from Telengāṇa to Andhra. The *Kshatriyas* in Andhra were known as *Rāchavāru* or *Rājus*. The *kshatriyas* falling in line with the Brahmins adopted *gōtras* like Kāśyapa, Dhanunjaya, Vashishta and Kaundinya. The Kākatīyas and Kōṭas who were *Kshatriyas* belonged to the *Kāśyapa* and *Dhanunjaya* gōtras.[33] It appears that four Rajput tribes belonging to Vashishta, Dhanunjaya, Kaundinya and *Kāśyapa gōtras* migrated to Telengāṇa from Andhra under the leadership of Mādhava Varma, the Anumakoṇḍa inscription of Prola II throws valuable light. According to this inscription, Mādhava Varma was a great military commander and possessed a great army consisting of 8000 elephants, ten crore horses and unlimited infantry. Though these figures need not be taken in the literal sense they nevertheless suggest that Mādhava Varma had all the leadership qualities to lead a large number of immigrants in to Telengāṇa.[34] Thus it appears that many *Kshatriya* families migrated to Telengāṇa in search of better opportunities in political and administrative spheres.

Thus it appears that the *Kshatriyas* who distinguished themselves as rulers and great warriors played a commendable role in safeguarding the Kākatīya Kingdom. Though the *Kshatriyas* in coastal region had a chequered political career and could not build a powerful kingdom, the Kshatriyas of Telengāṇa were more fortunate. They not only proved themselves as successful rulers but also helped the Kākatiya rulers in resisting the Muslim invasions. Many of the Kshatriya families sacrified their lives on the battle field in an attempt to save the Kākatiya kingdom. It is likely that the remaining *Kshatriya* families after the fall of Orugallu in A.D. 1323 migrated to Vijayanagara and took up service under the rising Sangama Dynasty.

Vaisyas

The Vaisyas are generally referred to in the inscriptions as *Komatis* or *Śettis*. They like the Brahmins, adopted *gōtras* and *śakhas* which would indicate their social status. The *gōtras* of pure vaisyas are considered to be 102 out of which Nebela, Pennikala, Punasila, Venkula, Surukoti, Silakula, Puchchakula, Yeṛṛa settii kula, Bodakula, Vivarfisitla, Appanagatula, Murukula and Maddikula are mentioned in some of our records.[35] The assumption of the *gōtras* and *śakhas* by the Vaisyas suggests that they wanted to improve their status in the society by imitating the Brahmins. The Vaisya *Purana* states that Penugoṇḍa, Vengi, Denduluru, Ghantasala, Achanta, Nagaram etc., were the strongholds of this community. There were Kamma vaisyas, Mulikinānṭi vaisyas, Palnāṭi vaisyas based on the region of their habitation or may be regional sub-castes.

The trade guilds organized by vaisyas served as a catalactic in the process of shaping the economic life of the country. There were a number of mercantile organisations like the *Ayyavole* five hundred, *Nakharamu, Vīra-Balanja, Nānadesi, Ubhayanānāḍesi, Pekkandru, Teliki* 1,000, *Mummuridandas* etc., which throw a flood of light on the economic activity of the traders in the Kākatiya age. The existence of Nāñaḍesi guild in Sumatra and Burma and a colony of Tamil merchants (*Arava-Nakakharmu*) at Peruru in the Miryalagūḍa taluka of Nalgonda District indicate the mobility of the Vaisya community. These mercantile guilds consisted of not only the vaisyas but also merchants belonging to other castes. For example the Nānādēsi represented merchants belonging to various castes and communities but also various regions. But it is possible that the vaisyas whose occupation was mainly trade and commerce dominated the economic life of the period. The Mummaridandas that are referred to in many inscriptions of the Andhra and Karṇāṭaka regions might have been either the regular or the advance guard of soldiers of the Balanja merchants. Kannisetti is mentioned in an inscrption of A.D. 1249 as *Samaya Sēnādhipati*, the commander of the army of vaisya marchants. It is possible that the vaisya merchants maintained contingents of forces to protect the caravans from highway robbers and dacoits in the forests. Some of the merchants of the period are allowed to enjoy previlaged positions in the royal courts and also held public officers.[36]

Śūdra

The emergence of Śūdras as the ruling class is a unique characteristic of medieval Andhradesa. Most of the ruling families of the period belonged to *Chaturthakula* or Sūdra caste. The Kōṭas, the political successors of the Kondapaḍumaṭis, ruled the Velanāḍu six thousand country from the beginning of the 12th century to the last quarter of the 13th century A.D. They belonged to the *Chaturthakula* or the fourth caste.[37] The Natavāḍis who ruled the Natavāḍi *vishaya* which roughly corresponds to the region south of the river Krishna also belonged to the Śūdra Varṇa.[38] The Bayyāram tank inscription of Kākati Mailama, daughter-in-law of Natavāḍi Buddharaja records that both the families were of the same Śūdra descent.[39] Recherla Reḍḍi chiefs,[40] Cheruku Reḍḍi chiefs, Gona chiefs and Velama chiefs belonged to the fourth caste. The Malyāla chiefs[41] and Viriyāla chiefs[42] claim to be Śūdras born in the line of Durjaya. The Kāyastha chiefs claim to be *Kshatriyas*, but in the opinion of B.N. Sastrty they were brahmins.[43]

The Śūdra rulers not only styled themselves as Kshatriyas after acquiring great wealth and power but also went to the extent of inserting mythical and semi-mythical personalities in the geneological lists in order to strengthen their borrowed lineage. The semi-mythical and mythical personalities that are often referred to in the Kākatiya inscriptions are Durjaya, Karikāla Choḷa, Sun, Manu, Ikshāvaku, Sagara, Brihaspati, Kakustha, Dilipa, Daśaratha, Rāma etc., Many minor ruling dynasties of medieval Andhradesa, viz., Chāgis, Kondapaḍumatis, Natavāḍis, Parichchedis, Kandravāḍis, Viriyālas, Velanāḍu Choḷas etc., claimed descent from Durjaya. Thus the Śūdras caliming *Kshatriya* origin and referring to semi-mythical and mythical persons as their ancestors would demonstrate a tendency on the part of the Brahminical society to absorb rulers of lower castes into the Kshatriya fold. Further the Śūdras who remained Śūdras but exercised their rule over some regions as subordinates of the powerful dynasties, at least imitated their overlords by referring to mythical persosn as their ancestors in their genealogical lists.[44] During this period the Recherla Reḍḍi's Nāgulapadu inscription referred to the eighteen commuinities but unfortunately it is damaged and we cannot find anything more than a mere mention of *Kōmaṭies*, taddy-sellers, shephereds, goldsmiths, weavers etc.[45]

With the land reclamation and foramtion of new villages and the powers enjoyed by the village assemblies, and proliferation of occupations different sub castes arose in the Śūdra varṇa. Of the higher Śūdras during the Kākatiya period the Reḍḍis, Velamas, Padmanāyakas, and Kammas were prominent. There were several sub castes in lower Śūdras, who contributed to the economy and well being of the socieity.

The caste system was not rigid, at least in ruling classes. Y. Gopala Reddy observes that the matrimonial alliances among the ruling families that were contracted during the period under consideration throw some welcome light on the part played by the caste in the society. The Natavāḍis belonged to the fourth caste. The daughter of Natavāḍi Rudra, Bayyaladevi, was married to Kōṭa Keta III who belonged to the fourth caste. Gaṇapatideva after reducing the Ayya chiefs of Divi to subjection, married Nāramba and Pēramba, the daughters of Piṇa Choḍa and took Jayapa, one of the three sons of that chief, into his service. Gaṇapatideva had two daughters, the elder called Rudrāmba or Rudrāmadevi and the younger named Gaṇapāmba or Gaṇapamadevi. Rudrāma was married to Virabhadra, a *Kshatriya* Prince who belonged to the Niḍadavole branch of the Chālukyas. Indulūri Annaya, son of Peda Gannaya, a brahmin by caste, married Ruyyāma, the daughter of Rudrāmadevi. The Alapāḍu grant of Yellanadeva, dated A.D. 1264, states that the queen Rudrāma gave her second daughter in marriage to Yellanadeva. It is evident from the above information that the matrimonial alliances were effected between the śūdras, śūdras and *Kshatriyas* and Śūdras and brahmins in the Kākatiya age. These inter marriages saw horizontal and vertical social mobility in the *varṇa* divided society of medieval Andhradesa. This social mobility largely improved the actual social status of the śūdras.[46]

All of the foregoing suggest that the *Kshatriyas* and *Śūdras* dominated the polity of the Kākatiya age. The *Sāmantas*, and *mahāsāmantas* who emerged as powerful political factors mostly belonged to the fourth caste. The *mahājana* institution which controlled the *agrahāra* administration was practically dominated by the Brahmins. Ketana's *Vignanēśvariyam,* a work based on *Mitākshara*, States that the Brahmins were exempted from trial by ordeal and physical torture. But this is not supported by any epigraphical evidence. The wide spread practice of making grants of land to the Brahmins by the kings, queens, feudatories etc., paved the way for the raise of Brahmana landed magnates, wielding considerable economic and political power. The functions of the collection of taxes, regulation of mines, agriculture etc., together with those of the maintainance of law and order and defence which were hitherto performed mainly by the other castes now step by step went into the hands of Brahmins. This may be taken as a presage of feudalism. The vaisyas enjoyed a privileged position as the heads of corporate bodies and looked after the internal and overseas trade. They even enjoyed immense judicial authority and rendered military assistance to their overlords.[47]

Women

Women of the age, though the foundations of society were based on patriarchal system, enjoyed equal status with men. The ideal womanhood was *grihalaxmi* and *ardhāngi*. Her aim was service to husband and devotion to god. She propitiated the gods and the goddesses for the bestowal of happiness, health and prosperity for her family and herself. The history of the period reveals ideal wives, mothers, lady ministers, generals , administrators and benefactors. Some princesses and private ladies under took works of public untility, built temples and endowed them with rich gifts. Some women were learned in fine arts. Women in general participated along with their husbands in religious ceremonies, festivals etc. Some women occupied highest posts and proved themselves equal to men. We know Rudrāmadevi, daughter of Gaṇapatideva ruled Kākatiya kingdom after her father. Gaṇapamadevi another daughter of Gaṇapatideva who was married to Kōṭa Betarāja took the responsibility of governing the Kōṭa Gaṇapamadevi *ammangāru* in the Mogulutla copper plate and in some other stone inscriptions. Like the other Kōṭa kings, Gaṇapamadevi also styled herself in the inscriptional *praśastis as śrimat trinayana Pallava Prasādadi to Krishṇa venna nadi dakshina shātsahastra vani vallabha bhya lobha durlabha, pratāpa laṅkēśvara, ganadabhērunda, nandi martānda, śrīman mahā manḍalēśvara* etc. She administered the Kōṭa region for forty five years after the death of her husband. The *praśastis* of the inscriptions show that her claims to the kingship were accepted and legitimised.[48] Viriyāla Nāgasāni, wife of prola I was the feudatory ruler of Rembarti area. After her husbabd's death,her sons Malraja and Mummadiraja being young, Nagasani governed the fief. The Pammi inscription describes her as *Mahāsāmanta Viriyāla Nāgasānmma gāru.*[49]

We know that women of the age played key roles in political affairs. The Gūḍuru epigraph states that Kāmavasāni, wife of Eṛṛa took up the cause of young Garuḍa Beta and having approached the emperor established the line of Kākati, securing him the Anumakonda *vishaya* as fief.[50] On the basis of the information given in the Chronicles *Siddhēśvara charitra* and *Pratāparudra charitra*, it becomes obvious that Viriyala Kamavasāni acted as regent upto A.D. 1000. Afterwards Garuda Beta, her nephew, succeeded to the throne.

Women of the age not only occupied prestigious positions, but also rendered service to the cause of people by building tanks, erecting temples and making munificent grants. Epigraphical evidence is abundant in this respect. Two instances are sufficient in support of this. Pillalamarri inscription of Erakasani states that *Recharla Pillalamarri Betirreḍḍi pendlāmu sakala guna ganālankrtyaina Erakasāna ammangāru saka varshamulu 1130 gu vibhava. Samvatsara Jyestha suddha Tritiyayu Sōmavāarmu nāḍu pillalamarrini tana perana Erakēśvara dēvaram pratistha Sēsi a dēvaraku guḍiki gōparamunaku bagilimadu, manku baviki parvarmulaku maṭhamui naku aṁga-bhōga raṅga-bhōga adisamastapuka sidhyarṭ (t) hamai peramti eraka varamn nam= dama peram gathinchina eraka samudram etc.*, *Erukasān amman gāru* endowed with all auspiceious qualties, wife of the glorious Recherla Pillalamarri Beti Reḍḍi A.D. 1208, established the glorious god Erakēśvara in her name in Pillalamarri, and provided the temple, with gopura, doorway and well. Provision was also made for the members of the establishment, for the *maṭha*, and for worship. The west land and dryland under *Erukasamudram* constructed in her name in Erakavaram, were donated to the temple.[51]

The Bothpur inscription of Malyāla Kuppāmbika dated A.D. 1276 records the installation of *Linga* in the name of her husband and the grant of *vritties* under *Basamudram, Kuppasamudram, Gaṇapasamudram* etc.[52] In general, the status of women was honourable if not totally equal to that of men.

Sati

In Andhradesa, we find a few instances of the practice of *sati* during the medieval period. A record from Nidubrolu dated A.D. 1210 informs that the wife of a treasury officer of Gonka II proceeded to *Śivalōka* along with her husband. Few instances of *sati* are also found in the *Palnāṭivira charitra*. When Anapota died, his wife was also burnt on the same funeral pyre along with him. There is also another instance of *sati* in the same work. When Alaraju died his wife Peradevi is said to have jumped into the funeral fire of her husband. It is stated that Peradevi consoled her father-in-law and mother-in-law, offered prayers to lord Śiva and invited death by jumping into the flames. This suggest that Peradevi performed at her own will and not with the encouragement of the relatives.[53]

However it is not a general rule that every widow should commit *sati* on the funeral pyre of her husband. By and large in medieval Andhradesa this practice seems to be voluntary and not forced on women. The fact Rudrāmadevi, Gaṇapamadevi, Viriyāla Nāgasāni, Viriyāla Kāmavasāni and Malyāla Kupāmbika did not perform *sati* and lived along after the death of their husbands, shows that women were not forced to perform *sati*.

Sānis

During the medieval times, the five famous Śaivaite centres of pilgrimage located at Drakshārāmam, Sāmarlakōṭa, Bhīmavaram, Pālakollu and Amarāvati were widely known as the *panchārāmas*. These Śiva temples had expanded not only in size but also in terms of the proliferation and complexity in the nature of rituals performed in them and thereby emerged as the important socio economic institutions during the medieval period. The temple grils who were in service of the god were generally mentioned as *Sānis* in the temple epigraphs. This word is a derivative of the Sanskrit word *Svāmini*. To conduct the daily rituals and to perform festivals throughout the year, the temple employed a good number of servants male and female. Particularly, the performance of *aṅga raṅga bhōga* and other services were assigned to the female servants commonly know as *Sānis*. The word *sāni*, it must remembered, did not denote a derogatory meaning as it is now. Royal women, and house wives had the word *sāni* suffixed to their names as is evident by the names Erukasāni, Kamavasāni, Kuppavasāni etc. In the fertile river valleys and confluences of rivers, temples received a large number of endowments and so could maintain a large number of ladies in temple services, as is ordained in the scriptures. Temples in places like Juttiga, Kommuru, Chebrolu, Pālakollu and Drākshārāmam maintained *sānis* who organised themselves into guilds. The temple epigraphs mentioned some of the duties to be performed by the *Sānis*. Some of them are rituals like bathing the deity with sacred water, fanning the deity with chauries, carrying silver lampsteads during the *ratha yātra*, and singing and dancing at fixed times. There is a striking similarity between gods in temple and kings in the royal palaces, as both of them were served by women who were generally called courtesnas or *bhōga strīs*. To fulfil their duties as dancers and musicians, the temple girls had to undergo intensive training to master the arts of dance and music. According to the Chebrolu inscription[54] of Jāyapa *Nāyaka*, dated. A.D. 1213, some dancing girlswere serving the Nāgeśwara temple right from the age of eight years. These girls lived in separate quarters called *sānivāḍa* and were provided with all physical facilities by the temple. An inscriptin at Palakollu dated A.D. 1169 mentions that the *Vritti* (service tenure) of dancing (*AvajavaVritti*) was given to the head of the sāni-300 guild of Kshiraramesvara temple. This shows that it was the duty of the *sani*-300 guild to organise the dance and music rituals that were necessary in temples. An inscription at Pālakollu dated A.D. 1137 records the donation of Velanāṭi Ganna for setting up of a lamp in the temple, which was kept in the trust of the *Sānimunnurvuru*, guild of this temple. The *sānis* were suitably rewarded for their services to the temple. For instance an inscrpiton from Amarāvati mentions that out of the produce of the lands of the temple, one fourth share (*Chirukapālu)* should be given to the *Sānis* of the temple. But the *sānis* were also highly devoted to god and expressed their devotion by making donations to the temples. Thus, the temples during the period under review entertained a large numbe of *sānis* to conduct the *aṅga raṅga bōga* and other types of services to the gods and they were organised into guilds like the guild organisations of trade and commerce. These guilds of *Sānis* administered the endowments of trade under their trust by the donors and played a very important role in propagating *bhakti* ideology among the devotees through their music and dance performance.[55]

Education

The important centres of learning during the Kākatiya period were the *ghatikas, bhrahmapurīs, agrahāras*, temples and the *maṭhas*. It was customary for the kings and common people alike to grant gifts of villages and cash donations for the maintenance of these institutions as well as the teachers.

The teacher of *ghatikas* were referred to as *Ghadiya sasulu and Ghadiya*. Epigraphs present *bhrāhmapurīs* as the settlements of learned brahmins consisting of poets and philosophers. Land grant to a single or few brahamins is usually known as *bhattavrittis,* and when a whole village was settled by a number of learned brahmins, it was commonly known as an *agrahāra*, which are referred to as *Chaturvedi mangaḷams*. Education was greatly fostered by temples next to the *agrahāras*. While the instruction in the *agrahāras* was confined to the study of the Vēdas and other traditional Sānskritic learning, in the temple provision was made for the study of several branches of knowledge including fine arts. Like the *Vihāras* of Buddhist creed, a *maṭha* is a monastic establishment and was meant to propagate different religious creeds of Hinduism. Several records of the period reveal that they entertained students from far and near by providing boarding and lodging and imparted knowledge to them.

There are references to several Śaiva *maṭhas* and teachers in the Kākatiya inscriptions. According to an inscription at Kāzipet, Rāmeśvarapandita, the spiritual *guru* of the Kākatiya king Beta II, and his sons. Durgarāja and Prola II and the pontiff of Mallikārjuna Silamaṭha of Śrīśailam was proficient in the doctrines of *Lakulīśvarāgama*. Viśvesvara Śiva, Kēsiśvara Śiva, Santa Śiva Paripūrṇa Śiva Jnānōttama Śiva , Uttama Śiva and Sadā Śiva were some of the Śaiva teachers of *Gōlakimaṭha* in Andhradesa. These great Śaiva teachers commanded great influence on the Kākatiya Kings and their feudatories and received benefactions for the maintenance of the *maṭhas*. Consequently the *maṭhās* emerged as great educational institutions during the period under review. *Vidyāmanḍapas* are attached to the *maṭhas* for the maintenance of which the Kāyastha chief Jannigadeva granted a number of villages to Santaśivadesika of Abhinavagōḷakimaṭha of Śrīśailam for the maintenance of Vidyāmanḍapa and a feeding house. The Vedas, *vyākaranamu* and *tarka, Śaivāgamas* and medicine were taught in the Vidyāmanḍapas.[56]

Medical Facilities

Generally *maṭhas* and the temples maintained hospitals and extended medical aid to common people. The king, the feudal lords and the rich people made donations to the temple and *maṭhas* for the maintenance of hospitals. An inscription dated A.D. 1261 registers the gift of the village, Mandaram and of the village Velagapūḍi, together with an Island in the river by *Gaṇapatideva* and Rudrāmadevi to Viśveśvara Śivāchārya of the Gōḷaki *maṭha*. The donee amalgamated the two villages into one and founded a temple, monastery, a college, a choultry, a maternity home and a general hospital for the benefit of villagers. The

Malkapuram inscription speaks of preservation and preparation of medicines. Viśveśvars Śivāchārya established monasteries in other place such as Kāleśvaram, Ponnugam, Mantrakūṭam, Chandravalli, Nandapura, Kommuru, Eleśvaram, Nivritti, Sangameśvaram, Uttara Somasila etc. All these centres must have extended medical aid to the people as they already attained fame as great centres of medical importance. Not only *Śaiva maṭhas*, but also Jaina *basadis* maintained hospitals. *Basavapurāna* informs us that physicians were employed in the temple. Lands were also granted to temples for maintenance of gardens. Temples which were located near the forest area became famous medical centres in those days and among them, mention must be made of Śrīśailam, Tripurantakam, Eleśwaram, Drākshārāmam and Ālampuram.[57]

ECONOMIC CONDITIONS

The economic conditions prevailing in the areas ruled over by the subordinate chiefs were not different from those prevailing in the kingdom of Kākatīya rulers. A large portion of the kingdom was under the sway of the subordiante chiefs.

Agriculture

Agriculture was the main occupation of the people. Population was not so dense in medieval times as at present. The central zone of which large tracts of land were under the sway of Racherla Reḍḍi chiefs and Cheruku chiefs comprised of rocky soil dependent on rain fall which was inadequate. Similarly the third peripheral zone as well as the twilight zone were dense with thick forests. Most of the villages in those days were primarily the settlements of peasants who under th benefaction of the concerned chiefs brought as much land as possible under plough.[58] So the twin tasks before the rulers were land reclamation by clearing *jungles* and providing irrigation facilities and digging wells and tanks.

Land Reclamation

We know that the chiefs of Gona family were employed by Kākatīya rulers to clear and reclaim thick forests of the Kurnool district and Raichur doab. Gannaya Reḍḍi and his brothers got the *jungles* cleared and brought large tracts of land under cultivation. In the wrok of reclamation, Immadi Kāṭa Reḍḍi, son of Kāṭa Reḍḍi was helped by Buddha Reḍḍi, a resident of Aiza village. The Kākatīya general Immaḍi Kāṭa Reḍḍi was very much pleased with the services of Buddha Reḍḍi and got him appointed as Naḍa gouda over Manuva, Beludoni, Raichur, Mosulkallu, Ālampur, Āḍōni, Aiza *Seemas* by king Pratāparudra in A.D. 1290.[59]

The local tradition preserved in the *kaifiyats* of several villages throws some light in the aspect. It is said that Pratāparudradeva in his campaign against Ambadeva reached Kocherla Kōṭa and ordered his officers to cut down the forest which than covered the adjacent area.[60] The region to the west of the Śrīśaila mountain corresponding to a large portion of the present Nandikotkur taluk in Kurnool district was also at that time covered by dense woods which were cleared at the instance of the king.[61] The Hanumkonda inscription dated A.D. 1163[62] and the Tripurantakam inscription[63] dated A.D. 1252-53 refer to the clearance of forests and the construction of tanks.

The Kākatīya rulers ordered their subordiante chiefs to carry on land reclamation, from the economic point of view, to increase food production in proportion to the increasing population. It was followed in two ways 1) clearance of waste or land covered with *jungles* and bringing it under cultivation for the first time or of the land under cultivation but later deserted, 2) foundation of new villages.[64]

In granting *agrahāras* and founding new villages the motive might have been acquisition of religious merit, but it also fulfilled a real economic purpose, for a new settlement invaribly meant increase of cultivable fields. The Pālampet inscription[65] dated A.D. 1213 records that Recherla Rudra built a town called Nekkonda and granted it to the Rudreśvara temple at Orugallu.

By granting *agrahāras* and laying out gardens, the Kōṭas encouraged agriculture. The *agrahāras* were assigned to Brahmins named after themselves, their relatives or after their titles. Bhima II granted twelve villages in the region of Gaṇḍanatavāḍa,

Kondapaḍumaṭi and Doddikandravāḍi and converted them into four towns Subbambikapuram, Bhimavaram, Chodavaram and Jagamecchuganḍapuram, after his mother, brother, father and named after his title. Keta II granted 24 *agrahāras* and another 70 *agrahāras* on the banks of river Krishna. Keta III, Keta II and Gaṇapāmba donated agrhāras, and laid many flower gardens.[66]

Buddha, son of Natavāḍi Rudra founded the Village Budhapura after his name clearing the forest and furnished it with a tänk.[67] Similarly the village of Kundavaram in the Chennur taluq, Adilabad, district and a tank *Kundasamudra* were built by Kundāmba, wife of Natavāḍi Rudra I and sister of Gaṇapatideva, after reclamation of the land.[68]

Irrigation Facilities

The subordinate chiefs of Kākatiya rulers like their overlords paid much attention to the irrigation facilities for the purposes of agriculture, which was the main source of the country's prosperity. The main feature of it was establishment of a network of tanks or reservoirs in which rain water was caught and stored for utilization in the cultivation of soil. Excepting the first two pheripheral zones which are watered by the channels dug from the rivers like the Pennar, the Krishṇa and the Godavari the other zones had to depend on storage tanks and on wells sunk deep in the earth. Every village in the country had one or more tanks, according to the extent of its arable land and conditions of the crops raised there on. Before the rise of the Kākatīyas the tanks were small, the irrigation facilities were quite inadequate, and the area under cultivation was usually very limited in extent. But the Kākatiya rulers realised that red and sandy soil of Telengāṇa was extremely fertile and eminently suitable for wet cultivation and constrcution of tanks in every village.[69]

However, the state undertook no direct responsibility for the construction and maintenance of irrigation works. The construction of tank was regarded as an act of charity which would endow great religious merit. It was one of the *Saptasantānas* or seven acts of righteousness namely one's own son, a temple, a garden, a tank, an agrahāra, a literary work and treasure, which would perpetuate the name of the donor and establish his fame permanently in the world. Influenced profoundly by this brief, the kings and the *Sāmantas*, nobles and officials, religious leaders and merchants, and wealthy men in general all busied themselves in the construction of tanks, and thus the whole country was provided with an adequate irrigational system. Two noble families of Telengāṇa, viz, the Malyāla and the Recherla, deserve special mention in this connection, since many of the surviving tanks which secured the name of 'tank district' for the region in later ages were the fruits of their enterprize and activity. The *Chaunḍasamudram, Bāchasamudram* (*Bassamudram*), *Gaṇapa-samudram, Kuppasamudram, Buddhunikunta, Kuppāmbakālva, Poli Reḍḍi Kālva, Dadla kālva,* and the great tank at Pakhal were all excavated by the Malyāla chiefs while *Subba-samudram, Nāma-samudram, Viśwanātha-samudram, Gaur-samudram, Eṛṛa-samudram, Laluma-samudram, Kuḍi kuḍiya cheruvu, Katyare-Cheruvu, Neredla-Cheruvu, Eṛṛamārju-kuṅṭa* were constructed by the Recherla chiefs. In the south, the Kāyastha princes, especially Ambadeva and his subordinates also developed agriculture. Ghōḍayarāya Gangayadeva, the famous *mahāpradhāna* of Ambadeva, caused two tanks called *Ambasamudram* to be excavated in the name of his master at Bali (Obali) and Uṭukūru respectively. He also had a canal called *Rayasahasrāmalla-kālva* dug from the river (Cheyyeru) at Lembaka and named *Gaṇdapendara-kālva* excavated at Tadlapaka.[70]

The other nobles also did not lag behind in the construction of tanks. Malla of Viriyāla family founded a tank in the village of Gumuduru.[71] It is recorded in the Kaṭukūru inscription that Viriyāla Sūra built a tank in the village of Ayyanavōlu.[72]

The subordiante chiefs also realised the importance of the construction of tanks at proper and promoted agriculture in their regions. Annaya of Indulūri family is said to have constructed many tanks along the banks of the river Krishṇa and Godavaṛi respectively.[73] Kōṭa Gonka and Kāma II constructed many tanks and dug ponds in gardens. Rompicherla may be identified with Rampicheruvu and Pankatatakapuram probably derived its name after some big tank in its vicinity.[74] The tanks of Rudra-*samudram* are mentioned in Nadurupadu inscription of the Natavāḍi chiefs.[75]

Rain was no doubt the sole source from which most of the tanks derived their water supply. Water collected during the monsoon in the catchment area flowed into the tanks through streams lets called *Vāgus*. Tanks situated in the vicinity of the rivers were fed from them by means of canals excavated for the purpose. The *Mūseti-kālva*, the *Immagāḍi kālva* from Perakamma, the Krishṇaveni-kālva from the Cheyyeru excavated by Ghodeyarāya Gangayadeva at Lembaka and others referred to in the inscriptions of the period, probably conveyed waters of the said rivers to the tanks of the neighbouring villages.[76]

Drawing water by means of *ētāmu* or *mōṭa* was also in vogue in those days. They were called *ratanas*. Bullocks were generally used to lift the water from deep wells. An inscription at Dōsapāḍu dated A.D. 1176, records the gift of *ratana* with necessary wood and bullocks. But where water is not very deep man also used to lift it from canals and wells. Reference to *ratanas* that is lifting water by pulley device is very common in inscriptions. It seems that these *ratanas* were let out for rent by the owners of the wells to the neighbouring land owners who did not possess wells.[77]

Tenures-Proprietorship of the land

Dr. P.V. Parabrahma Sastry observes that the basic proprietorship of the land rests with the king, while the individual possesses only secondary ownership. For the sake of peaceful administration the king never disturbed the cultivators so long as he got his annual revenue regularly. Therefore, the ryot can either sell, denote or mortgage his land with the same rights what he hitherto is enjoying over it. The king or any government is least worried with such kind of transfer, because it did not make any difference whether the dues were paid by the old owner or the new owner.[78] While the king is the pimary owner of the land, the subordinate chief gets the deputised rights over the land. He acts on behalf of the king. He is neither the primary ownership of the land at the pleasure of the king.

Deva Vritties, Agrahāras and Service Tenures

While the feudatories are permitted to grant *dēvavritties, agrahāras* and service tenures, they acted only on behalf of the king. Gaṇapāmba, wife of Kōṭa Betarāja and daughter of Gaṇapatideva expressly states in her record that the one forth the taxes and other levies due to the king should be paid to the donee alone.[79]

Taxation

The main source of the income of the feudatories is taxation. Agriculture was the chief and most important occupation of the people. Hence, land tax was an important source of revenue. Next to it come the taxes levied on trade and industry and also on the assessments of forest and pasture lands, on their yield of timber and value of grazing rights. Taxes were collected by regular officials. There also must have been *Dariśanamu, Appanamu and Upakriti*,[80] the traditional gifts or *Kanikas* being rendered to the subordinate chiefs as in the case of the king.

During the times of Kākatiya monarchs the extent of arable land rapidly increased by land reclamation and improvement of agricultural facilities. The land under the feudatories was also classified, as dry (Veli-*volamu or Veli-chenu or Veli-bhūmi*), wet (*Nīru-nēla*) and garden areas (*toṅta-bhūmi or toṅa-polamu*) for purpose of assessment in accordance with the nature and fertility of the soil. There were regional variations on the standard length of the measuring pole. The wet land was measured in marthuru or matter, and its sub divisions, while the dry land was reckoned in *Khanduva*, *Khanduka* or *putti* or its component parts. *Cheluka or Chelika bhūmi*, fallow land which had been newly brought under cultivation, was taxed progressively in proportion to the yield of the crop after a period of three or four years had passed, no tax being levied during initial years. The expression at the rate of one *Chinnamu* per *marturu* of sowable ploughed field and one *Chinnamu* per *putti* of dry land occur in inscriptions of this period. The tax on wet land was accepted both in cash and kind. The tax on dry land and garden land was always paid in cash and was respectively known as *putti-pahindi* and *touta Sunkamu*.[81]

Taxes in kind were generally paid to the government in two instalments, one in the month of *Kārtika* (October-November) and the other in the month of Vaisākha (April-May) evidently being the two main crop seasons. The officers of the king or the subordinate chiefs went round the villages to collect the government share of grain from them. There was *Kolakāndru* (officials engaged in measuring grain) and also *tirparulu* (assessors) to do the job. The government's share of house holder's income in kind was called *putti-koluchu* and that of their share in cash, *putti-pahidi*. The government also collected nominal rent on lands which had been granted to gods and brahmins. That which was collected from wet land was called *para* and that from dry land was called *pangamu*. The general term used for land tax was *ari* and the tax paying ryots were called *arigapula*.[82]

Sunkamu is a term of broad import. It is used in inscriptions to denote taxes on garden lands, duties on exports and imports, customs duties collected on articles of merchandise brought to and taken from the *pēṭas* or market towns or places, and excise duties. The tolls, either customs duties or others, collected on articles of trade, including salt, were farmed out to merchant guilds or associations comprising members of the trading community like the Vīrabalanja *samaya* or the *Ayyavali* guild of merchants, on payment of a fixed sum to the government. It is not known whether the right of collecting taxes was sold by auction, or the length of the term. The tax farmers had their own branches in different localities, and their own officials, office establishments, and accountants to keep records of their transactions, receipts, and remissions in the course of the collection of tolls and duties. The tax collectors were called *sunkarulu* and their accountants *sunkukaranālu*. Probably with the common consent of the members of the local branch, the money collected as duty on certain articles of trade in the locality was sometimes bestowed as a gift for charitable or religious purposes such as the setting up of light before gods in temples and other places. The duty collected on sales effected in the *pēṭa* on articles of trade was called *peṁṭa sunkamu* or *magama*. The guilds of the tax collectors were held allowed full freedom to manage their own affairs without any interference by the government or its officials.[83]

Sunkams with varying designations such as *ammubādi-sunkamu, ammukāḍa-sunkamu, peruka-eḍla sunkamu, ganuvula* (oil mills), *mudra-sunkamu, ganuvuku-ari-sunkamu, and uppu-perika-sunkamu* and others find mention in the records of Kākatiya period. These were all duties collected by toll formers and merchant guilds in market places, in places of pilgrimage, and in the precincts of shrines and celebrated temples. Ammubāḍi-sunkamu and ammukāḍa-sunkamu appear to be equivalent terms of the same import. If it is argued that they were infact seperate fiscal dues, then the former may be the duty collected at some specified rate, not unknown, on sales effected, and the latter the duty levied on each shop. The tax on pack oxen *(perika-eḍlu)* laden with sacks containing articles of trade, was called *perika-edla-sunkamu. Gānuvula-mudra-sunkamu* was probably the duty on oil mills paid as a registration fee, semi-annual tax payable on an oil-mill as such. Tolls were collected not only on the sale of all goods, but also on the possession of many other commodities such as carriages (*banḍi*), slaves (*bānisa)* and horses.[84]

Salt was probably a monopoly of the state. Pedda Ganjamu, Pinna Ganjamu (China Ganjam), Kakakudura, Chomperla, Kanaparti, Devaramupalli and Pamdorti all on the sea coast were some of the places known from the records where sale was produced during the Kākatiya period. These salt pans were either managed by Government officials like the accountants who collected the duty on salt or were farmed out to marchants as explained above since this is a commodity which has to be measured as explained above since this is a commodity which has to be measured like grain. There were also officials called *Kolakandru* and *Tirparulu* to regulate the manufacture and sale of salt. Another sources of income for the state was the *pullari*[85] collected from pasture lands (*pullu*=grass and *ari*=tax) of the Government attached to each village. Besides, *pullari* there is also the mention of another *sunkamu* called *addavatta sunkamu*. Its nature is not clearly known. It may be a tax on herd of sheep.

Besides those mentioned before, there are other taxes such as *gadduga-māḍa, gadduga-kanika, upakshiti, pannu* and *banṭela* (*banṭula-āyamu*).

But, it is not known how the king and his subordiante chiefs shared the state income. It is also not known whether the officials deputed to collect taxes were of subordinate chiefs or of the king. It can be assumed that Central Government did have a wide network of revenue officials, but employed the officials of the subordinate chiefs to collect revenue in the feifdoms. That would be an easier task. The subordiante might have retained his portion of the revenue and sent the rest of the king.

RELIGIOUS CONDITIONS

During the period Śaivism was a dominant religion which greatly influenced the life of the people. Vaiśṇavism was next to it. To a limited extent Jainism and Buddhism also flourished.

Śaivism

Śaivism with its different schools was at its zenith during the Kākatiya period. Kākatiya rulers built many temples to lord Śiva and the Kākatiya feudatories followed the footsteps of their over lords.

The Recherla Reddis described themselves as *parama mahēśwaras*.[86] They built several temples of lord Śiva, *maṭhas*, and donated lands for their maintenance. Erakasāni, wife of Beti Reddi built Erakēśvarālaya after her name and donated lands. She also constructed Komarēśvara and Erakēśvara temples after the names of her parents.[87] Nami Reddi built Trikūtēśvara temple after the names of his parents. In his own name he built Namēśvara temple at Pillalamarri, granted villages and opened a choultry for feeding the poor and the needy. Rucharla Rudra *Sēnāni* built the famous Rāmappa temple besides other temples at Elkurti and Orugallu. His son Kātreḍḍi donated lands to a great Śiva scholar Mahadēvamanchi. Kāṭaya, son of Rājanāyaka, minister of Recherla Rudra built Trikūtēśvaralaya at Goḍisāla.[88] Natavāḍi chiefs were also Śaivaites. Pakkidi Rudra's wife Mailāmba installed Mailāmbikēśvara at Tripurantakam and donated lands for the lord's *naivēdya.*[89] Kundānba, wife of Natavāḍi Rudra I consecrated god Rudreśa after her husband's name, Mahadēva, after her father's name (Kākati Mahadēva), Sūrya and Gaṇapati after her brother Gaṇapatideva and endowed them with a part of the village Kundavaram. This shows that Kundāmba's patron diety was Śiva and as she was specially devoted to Śiva she constructed temples to the god Śiva at Kālēśvaram, Jeedikallu, Śriśailam and Mantrakūṭa.[90] The Cheruku chiefs, though Śaivaites, were tolerent towards other sects. They built and endowed lands to Śiva and Vaiśṇava temples. The temple of Kēṭēśvara, Māreśvara and Sūrya built by Cheruku Bollaya Reḍḍi were living symbols of the memory of his family members.[91] Similarly the temples of Bollēśvara, Mallēśvara and Ganapēśvara came into existence to cherish the memory of Immadi Viswanātha's parents and brother. Care was also taken to provide for their maintenance with lands situated at Rempadi village.[92] The *praśasti* of Kōṭa rulers of Dhānyavati claims that they were devotees of Amarēśvara of Amarāvati.[93] Kōṭa Gaṇapāmba, a devotee of Śiva is credited with the construction of many Śiva temples and the installation of golden *kalaśa* on the *śikhara* of the Amarēśvara temple at Amarāvati. She constructed at Enamadala Bēṭeśvara temple after her husband's name. She built Gaṇapeśvara temple at Amarāvati in her name as well as in her father's name.[94] The Kāyastha chiefs were also Śaivaites.* They built several temples and endowed them with *agrahāras.* Ghoderāya Gangayadeva, a great Śaiva, teacher and Ambadeva's minister, established Ghoderaya, *gurupiṭha* or a *Maṭha.* His son was Siddhēśvara. The Śaiva āchāryas Nanda Śiva, Trayambaka Śiva Kumāra Śiva, Rudra Śiva, Santapura Śiva, received gifts of villages from the Kāyastha chiefs for the maintenance of *maṭhas* and *Vidyāpīthas.*[95] Itigullapāḍu epigraph of Jannigadeva refers to a gift made to Santaśivadēśika of the Abhinava Gōḷaki-maṭha, at Śrīśailam for the maintenance of *Śivalinga maṭha, Vidyāmaṇḍapa*, and a feeding house. Another record of Jannigadeva from Pondaluru record the grant of Purundaluru (Pondaluru) in Potttapinadu to his spiritual guru, Santa Śiva Dēsika of Abhinava Gōḷaki *Maṭha* of Śrīparvata for the maintenance of *Vidyāmaṇḍapa* and feeding house attached to *Śivalinga maṭha*, at Śrīśailam.[96] As these *maṭhas* were considered to be of the *Pāśupata Śaivasm*. The Indulūri chiefs were also Śaivaites, though much is not known about their patronage of Śaivaites for want of epigraphical evidence. Recharla Velama chiefs were Śaivites initially, in tune with their Kākatiya overlords, but later adopted Vaishṇavism.[97] The Chalukya Chiefs of Niḍadavole were Śaivaites who consecrated temples to Śiva and provided for worship and festivals in them.

Among the several schools of Śaivism like the Kālamukha Kāpālika, Pāśupata, Āradhya Śaiva, Viraśaiva etc. Pāśupata gained prominence during the Kākatiya period. It is well known that the followers of Kālamukha Śaivism adopted the Pāśupta philosophy as they do not have a specific philosphy of their own. The early rulers patronised the Kalamukha school of Śaivism. Beta II is said to be the best pupil of Rāmeśvara Pandita, proficient in *Lokulēśvara āgama mahā siddhānta*. The Śanigaram inscription records that Prola I, Beta II and Prola II were *Parāma-mahēśwaras*. Rudradeva was a Parāma Mahēśvara. Thus upto the end of 12th centry Kālamukha Śaivism spread throughout Andhradesa because of the patronage of the Kākatiya rulers. This is evident from the innumerable temples and *maṭhas* that came into existence and the patronage extended to the Śaiva teachers of the Pāśupata school. During the reign of Kākati Gaṇapatideva, the Pāśupata Śaivas belonging to the Gōlakti *maṭha* in the Dahala Country on the bank of Narmada, gained popularity among the masses as well as the rulers. While the names of Kālamukha ascetics end with rasi, pandita and sakti, the names of Pāśupata end with Śiva, Śambhu, Pandita and Rishi.[98] According to Malkapuram was Viśvēśvara śiva of the Gōḷaki maṭha. The epigraph furnished interesting and detailed account of Śaiva teachers of Gōḷaki maṭha. It records the grant of Mandaram of Manaḍam village on the bank of river Krisṇa to Viśvēśvara Śambhu in A.D. 1261 who built a temple to god Śiva, a monastery and a feeding house. It also mentions other charitable gifts and benefactions which Viśvēśvara Śambhu made at other places. The Kākatiya period is also noted for another school of Śaivism called Āradhya Śaivism.[99]

Supporting Śaivism, Dr. B.S.L. Hanumaṭha Rao disagreed

that Viraśaivism dominated the Kākatiya period.[100] The frequent mention of 18 *Samayas* in inscriptions of the times and references in the local records to the growing jealousy and rivalry between the two principal fighting communities, the Velama and Reḍḍis of the Kākatiya court only prove the failure of Viraśaivism in bringing about a change in the traditional outlook of the rulers as well as of the people. It is therefore reasonable to think that Vīraśaivism was not universal and found favour among a few communties in the population, the *Āradhyas* among Brahmins and the *Jangamas* and some sections of the *Sāles* (Weavers) and *Balijas*.

Vaishṇavism

Vaishṇavism made steady progress during the Kākatiya period. Inspite of the preference to Śaivisim, the Kākatīyas were in no way opposed to Vaishṇavism and continued to have the sacred boar (Varāha) and the Divine Mount (*Garuḍa)* as the crest and banner of their family. In temples they installed both Śiva and Vishṇu deities and made provision for their daily worship.[101]

Some of the Kākatiya subordinates like Viriyāla[102] and Malyāla[103] families were devoted to Vishṇu. The Gona chiefs were Vaishṇavites. For instance the *Ranganātha Rāmāyana* composed by Gona Buddha is sufficient proof of the devotion of the Gona chiefs to lord Rāma and the epic Rāmāyana.[104] The Cheruku chiefs also built temples for Vishṇu. The Velama chiefs in later period adopted Vaishṇavism.

Vaishṇavism, appears to have won the allegiance of large sections of people from all classes, because of the appeal of the doctrine of *Prapatthi*. the liberal outlook of Vaishṇavism and the *bhōga* concept of Vaisṇavism.

Jainism

The life of Mallikārjuna Panditārādhya was a saga of fierce campaign against Buddhist and Jainas. An inscription from Pudur near Gadwal in Mahbubnagar district bear testimony to the destruction of Jains by Śaivaites in the time of Gaṇapatideva. The Kākatīyas started their political career as vassels of the Chālukyas who were followers of Jainism and so the early members of the family were not opposed to, if not actually professed Jainism. From the time of Prolarāja II, the Kākatīya took advantage of the growing weakness of their Chālukayan overlords and made a bid to build an empire. The realisation of their ambition necessiated the rulers destruction of all religious beliefs and institutions that were sanctimonius to the Western Chālukyas. Simultaniously, the Viraśaiva movement was making vigorous progress to the advantage of the Kākatīyas. Gaṇapatideva took advantage of the growing popularity of Vīra Śaivism vis-a-vis Jainism and to wipe out Jainism. In spite of such fearful compaign of persecution, Jainism did not completely die out in Andhra. It lingered on for a considerable time at places like Penugoṇḍa and Adōni, and was completely wiped out during the Muslim invasions.[105] In such an atmosphere, there is no possibility for the feudatory chiefs to either protect or profess Jainism, which in course of time died its natural death lacking succour.

Buddhism

Buddhism was in its declining phase during the Kākatīya period. Shorn of its glory and grandeur, the worship of Buddha continued in Andha till about the close of the 12th century A.D. An inscription from Abhur dated in the year A.D. 1182 records the gifts made by Kōṭa Ketarāja of Dharanikōṭa and his courtesans to the Buddha. But it may be added that Ketarāja and his courtesans worshipped Buddha as an Avatara or incarnation of Vishṇu. The last blow at the remnants of Buddhism in Andhra was delivered by Vīraśaiva movement under the leadership of Mallikārjuna Panditārādhya. His biography in Telugu by Pālkurki Sōmanātha records disputation between the Buddhists and Pandithārādhya in the court of the Velanāṭi Chief Rajendra Choḷa at Chandol which resulted in the murder of the Buddhist *Āchāryas* and destruction of their monestory. The antagonism and hostile attitude of the Śaivas gave a death blow to Buddhism which gradually disappeared in Andhradesa.[106]

However, it must be admitted that the sectarian conflict between the Vīraśaivas and followers of other faiths did not assume serious proportions as in Karṇāṭaka during the period. Mallireḍḍi in his Bekkallu inscription[107] states that the four *samayas* namely Śaiviam, Vaishṇavisim, Jainism and Buddhism are mere superficial differences which give rise to undue suspicion. Believing god in reality to be one, althogh their family religion was Jainism, he constructed several Śiva temples. It bear testimony to the religious hormony during the period.

REFERENCES

1. Y.Gopal Reddy "Varṇa in Relation to polity and Justice under the Kākatīyas of Warangal", *A.H.R.S.*, 38. Pt. II, p. 115.
2. A.L. Basham, *The Wonder that was India*, London, 1954, p. 137.
3. Y. Gopal Reddy, *op. cit.*, p. 116.
4. *Siddhēśvara Charitramu*, Hyderabad, 1960, p. 217.
5. *S.I.I.*, X, 464 & 470.
6. Y. Gopal Reddy, *op. cit.*, p. 116.
7. *Corpus*, No.43.
8. P. Kanakadurga: *Kākatiyulanati Sāmajika Jeevanamu*, Vijayawada, 1992, pp. 23-24.
9. *Ibid.*, pp. 24-25.
10. *A.P.R.E.*, 1966. No. 326, *I.A.P.* Wg. No. 58
11. Y. Gopal Reddy, *op. cit.*, p. 124.
12. *Ibid.*, pp. 124-125.
13. *Ibid.*, pp. 125.
14. P.V.P. Sastry, *The Kaktiyas*, Hyderabad, 1978, p. 212.

14A. R. Narasimha Rao, *Corporate life in Medieval Āndhradeśa*, Hyderabad, 1967, p. 86.

15. Y. Gopal Reddy, *op. cit.*, pp. 126-127.
16. *Epigraphia Andhrica*, IV.
17. B.N. Sastry, *Cheruku Vamsha Charitra Śasanamulu,* Hyderabad,
18. P. Kanakadurga, *op. cit.*, p. 29.
19. M. Rāma Rao (ed) *Kākatiya Sanchika*, (Śivayōgasāra), Hyderabad, 1989, Ins. No. 10.
20. *Ibid.*,
21. *Ibid.*,
22. B.N. Sastry, *Tripurantaka Devalaya Śasanamulu*, Hyderabad, 1984, No. 51.
23. P.V.P. Sastry, *op. cit.*, p. 163.
24. M. Rāma Rao (ed), *op. cit.*, pp. 342-351.

25. *E.H.D.*, p. 674.
26. *S.I.I.*, IV, No. 1117.
27. *I.A.P.* Wg., No. 55 & 56.
28. B.N. Sastry, *Recherla Reddi Vamsa Charitra Śasanamulu*, Hyderabad, 1989, Ins. No. 27.
29. B.N. Sastry, *Kāyastha Rājulu*, Hyderabad, 1991, Ins. No. 3.
30. *A.R.E.*, 406 of 1911.
31. *Rāmavilasanu*, I, Introduction.
32. Sr. Na. I. V. 32.
33. M.S. Sarma, *History of the Reddi Kingdoms*, Śrisailam, 1993, p. 267.
34. *E.I.* IX, p. 264.
35. *J.A.H.R.S.*, XXX, p. 15ff; S.I.I, X, Nos. 114, 264, 299, 737, IV No. 660.
36. Y. Gopal Reddy, *op. cit.*, p. 131.
37. *J.A.H.R.S.*, XIX, pp. 60 ff.
38. *I.A.P.* Wg., No. 49.
39. *Epigraphia Andhrica*, I, pp. 71ff.
40. B.N. Sastry, *op. cit.*, 1989, Ins. No. 3.
41. *Corpus*, No. 8.
42. *I.A.P.* Wg., No. 27.
43. B.N. Sastry, *op. cit.*, 1984, p. 5, Ins. No. 19.
44. Y. Gopal Reddy, *op. cit.*, pp. 120-121.
45. *Corpus*, No. 30.
46. Y. Gopal Reddy, *op cit.*, pp. 127-128.
47. *Ibid.*, pp. 135-136.
48. M. Krishna Kumari, *Social and Cultural Life in Medieval Andhra*, New Delhi, 1990, pp. 30-35.
49. B.N. Sastry, *Andhradeśa Charitra Samskriti*, Hyderabad, 1992, pt. II, p. 243.
50. *I.A.P.* Wg., No. 27.
51. *Corpus*, No. 42.
52. *Ibid.*, No. 50.
53. *Epigraphia Indica*, V, pp. 142ff.
54. M. Krishna Kumari, *op. cit.*, p. 37.
55. *Ibid.*, pp. 43-51.
56. *Ibid.*, pp. 67-71.
57. P. Hymavathi, " Medical Facilities under the Kākatīyas", *Cultural Heritage of the Kākatīyas*, Warangal, pp. 77-79.
58. P.V.P. Sastry, *op. cit.*, p. 197.

59. M. Rāma Rao (ed), *op. cit.*, p. 261.
60. *E.H.D.*, p. 681.
61. *Ibid.*,
62. *Corpus,* No. 3.
63. *S.I.I.*, X, No. 340.
64. Y. Gopal Reddy, "Agriculture under the Kākatīyas of Warangal" *Itihas,* Hyderabad, 1973, p. 65.
65. *I.A.P.* Wg., No. 50.
66. *J.A.H.R.S.* XXV, pp. 79-80.
67. *I.A.P.* Kn., No. 28.
68. *A.P.R.E.*, 1966, No. 5.
69. *E.H.D.*, pp. 677-678.
70. *Ibid.*, pp. 678-679.
71. Pratāpacharitra, p. 81.
72. *I.A.P.* Kn., No.
73. M. Rāma Rao (ed), *op. cit.*, p. 33.
74. *A.R.E.*, 299 of 1915.
75. *J.A.H.R.S.*, XXV, p. 83.
76. *E.H.D.*, p. 680.
77. P.V.P. Sastry, *op. cit.*, pp. 206-207.
78. *Ibid.*, pp. 200-201.
79. *Epigraphia Andhrica*, IV, p. 97.
80. *S.I.I.*, X, 427, 499 and 509.
81. *S.I.I.*, X, 509, 530.
82. *E.H.D.*, pp. 683-684.
83. cited in *E.H.D.*, p. 686.
84. *S.I.I.*, X, 358 cited in *E.H.D.*, p. 686.
85. P.V.P. Sastry, *op. cit.*, p. 222
86. B.N. Sastry, *op cit.*, 1989, p. 24.
87. *Ibid.*, p. 6.
88. B.N. Sastry, *op. cit.*, 1992, pt. II, pp. 100-101.
89. B.N. Sastry, *op. cit.*, 1984, Ins. No. 11.
90. *I.A.P.* Wg., No. 57.
91. B.N. Sastry, *op. cit.*, 1989, Ins. No. 1.
92. *Ibid.*, No. 3.
93. *J.A.H.R.S.*, XII, p. 60.
94. M. Krishna Kumari, *op. cit.*, p. 34.
95. B.N. Sastry, *op. cit.*, 1992, Pt. II, p. 156.
96. P.V.P. Sastry, *op. cit.*, p. 279.
97. B.N. sastry, *op. cit.*, 1992, pt. II , pp. 365-366.

98. K. Sarojinidevi, *Religion in Vijayanagar Empire*, New Delhi, 1990, p. 52.
99. P.V.P. Sastry, *op. cit.*, pp. 274-279.
100. B.S.L. Hanumantha Rao, *Religion in Andhra*, Hyderabad, 1993. p 302.
101. *Ibid.*, p. 269.
102. *Corpus*, pp. 31-35.
103. *Ibid.*, pp. 50-53.
104. *J.A.H.R.S.*, p. 24.
105. B.S.L. Hanumantha Rao, *op. cit.*, pp. 199-201.
106. *Ibid.*, pp. 137-138.
107. P.V.P. Sastry, *op. cit.*, p. 281.

Chapter-VI

CONTRIBUTION OF SUBORDINATE RULERS TOWARDS LITERATURE, ART AND ARCHITECTURE

LITERATURE

Like their overlords the subordinate rulers patronized scholars and promoted literature. They also contributed to the development of art and architecture. They appointed eminent personalities in their courts. Several notable Sanskrit writers and poets who produced works of great literary merit flourished during the age of Kākatīya rulers. Some of them figure as the authors of inscriptions which must be taken into consideration, on account of their literary excellence and manner of composition, as being *Kāvyas* in miniature.

Sanskrit

One of the great poets Īśvara Sūri or Īśvarabhattōpādhyāya adorned the court of Malyāla Gunḍa who obtained a *marturu* land as a gift from his patron.[1] Malyāla Gunḍa held Īśvara Sūri in high esteem and gave him some land as *Ubhaya mukhi dakshiṇa* during an eclipse besides eleven *marturus* of wet land behind Kuppasamudram and ten *marturus* of dry land. Īśvara Sūri continued in the service of the family after Gunḍa's death and composed an inscription on behalf of Gunḍa's wife Kuppambika.[2] Īśvara, was the son of Mayurārya on the Taranikanti family, who appears to have been himself a notable scholar. He mastered Paṇinīya grammar and also the Yajur Vēda together with its *pada krama*, and was an adept in the *Chitra Kavitva*. The Bothpur inscription which contain verses composed without gutturals (*Nish kaṇthya*), or without palatals (*Nish talavya*), or without carebrels (*Nir mūrdhanya)* or dentals *(Nirdantya)* or labixals *(Nir-Ōshṭhya)*, as well as *bhramakas* and *bandhas,* may be taken as examples of his skill in poetic composition.[3] He appeared to be well acquainted with *Tāntric* literature and could construct various *bandhas*, such as *Padmabandha* and *Chakrabandha*.[4] In *Chakrabandha* the four lines of the verse can be arranged in three diameter and circumference of several concentric circles. Another feature of the verse is, it contains in the second circle the title of the record as Taḍāga śāsana in the fourth circle *Gunḍaviranuti*, in the seventh circle, the name of the composer Īśvaraya Kritamu. This *Bandha* is named as *Kavi Kāvya Kathā nāyaka chakra*.[5]

The Velpuru and Amaravati inscriptions of the Kōṭa Chiefs display the difficult compostions like *Anuprāsa, Pratilōmya* and *Yamaka* using words of only select endings.[6] Bālabhārata kavi was a court poet of the Natavāḍi Chief Rudra I. Even after the death of Rudra I, he appears to have been patronised by Kundāmba, wife of Natavāḍi Rudra I. Her inscriptions from Kundavaram,[7] Chennuru and Niḍigoṇḍa[8] testify to his poetic skills.

We have no record of authors of poetical works patronised by the Kākatīya subordiante chiefs. Among the prominent works on grammmer the contribution of Kolani Rudradeva, the Indulūri chief, and the son of Manuma Ganna is worth mentioning. It is a commentary on the *Ślōka Vārtika* and styled *Ślōka Vārtika Vyākhya or Rājārudrīya* after the author. It is an interesting work in grammer being a glossary on the *Ślōka Vārtikas* i.e., metrical dicta of a *vārtika* character quoted by Patanjali.[9]

Telugu

Telugu literature appears to have suffered an eclipse for nearly a century (A.D. 1060-1160) after Nannayabhaṭtu. Literary activity, however, did not completely cease. The evidence of inscriptions, several of which were composed partly or wholly in Telugu verse indicates that poetry was still cultivated, and that the rulers and feudatories of the age still favoured Telugu learning and extended their patronage to men of letters. Contemporary records frequently allude to the feudatoy princes and their ministers as patrons and protectors of poets. Unfortunately on may occasions the names of individual writers or literary compositions by means of which they rose to distinction and fame are not available. Occasionally, however, the name of a Telugu poet does occur here and there as the author of an inscription.[10] Much of Telugu literature could only be gleaned from epigraphs of the period.

The inscriptions of the Recherla Reḍḍis bear testimony of their patronage of eminent poets, who composed commendable works in both Sanskrit and Telugu. Great scholars and poets like Hariharārya, Evaturi Somana, Manchirāju alias Bālasarasvati, Pradakshinamu Mahadēva manchi, Soma mantri and others were patronised by the Recherla Reḍḍi Chiefs. The Telugu inscriptions of Recherla Reḍḍis located at Somavaram, Pillalamarri, Nagulapāḍu, Annavaram, Tāḍuvāi, Tripurantakam, Dicchakunta, Machapur etc,. provide an insight into the literary genious of the poets who composed inscriptions and handed over to the posterity living examples of the spoken languages of the people.[11]

Of the Viriyāla records, we come across with the name of Sutradhāri Kommaju, the writer of the record of Gūduru in Jangoan taluq, Warangal district.[12] His narration of Kāmavasāni's efforts to establish the line of Kākati speaks of his poetic excellence.[13]

Earlier, we have spoken of Īśvarasūri, a court poet of Malyāla Gunḍa. Though his inscriptional compositions are mostly in Sanskrit verse, they are interspersed with long passages in Telugu prose which show that he was as great an adept in the vernacular as he was in the classical language.[14] Kuppāmbika, wife of Malyāla Gunḍa, daughter of Buddhaya of Gona family, is credited with the composition of *Ranganātha Rāmāyana*. Gunḍaya and his wife Kuppāmbika extended patronage to men of letters. Some of whom were qualified as *Ghaṭaśāsins* i.e. professors in a *ghatika* or an institution for higher education in various *śāstras,* and received gifts of villages and cash from the feudatories.[15]

One of the poets of the Natavāḍi court was Bālabhārata kavi, the composer of Kundavaram (of Warangal and Adilabad districts) and the Niḍigonḍa inscriptions. It is stated that his verses shone like pearls.[16] Though the records are drawn in sanskrit, he must also have been a great scholar and poet in Telugu.

None of the works of the poets patronise by the Cheruku Reḍḍi chiefs are available, and their names are also not known.

Most of their inscriptions are engraved in Telugu. The Kurella inscriptions stated that Laxmidhorappana, the spiritual *guru* of Cheruku Rudradeva donated villages to scholars well versed in literature.[17]

The title *Kavigalamogaḍa Kaibedu varigiva kaigandara ganda* in the *praśasti* of the Kōṭa Chiefs attests to their patronage of scholars. The Kannada language adopted in the *praśasti* speaks of the influence of Kannada over Telugu and the place of Kannada poets in the court of Kōṭa Chiefs. King Keta I was himself a scholar. His daughter-in-law Sabbama patronised poets. Keta II was a patron of scholars. Bayyaladevi, a scholar herself is compared, with th sun to the lotus tank i.e., scholars. Some of the poets of the period were Ubhayakavi Narasimha and Varakavi Gunḍa belonging to the reign of Gaṇapati Narasimha bhattōpādhyāya was the composer of the Yanamadala inscriptions of Gaṇapāmba.[18] However, none of their literary works are available. Bhimaya Panda, who is mentioned in an epigraph at Chebrolu in Gunturu district dated A.D. 1145, is said to have been a poet capable of producing verses both in the *mārga* and the *deśi* styles as the ancient had done. He was probably the author who composed the *praśasti* embodied in the record.[19] The Mogulutla copper plate grant of Gaṇapama devi speaks of brahmins who were *ghaṭa śāsins*.[20] Nothing is known of the patronage extended by Kāyastha chiefs to the cause of literature. They have mostly encouraged learning by making substantial grants to religious teachers and *maṭhas*.

The literary and artistic activities of the Induluri family are known from *Śivayōgasāra* by Kolani Adi Gaṇapatideva. Soma, son of Peda Malla was learned in *vēdas* and *Śāstras*. Kolani Rudra was a scholar, proficient in *āgamas*.[21] A family of ministers in the service of the Chālukyas of Niḍadavole patronised arts. Nandamiya of Karamchedu was learned in the Vēdas, *Śāstras* and allied branches. His son Narayana was like *Kāmadhenu* to poets. Narayana's son was Bolla and daughter-in-law Nāgamba were praised by poets because of their benevolence to learned people.

According to the Raichur inscription,[22] Ganna at Vardhamanpura and his *rājya rakshmaṇi* Vithala at Raichur enjoyed scholarly discussion in the court in the company of learned men. It is stated that the court of Vithala was adorned by experts in *Puranās, Śāstras, Kāvyās, Nāṭakas*, besides ministers, priests and friends.[23] Gona Buddha and his sons Kācha and Vithala were the authors of *Ranganātha Rāmāyana*, The authorship of this Rāmāyana especially *pūrvakānḍa* is a matter of controversy and consequently plently of literature has grown around it. But the colophon of the poem and other evidences decide it infavour of Budharaja who traceed his descent from Vithala, Buddha and Rudra, his father, grand father and great grand father respectively of the Gona family. *Ranganātha Rāmāyana* is considered to be the best of the Telugu *dvipada* poems.[24] Simple, beautiful and faultless in style, *Ranganātha Rāmāyana*[25] is the best of works in couplet metre. Buddha in the begining of work says that he would narrate *Śrīrāma Charitra* in the way narrated by *Ādikavi Vālmiki* to the liking and pleasure of the deserving persons. But he was the first among Telugu poets to have made major changes in the main story while rendering Sanskrit work into Telugu and deviated from the original. He introduced some new stories, not found in the original but found perhaps in *Padma purāna*, *Navavidha Rāmāyana* and soforth, and sung as songs and ballads by people. His interpolation of anecdotes from folk songs gave it *deśilakshana* or indigenous character. Almost every *kānda* has a new anecdote not found in Vālmiki *Rāmāyana*. In *Bālakānda* he narrates how Ahalya in the form of stone came back to life by the touch of Rāma's feet. *Āttrivrittānta* found at the end of *Ayōdhyakānda* in the Vālmiki and *Bhāskara Rāmāyanas*, is given in the beginning of *Aranyakānda* in this work. The anecdote Jambavati in *Aranyakānda* is found in Vālmiki Rāmāyana but is found in Bhāskara Rāmāyana. The stories of Kalanemi, Sulochana, Kaikeyi, the display of splender of Ravana in the battle field, the conversation between Kumbhakarna and Vibhishana in the battle field and the laughter of Soumitri all in *Yuddhkānda* are not found in other *Rāmāyanas* and add to the beauty of the work. The laughter of Lakshmana borrowed from *Lakshmanadevera navvy*, songs connected with *Lakshmanadevera mūrccha, Ūrmilanidra, Lankayāga* and soforth were popular prior to the composition of *Rāmāyana* in Telugu. The major difference between the *Rāmāyana* of Vālmiki and that of *Ranganātha* is that the latter gives a true picture of the Paulastya family. Buddha's greatness lies in striking a balance between *mārga* and *deśi* styles.

Regarding the inception of *Rāmāyana*, Buddha stated that one day in Vithala's court. While scholars were discussing *Bhārata* and *Rāmāyana*, the king asked, " who is the fittest in the world to do *Rāmāyana* in Telugu in Kāvya style? The *sabha* replied that his son Buddha, a *sarvajna, kavisārvabhauma*, *kavilōka bhōja*, expert in *sabda, artha* style and the intricacies of the *Rāmāyana* was the fittest. Then he sent for Buddha and asked him to render it in Telugu. Buddha claims that his work is unsurpassed in pada, *artha, bhāva, gati* style, meanings, *yati, rasa, gurubhavas, prāsa, alamkara* etc.

Though the *Utharakānda* of *Ranganātha Rāmāyana* on the basis of name, is attributed to *Ranganātha*, internal evidence suggests that it was the combined work of Kācha and Vithala. Both the *Rāmāyanas* together from *Sampūrna Rāmāyana* composed under Buddha's command. *Uttarakānda* belongs to the same period as the *Pūrva Rāmāyana*, The style is faultless, sweet, flowing and continuous. It appears that from internal evidence that Buddha himself wanted to write the complete life of Ramachandra, and acquire fame, prosperity and praise from people. But when he worshiped his favourite deities, Vishnu appeared before him and said thus," I am pleased with your devotion; your sons are capable of fulfilling your deśire, ask them; they would respond to your call with due respect." So Buddha sent for his sons and praised them as royal poets like *Kavi Bhoja*, possessing knowledge in many *puranās,* and arts, lights of his lineage and asked them to compose the *Kathā* which he wanted to undertake for the satisfaction of all.

PAINTING

Painting the monuments with religious themes and decorative motifs is an ancient tradition in the Deccan, as is evident from the mural paintings of Ajantha and Sittennavassal. However, mural art in temples seems to have come to an end by eleventh century in medieval times throughout the South despite prolific building activity. But mural art traditions continued to survive in Andhra, though it did not receive much of patronage. The surviving wall paintings in the temples of Pillalamari and Tripurantakam attest to this fact.

There are paintings in the *Maṇḍapa* and temple on the hill top at Tripurantakam in a state of decay. They are found in obscure corners and their conditions is such that no systematic study can be undertaken to pass any judgement. The Pillalamarri temple has a fragmentary painting depicting the scene *Kshīrasāgara-mathana*. The painting presents both gods and demons pulling the churning string, the great serpent *Vāsuki*, twisted around the churning stick, the mount *Mandara* and churning the milk ocean to obtain nector. After surface treatment of the area, the picture was drawn in outline with suitable foreground and background composition. Colour were applied then. Ochre colours are used mainly in their original shades and less effort is made to produce other secondary shades by mixing the primary colours in different proportions. Important colours used are Red Ochre or Terra verts, Yellow Ochre, blue, lime white and lamp black. Perfect line, well proportioned drawing, lucid composition and talented execution with balanced colour scheme are the characteristics of the painting as a whole. The drawings are full of life, vigour, movement and action in different poses. Even in the cases where the human figures were introduced together, the artist was not ambiguous in accommodating them and adjusted the space by introducing the suitable natural including landscape and seascape. In this effort the traditional style in depiction and perfection of drawing and execution of the work with different colour combination is observed. This is comparable in style with other early paintings of Bādami and the sculptural representations in the later Chālukyan as well as Kākatīya monuments. In particular the sculptural representation of this scene is noticed in the Kākatīya temple at Mācherla. However, in technique this does not indicate any progressive development in art during this period.[26]

The only two examples of mural painting at Pillalamarri and Tripurantakam indicate that art did not die out but later flourished during the Vijayanagara period.

ARCHITECTURE

A comparative study of the styles of the Kākatīya art and architecture with that of the Hoyasalas, reveals that both of them derived from a common source of later Chālukyan art and architectural style. But both of them developed a few individual characteristics of their own in as much as they share some common features. Following the later Chalukyan architectural tradition, the Kākatīyas as well as their feudatories carried on the construction of temples, as that is the main source to glean the architectural styles of the period. Despite their preference to Śaivism, the Kākatīya rulers were not begots and encouraged people to follow their form of worship and build shrines to the dieties of their choice. Among the subordinate chiefs, the Recherla Reḍḍis, the Natavāḍi, the Cheruku, the Kōṭa, the Kāyastha, the Indulūri, the Recherla Velama and the Chālukyas of Niḍadavole were Śaivites, while those of Malyāla, Viriyāla and Gona families were Vaishṇavites.

Following the line of their overlords, the subordinate Chiefs as well embarked upon liberal construction of different temple forms invariably associated with water tanks thus realising the twin objectives of *puṇya* and *purushārtha*. These temples partake of the forms of *Ekakūta, Dvikūta, Trikūta* and *Panchakūta*, depending upon the numbe of shrines put up together on a common plinth with a common *rangamanḍapa*.[27] *Ekakūta* temples are generally seen with *garbhālaya* and *ardha manḍapas*. *Dvikūta* or *yugala* type consists of two temples either facing each other, or standing side by side in 'L' shape connected by a common *manḍapa* as seen at Mallēśwaram in Mahaboobnagar District. *Trikūta* type of temple are quite common during this period. In this category, the main shrine being in the centre, the remaining two are on either side connected by a common *navaranga manḍapa*. The *Trikūta* temple with three shrines all in a row with a common front *manḍapa* is also noticed at Kūsumanchi in Khammam district. There are also *Pañchakūta* variety of temples during this period. Earlier we have some examples of *Pañchāyatana* and *Ashtaparivara* variety of temples. In *Pañchāyatana* variety, all the five temples are built on a common plinth with the main shrine at the stylobate with sub-shrines for Durga on the north-east, Gaṇēsha on the south-east, Sūrya on the south-west and Vishṇu on the north-west with Śiva as the main presiding deity. The earliest temple with *Astaparivara* is found at Mukhalingam. At Gangāpur in Mahabubnagar district, the *Pañchāyatana* temples are raised over a common plinth. The lone *Pañchakūta* or Pañchāyatana temple is located one kilometre away to the north-east of Rāmānujapuram village on Mulugu Ghanpur road, four kilometre away from Pālampet and is locally known as Yerukala nānchariguḍi.[28] We shall now make a detailed study of one or two examples of each variety of these temples.

Ekakuta or Single Shrine Temples

There are two temples in Pillalamarri, one situated on the southern side in a compound inside the village and the other situated outside the village. The main temples at Pālampet with three porches also comes under this variety and the northern temple at Nagulapāḍu is also of this kind. Pillalamarri is a small village situated about three miles north-east of Sūryapet. It was the headquarters of Recherla chiefs. An inscription of Erakasāni, wife of Recherla Beti Reḍḍi, date 1208 A.D. records[29] The construction of the temple in honour of the glorious Erakēśvara in Pillalamarri and along with the *gōpura,* the doorway etc. The Erakēśvara temple situated outside the village is the most imposing of all the three temples at Pillalamarri. Placed on a *upapīṭha* it commands a panoramic view of the entire neighbourhood. The temple faces the east. It is built of basalt of a light grey colour.

The temple is cruciform in its plan with a central hall having four projections constituting three porches in the east, north and south and *garbhagriha* on the west. The hall is in two squares, one inside the other, the inner square being formed by four finely carved grantie pillars. The *upapiṭha* is 4' 6" high and runs around the temple. It consists of seven flat bands and six deep recesses in between them. There are steps to the platform on the east, north and south. The platform has four projections emanating from one another and each marking off the *grabḥagriha*, the portico, the hall and the entrance situated in front of each other in the west-east direction. While the *antarāḷa* is divided by tall narrow pilasters into three compartments, *garbḥagriha* is divided by six pilasters into six compartments. The projecting roof on its inner side contains alternating rows of lotus buds and garlands of three stringed beads. The *śikḥara* which rises above is of brick and lime construction and consists of the main structure and the antefix towards the east. It is decorate all over by miniature turrets of northern type. In the centre of its northern, western and southern faces is a wide tapering band. The projection to the east of the *śikḥara* emanating from the central towar is also decorated and has the form of a *śāla,* with big ornamental gable. The hall is square and is reachable by five steps from the top of the lower platform through the portico in the east. It has slightly carved pillars all round supporting the roof. The centre of the hall contains a square formed by four richly carved granite pillars placed in the four corners of a square. The floor of this square is slightly higher than that of the hall. In side the square there is a circular elevation. The southern face of the northern pillar has on its *aśvapāda* a woman standing in a graceful pose in a niche surmounted by *kīrtimukḥa*. The second band from the base has has a fine female figure in the *tribanga* pose. The fourth band has the figures of Brahma, Vishṇu and Śiva with attendants on either side. The *aśvapādas* of the other faces of the pillars have similar niches. Many sculptures on the pillars are defaced. The ceiling of the hall divided into nine compartments of which the central one is situated above the four granite pillars is richly carved. The three beams connecting this central part with the *antarāḷa* and the architrave of the doorway of the *antarāḷa* contain paintings depicting the *purānic* episods of the churning of milk ocean. The doorway of the *antarāḷa* has side screens of exquite fret work admitting plenty of light in. Its *Sakhas* are adorned with floral design and spirited figures in dancing poses. The *bhuvangama* contains miniature *vimānas*. The lintel has a central projection connecting the image of Gajalakshmi. The architrave above it is exquisively carved with row of turrets interspered with circles vertically arranged and containing women in graceful poses. There is a *sahasra linga,* to the right of the doorway of *garbhagriha* which is carved like that of *antarāḷa* though less elaborately.[30]

The identification of the builder of the *ēkakūta* temple inside the village is difficult, but is certainly built by Recherla Reḍḍis. This is most richly carved of all the temples at Pillalamarri. Unlike in the Erakēśvara temple outside the village, this shrine seems to have escaped the notice of the armies of Allauddin, the Bahamani Sultan, and therefore the beautiful sculptures found on the pillars of this temple are in tact. The simple plan of the shrine consists of a portico facing the east, a hall behind it and the *antarāḷa* and *garbhagriha* to the west of the hall. The walls of the shrine are plain and built of large blocks of stone. The super structure over the shrine is mostly ruined. On the edges of the roof is built a long row of miniature turrets resembling the turrets on *śikhara.* The hall contains sixteen pillars moderatly carved. In the centre of the hall there is a square elevation with richly sculptured grantite pillars at its four corners and a higher circular elevation inside the pillars. There is a profusion of figure sculpture on each of these four pillars. The sculptural decoration of the pillars consists of *kīrtimukhas*, bead garlands, swans, lions and other decorative patterns. The beams over the pillars and the ceiling supported by them are profusely carved. The ceiling is covered by *kaḍalikākarana* process. The doorway of the *antarāḷa* is also profusely carved. Its bottom piece contains miniative *vimānas.* The base of the jambs contains *dvārapālakas* in fine poses with an attendant on either side. The jambs on each side contain a fine pilaster and fret work. Lintel has in the centre the figure of Gaja lakshmi. The architrave has miniature turrrets interspersed by vertical rows of circles with women in fine poses and in the centre is a good figure of *Śiva tāndava*. The *garbhagiha* contains a *liṅga* on a finely carved pedestal.[31]

The famous temple of Pālampet consecreated to Rudrēśvara was built by Recherla Rudra, the well known Kākatīya general in 1213 A.D, now known as Rāmappa Temple. The main temple, the construction of which is ascribed to general Rudra of cruciform with *garbḥagriha* preceded by an *antarāḷa* on the western side and porticos towards the east, north and south. The *upapīṭha* of 6' 4" high is divided into a number of mouldings horizontally. The *pattika, padma* and *tripatta* of various sizes are repeated alternate with recesses. The *upapiṭha* with a ten feet width of space all round the temple provides the *pradakshināpatha*. The *adhiṣṭhāna* is also similarly moulded. The *pabhāga* is moulded with elephants, deities and other motifs carved on top band. The walls are broken up by *ratha* off sets and spaced at regular intervals by pilasters. The recesses, thus formed are filled up by structural motifs as *Kudu, Panjara* and ornamental pilasters. Each of the three walls of the shrine has a triple storeyed niche in it, with a balcony and a cell in each storey of the niche. The section divided into a number of compartments with dancers, deities and musicians carved on them. The roof projects over the walls carved with rows of small pendants and other ornaments on its carving under sides. The temple is famous for its bracket figurines nominally supporting the ponderous *chajja* slabs. There are about thirty eight of them. Some are *alasa kanyas* and some *gaja* vyālas. They pyramidal storeyed superstructure has four *bhūmis*, each with pilasters surmounted by roof and forming pavilions. The recesses and projections of the tower correspond to the offset and recesses on the walls of the *grabhagriha*. The tiers of pilasters give the structure a vertical theme, while the railings and bold cornices the horizontal theme. The superstructure is build of light spongy bricks probably to reduce the weight over the building. The hall entered by any of the three porches by climbing several steps, has a square compartment enclosed by four exquisitely carved pillars in the middle. A platform about 3' 6" high runs round the hall with eight small cells built for accommodating the images of deities, which are now in a mutilated condition. The arrangement of the pillars has divided the ceiling into several compartments, each of which is superbly carved, from the full blown lotus to the most intricate honeycomb scroll. The ornamentation of the four central pillars of the hall and the *purānic* episodes are found there. The *antarāḷa* and the *garbḥagriha* are entered through door ways which are of the most ornate ones met within Telengana. In the *garbhagriha* stands the *linga* on a high pedestal of black basalt.[32]

The northern temple of the times of Recherla Reḍḍis is situated on an *upapīṭha* approached by a flight of seven steps built in each of its sides towards the north, east and west. It has mouldings similar to the *trikūta* at Hanamkonda and the main temple at Palampet. Its top is paved with large slabs of masonry. The temple has porticos on three sides corresponding to the steps of the *upapiṭha* and is to be enterd by five more steps from the latter. It has a hall, an *antarāḷa* and a *garbhagriha*. The roof of the porticos and hall have fallen down. The surface of the temple wall have been divided both vertically and horizontally by most becoming devicess comprising a series of projecting pilasters adorned vertically with a lacework of crisp mouldings and fine sculptures.[33]

Trikūṭa or Triple shrine Temples

In temple architecture, the architects adopted different structural forms, among which *trikūta* form dominates. *Trikūta* temples is an extention of *chaturasra* form distributed on three sides of a central *maṇḍapa,* thus giving a structural unity on plan as well as in elevation. *Trikūta* or triple shrine is a popular style of temple architecture which flourished in Telengāna and other parts of the Deccan during the period from A.D. 10th century to early A.D. 14th century. The Western Chālukyas patronised this type of structural temples in this period and later the Kākatīyas and Hoyasalas followed, favoured and popularised this *trikūta* form. 'Trinity' is the most respectable concept of Hindu worship. The three great gods Brahma, Vishnu and Mahēśvara are placed in highest state of divinity in Hindu mythology. Though, the *trikūta* form was not developed along the worship of the trinity but certainly the evolutionary stage of the style coincided with the worship of the trinity. Most of the early triple shrines are dedicated to the trinity. Worshiping of trinity was popularised by the Pallavas and structural evolution of temple also took a major turn under the region of the Pallavas. The cave temples of Andhra Pradesh at Mogalrajapuram, Vijayawāda and Undavalli have the formative features of the later *trikūtachala* temple forms. Kalyāni Chālukaya's admiration for the unique forms known to us from their *trikūtas* at Rattepalli, Harchalli in Karṇataka and Mallēśvaram, Raikal, Valigonda, Chivalakodur. Tandur in Andhra Pradesh. As subordinates and successors of the Western Chālukyas of Kalyāni, the Kākatīyas cultivated and adopted many of the architectural styles that were more prominent under the former. The Kākatīya subordinate chiefs followed suit. They added some more structural features by large *upapīṭhas,* high *adhisthāna* recesses and projections in wall decorations etc., all giving perfect horizontal and vertical distribution of the architectural form. These temples are well known for their interior decoration and especially for their lathe turned pillars. The Kākatīyas and their subordinates left many *trikūta* shrines which still remain in Teleṅgāṇa and other regions. They are found at Hanamkonda, Panugallu, Pillalamarri, Nagunuru, Kalabagur, Kondapaka, Nagulapāḍu, Gārla, Kūchimanchi, Upparapalli, Kaṭkūru, Mutharam, Manthani, Vilasagar, Chittapur, Timmapur in Teleṅgāṇa region and on *trikūta* at Pushpagiri in Cuddapah district which are the best standing examples of this unique architectural form. Three shrines located on the three faces of a common *mukha maṇḍapa* is the most common feature in the temple layout of *trikūta* style of architecture. At some places three shrines are planned in a single line parallel to each other with a common *manḍapa* in front. This form of layout is also described as *trikūta* form of architecture. Among the Kākatīya temples, all the *trikūta* temples were built in cruciform ground plan. The exception is the temple at Kūchimanchi which have a rectangular *manḍapa* with three shrines in a row on one side.[34]

An inscription dated 1195 A.D. at Pillalamarri records that Recherla Nāmireḍḍi established three *liṅgas* of Śiva Kāmēśvara for his father, Kāchēśvara for his mother and Nāmēśvara for himself.[35] These three were established in *trikūta* style. With a cruciform plan it has a square hall in the centre with three shrines projecting to the north, west and south and a portico projecting to the east. The temple faces the east. The wails of the three shrines are constructed with large blocks of stone. They are all plain with no carvings. The superstructures on these shrines have fallen down and only a few bricks remain. The porticos has a flight of four steps with elephant trunk on either side. The hall is square and contains 16 pillars. In the centre of the hall there is square is circular elevation. The ceiling is covered by *kadalikākarana* process. There is in the hall a finely carved and polished *Nandi* of whitish grey stone. All the three shrines are likely and consist of an *antarāḷa* and a square *garbḥagriha*. The doorways are comparatively less carved. The *bhuvangama* is cut into five carved projections. This lintal has Gajalakshmi in its centre. Above it is the architrave containing a row of turrets of the northern type. The door jambs are plain with *dvārapālakas* at the base.[36]

There is a *trikūta* temple at Nidikoṇḍa, eight Kilometers away from Jangaoan on the Hyderbad Warangal highway. They are locally called as "*Kummarigullu*". The Nidikonda inscription dated A.D. 1219 records the construction of the *trikūta*, consecreted to Rudrēśvara, Mādhava and Gaṇapati Sūryadeva, by Kundamāmba wife of Natavāḍi Rudra after the names of her husband, father and brother respectively. It is said that she, who saw the *trikūta* temple at Hanamkonda, now called the thousand pillared temple, was inspired to build a *trikūta* at Nidikoṇḍa. Each of the shrines consists of a *garbḥagriha* and an *arthamanḍapa* enjoyed by a single *navaranga manḍapa,* with enterance on the north. Except the shrine of Mādhava, the other are in a state of ruin. Only nine pillars are remaining in the *navaranga manḍapa*. The remains of foundation layers denote the existence of compound wall around the *trikūta*. The whole temple was built on a high *upapīṭha,* which serves as a *pradkshināpatha*. It contains *adhistāna*, *padavarga* and *prastāra*. The brick bats present around the foundations clearly testifyies that there was *Vimāna* on the roof which was fallen due to lack of proper maintenance. *Upāna*, *padmajagati*, *kumuda* and *kapota* are moulded in later Chālukyan style. All the three shrines and the *navarangamanḍapa* hava a common *aḍhistān*. The pillars are carved with *vēdika, aśvapāka, aśvapāda, kalaśa vritta* and *phalakapadma*. The *aśvapāda* and the *vēdika* below it run around the whole temple. The walls of the temple are plain. The doors of *arthamanḍapa* are carved with beautiful figures of *dvarapāla*. There are beautiful carvings on the four inside pillars of the *manḍapa* and aslo on the ceiling.[37]

Kata of Malyāla family built a *trikūta* temple dedicated to Śiva, Kēśava and Prōlēśvara, as per the inscription dated A.D. 1241 at Konḍparti which is situated at a distance of the ten kilometers from the Warangal railway station. According to the inscription, it has *prākara* wall. The *śikḥaras* of the shrines are built with brick in stepped pyramidal type. The temple is similar in style to those of the temples in the Warangal fort.[38]

The *trikūta* temple at Pushpagiri in Cuddapah district stands as an examples for Kākatīya kingdom. The Vijayanagara architects turned their attention of high *gōpuras*, large *manḍpas*, multiple *prākaras*, sub shrines etc. Perhaps, the Vijayanagara architects preferred closed *manḍapas*. The shrine facing main entrance can only get the light and the presiding deities of other two shrines remain in darkness.[40]

Panchakūta Temple

A Panchakūta temple at Rāmānjapuram village on Mulug Ghanpur road located four kilometers away from Pālampet is quite interesting for its plan. Though it is certain that it was built during the Kākatīya period, no information is forth coming whether any feudatory chief is involve in its construction.

Here all the five shrines are raised over an *aḍhistana* of *manchaka* type with a common *manḍapa*. The central shrine faces the south and is flanked by a pair of shrines in a row on either side. The entire complex has its entrance to the south with a four pillared *manḍapa* as *dwāra*. All the shrines are enclosed by a *prākara*. Occurance of brick bats around this *manḍapa* as in the case of Hoyasala temples. Each shrine consists of a square *garbḥālaya* and an *arthamanḍapa*. The rectangular *rangamanḍapa* is well planned and supported by eighteen pillars. Exquisitely carved pillars with *aśvapāda*, shaft *Kutam, phālika padma* and *poduka* are at the centre. Where as dwarf pillars devoid of *aśvapāda* are crected on the common platform. The ceiling on *manḍapa* is plain. The roof of the shrines and the central bays of the *rangamanḍapas* are raised in four tiers by stepped up triangular slabs. Miniature shrines to house *parivāra dēvatas* are built on the stylobate in between the subtemples and at the corners of the *rangamanḍapa*. The *aḍhistana* consists of *upāna*, *padmajagati* and interestingly a few mouldings like *kanṭha* and *kapōta* are adopted to in between the sub temples and at the corners of the *manḍapa*. Over the *aḍhisthana, kakshāsanas* or *asanapattis* are arranged. Two beautifully carved elephants with riders are arranged on either side of the entrance of the *rangamanḍapa* probably to serve as balustrades. The *pādavarga* or superstructure of the temple is plain which is super imposed by a *prastāra* comprising of *uttara*, *kapōta* and *vyālavarga*. Evidence is there is to prove that the main temple was dedicated to Vēnugopala or Vāsudeva. The second shrine houses a *Śivalinga*. It seems the third shrine is dedicated to Surya. The fourth and fifth shrines contain *Śivalingas*.[41]

Thus, in the foregoing passages, an attempt is made to bring out various architectural pattern adopted by the architects of the period. Only a few temples built by the subordinate chiefs are saved from ruin and vandalism. There are beautiful temples built by the Kākatīya overlords themselves like the *trikūra* the thousand pillered temple at Hanamkonda, but they do not come under our purview to be described in detail.

SCULPTURE

Chalasani Prasada Rao states that Kākatīya sculpture can be broadly divided under four main categories based not so much on the stylistic grounds as on the subjects dealt with. The first is non representational decorative patterns which are found all over the temple. The second is figurative sculpture and friezes on the door ways, cornices and ceilings which depict Śaivaite mythology. They show much artistic skill and posses what may be termed as formal beauty. The third category is the sculpture on the walls, columns and in the corridars and halls outside the sanctum as also the entrance which are more beautiful and lyrical in conception. In addition to the above three types we can recognise a slightly different style in the innumerable serialised reliefs on the outside walls portraying dancers, musicians and other groups in scenic sculpture based on mythological legends as also contemporary social life.[42]

Chalasani Prasada Rao states that in the fourth category the sculptors of the day have carved scenes portraying social life which include wild animals, hunturs, hermits and rural population in various activities. What ever the sculptor did, whether he portrayed social life, animal or floral motifs or the Saivite legends, the purpose is to decorate the temple *vargams*.

Decorative Art

The lotus motif occupies a prominent place in the decorative patterns. The sculptors of the period had a special liking for it and used it for filling voids in their composition. The chief animal which they have popularised is that of *haṁsa* which has acquired a special sense of dignity and sensuous beauty at their hands. They were equally successful in the use of creepers and tendrils which were employed with great flexibility and imagination for achieving hormony of design in all their sculptures. Although they have chosen the crocodile in their animal sculpture like the Chālukyan artists, it did not fit into their concetpion of beauty and so crocodiles were usually depicted above lord Śiva in mamy places just to satisfy tradition. Every Kākatīya temple has a wide door was leading to the main sanctuary and these have been completely filled with relief sculptures based on plant and floral designs fused with sinuous curves of creepers and tendrils so as to give the impression of a delicate curtain rather than a prosaic entrance. The lotus figures within the intricate design were carved out skilfully with natural openings so as to provide light and ventilation while emphasizing their objectives so as to provide light and ventilation while emphasizing their objective. Here also, we find the invariable dancing figures in miniature in between these floral designs as an essential coponent of their over all composition. The lion and elephant figure prominently in the sculpture. Apart from the beautiful rows of elephants replacing tendrils in many friezes, they have been specilly utilised for door ways as also for filling up large spaces. Lions have also been carved out quite frequently in groups and in some cases we find a lion perched on an elephant. In some of the zoophorile, we find heroic ladies fighting the lions. The lion sculptures are more or less a traditonal design but the only surprise is that the sculptors have never thought of horse which officers more scope in a predominently rhythem based style.[43]

The doorways of the *antarāḷa* of Erakēśvara temple at Pillalamarri offers a side screen of exquite fret work admitting plenty of light in. The four grantie pillars of the hall are carved alike. The southern face of the northern pillars has on its *aśvapada* a women standing in graceful pose in a niche surmounted by a *kīrtimukha*. The ceiling of the *trikūta* is covered by *kadalikākarana* process. The sculptural decoaration of the pillars in the single shrine inside the village consist of *Kīrtimukḥas,* bead garlands, swans, lions and other decorative patterns. The beams over the pillars and the ceiling supported by them are profusely carved. The ceiling is covered by the *kadalikākarana* process.

The *pabhāga* in the main temple at Pālampet is moulded with elephants, deities and other motifs carved on top band. The walls are broken up by *ratha* offsets and spaced at regular intervals by pilasters. The recesses, thus formed, are filled by structural motifs such as *kuḍu*, *panjara* and *ornamental* pilasters. The parapet wall of the hall and the porches is divided into four horizontal sections. From bottom to top is the pattern of carving in the four sections, with rows of elephants, and vijrabandha decoration. The arrangement of the pillars has divided the ceilings into several compartments each of which is superbly carved with the decorations consisting of a variety of floral and geometrical patterns, from the full blown lotus to the most intricate honey comb scroll. The shrine situtaed to the south of the main temple at Pālampet has a ceiling with a fine carving, while the central compartment represents a full blown lotus. The Śiva temple at Pālampet has doors with *jāli* work and rows of *haṁsas* carved on entamblature. In a peice of parapet wall of the Kondaparti temple, the *kōlatūm* dance is depicted. The temple to the south of the mosque at Nāgulapāḍu has rich carvings of floral devices, architectural motifs and religious themes from the *Mahābhārata*, *Rāmāyana* and the *Purānas* on the ceiling of the hall.

Figurative Art

Figurative sculpture of the Kākatīya temples and other structures can be broadly divided for convenience into two groups viz., sculptures showing individual figures and those representing groups assembled for portraying any incident, narration or depiction of wider subject. Figurative sculpture of the first variety in which we find numerous examples of a fairly large size can be divided into dancers in characteristic poses or the main devinities and those dealing with minor figures inclusive of dwārapālakas and such other attendants.[44]

Divine Figures

Vishṇu was represented in various forms. The incarnation of *Nrisimha* is seen at the main temple at Pālampet. He is *sthāuna Nrisimha* depicted in the action of tearing out the entrails of Hiranya Kaśipa. The figure is found on the parapet wall going round the hall and porches on the southern side. Nrisimha is seated with the right let hanging down and left folded. The demon is placed horizontally across the lap of the god. The god has eight hands. The belly of the demon is being ripped open by the lower hand of the god. One of the upper right hand is holding the *makuta* of the demon and one of the upper left hand is holding down the legs. Two other hands, one right and one left are lifted upto the head of the image holding the drawn out entrails of Hiranya Kaśipa in the form of a garland.

From fairly early, the Śaivates, in general used to have *Śivalinga* as the principal object of the worship. There are two types of lingas *Sahasralinga* and *Mukhalinga*. *Sahasralinga* is one whose *Rudrabhaga* is carved into 100 emblems by incision of parallel horizontal and vertical lines and by chamfering the edges of the resultant crisscross sections. We come across this *Sahasralinga* at Pillalamarri. The form of Śiva which is most often represented in sculpture is that of Śiva in the dancing attitude of

Natarāja. Representations of this deity of the time of Kākatīyas are at Pillalamarri, Pālampet, Nāgulapāḍu and other places.

Lakshmi is one of the forms of Gajalakshim generally found on the lintels of door frames. The lintels of all the three Pillalamarri temples have a central projection containing the image of Gajalakshmi.

Madanikas

The *Śilpa Prakāśa* deals elaborately with *alasakanya* or Indolent Maiden. The text says *alasa* is indespensible in architecture. As a house without a wife, as play without a women, so without the figure of women the monument will of inferior quality and bear no fruit. The sculptures of *alasa kanyas* lend richness and beauty of temples.

The most beautiful representation of *alasa kanyas* is found in the main temple at Pālampet. Particularly the bracket figures of the temple are important. Among these bracket figures are representations of *nartaki* or dancer. Tradition says that these were carved in accordance with the dance poses mentioned at *Nrittaratnāvaḷi* of Jāyapasēnāni. But M. Radhakrishna sarma disputes with the tradition and says that it is an anachronism to suppose that the dance sculptures in the main temple at Pālampet construction in 1213 A.D. are carved according to the text *Nrittaratnāvali* written in 1253-4 A.D.[45]

Chalasani Prasada Rao observes "A closer inspection reveals that although many of these sculptures suggest dancing poses, none of them may be exact representations of dance sequences from the technical point of view. Inspite of the obvious suggestion of characteristic hand movements and footwork associated with dance, it is more appropriate to regard them as some beautiful poses which have impressed the sculptor from the artistic point of view instead of looking for their theoretical counterparts. The *tribhanga* pose itself is the most common form of figurative sculpture. There is no need to believe that the purpose of the sculptors was so specifically carve out dance items. Stylised figures described in theoretical terms do no offer enough scope for movement of rythm and the artist has to evolve his own conception to infuse life into them. For this purpose one need not rely all the time on the art of dance and in many cases the limbs and torso are conceived independently in a form of satisfying, rythm and balance."[46]

Of the 16 kinds of the *alasa kanyas* decribed in *Śilpa Prakāśa* there are three *alasa kanyas* seen at the main temple of Palampet. One is *dalāmālika* carved on the lower part of the door pilaster. The head is in the lower part of *tricheda* or triangle seen in beautiful profile. The second is *nartaki* who is seen turning her body and looking towards the right side. The arms are up raised. The third is *mārdala* (Drummer), as stated in the text her chest is on the middle line, cut across by the left arm. In the bredthe of the middle line a devinely beautiful mardala is carved.[47]

Speaking of the *alasa kanyas* Chalasani Prasada Rao observes "There are as many as twelve sculpture of dancing figures in Rāmappa temple...One particular one the famous nāgini... has gained special attention probably because it is the only example of a perfect nude with a few snakes alone serving as ornaments".[48]

Kākatīya sculptors have not shown much of difference with regard to the ornaments or decoration allotted to male and female figures. In both the cases the body is quite bare in the upper portion and the lower half has been skilfully covered by ornaments. Nevertheless a distinct difference can be noted between ornamentation and dress as such. We find a similar phenomenon even in the case of dancers also. As per the general convention and technique the sculptors also employed different types of decoration depending upon the status of the subject to emphasize the rigid heirarchy which is an unfortunate hangover when we think about gods.[49]

Sculpture in Groups

One of the skills employed by the Kākatīya sculptor was his way to draw our attention on the central figures against the background of their followers. With regard to the problem of differentiation between the divine and secular figures like dancers, they have utilized the marked difference observed in bodily proportions to emphasize the distinction.[50]

Adjacent to the *nāgini* sculpture, we find another figure in a dance pose, but in this particular case, we find at its foot a waiting maiden with a fly whisk and a monkey on the other side pulling off the skirt. In another sculpture, one finds a handsome bejewelled lady with a bow and an arrow accompained not by musicians as in previous cases but with a male figure plucking out a thorn from her foot. It is not difficult to conclude that she is a princess whose is on a hunting mission in the forest. These sculpture show that the Kākatīya sculptors could represent several types of 12 personages with suitable modification in dress, ornaments and such other minor details. On the cornices and doorways group sculptures are carved. In most of them lord Śiva is the central figure, though variations are introduced in minor details like hands or ornaments and the accompanying figures. One thing to be noticed in these figures of persons, human or divine, in these friezes is that the minor attendants of gods are of a smaller size. This is obviously to bring out their relatives importance since many of the figures might look otherwise quite alike. These decorative figures are not to mistaken for dwarfs since the bodily proportions are the same in all cases. In Rāmappa temple we not only find lotus relief in the central but also to fill up the voids at the corners, four triangular slabs with an eight armed Śiva on a bull in each. We found *gōpika vastrapaharana* scene on the columns of the temple. Even amidst a mass of miniature figurines, closer study reveals an impressive variety in posture and expression and distinct and independant groups which attract our attention by their beauty and imaginative skill. It is very rarely that we come across rhythmic friezes pulsating with life in any other branch of ancient Indian scupture. There are beautiful friezes in layers on the columns. Although none of these exceed four inches in size and carry at least ten figures in each layer, every single sculpture has received the utmost attention with regard to the detail apart from the overall rhythm in the entire compostion. In the central portion of a pillar, we find a scenic sculpture like that of *gōpika vastrapaharana* and in between we find dancers and musicians on all four sides.[51]

The above study reveals that the subordinate rulers under the Kākatīyas had patronized arts and letters as their masters did.

However, we cannot find any deviation in the style of arts and architecture i.e. The Kākatīya School of *Vāstu* and *Śilpa*.

REFERENCES

1. *Corpus*, No. 52, P. 145-146.
2. *Ibid.*, Part I, Introduction p. 10
3. *Ibid.*, No. 51 and 52; E.H.D p. 688
4. *Ibid.*, part I, Indtrduction p. 9.
5. P.V.P. Sastry, *The Kākatīyas*, Hyderabad, 1978, p. 293.
6. *Ibid.*, p. 293.
7. *I.A.P.*, Wg No. 58.
8. *Ibid.*, No. 57.
9. Raghavan's Introduction to *Nrittaratnāvaḷi*, p. 15, cited P.V.P. Sastry, *op. cit.*, p. 293.
10. *E.H.D.*, p. 991.
11. B.N. Sastry, *Recherla Reḍḍi Vamśa Charitra Śāsanamulu,* Hyderabad, 1989, pp. 59-0.
12. *I.A.P.*, Wg. No. 26.
13. *Ibid.*
14. *E.H.D.*, p. 691.
15. P.V.P. Sastry, *op. cit.* p. 51.
16. *J.A.H.R.S.*, XXVI p. 18.
17. B.N. Sastry, *Cheruku Vamśa Charitra Śāsanamulu,* Hyderabad, 1989, No. 11.
18. *J.A.H.R.S.* XXVI p. 17.
19. cited in *E.H.D.* p. 691.
20. *Epigraphia Āndhrica*, IV.
21. *J.A.H.R.S.*, XXVI p. 20
22. M. Rama Rao. (ed) *Kākatīya Sanchika,* Inscription No. 33.
23. *Ranganātha Rāmāyana*, Text pp. 3-4.
24. P.V.P. Sastry, *op. cit.*, p. 298.
25. V. Yosodadevi. The History of Andhra Country (1000 A.D. to 1500 A.D) Subsidiary dynasties, *J.A.H.R.S*, XXXVI pp. 51.
26. P.R.K. Prasad, 'The art of painting in Kākatīya Times' A paper presented at the National Seminar on *Kākatīya Art and Architecture*, Telugu University, Srisailam, 1991, (Cyclostyled).
27. S. Nagabhashana Rao (ed). Introduction, *Cultural Heritage of the Kākatīyas*, Warangal, pp. 3-4.
28. B. Subrahmanyam, and E.Śivanagi Reḍḍi, '*A Unique Panchakuta*

Temple of Kākatīya Period at Rāmanujapuram', *Cultural Heritage of the Kākatīyas* (ed.), S. Nagabhushana Rao pp. 47-48.

29. *Corpus*, No. 42.
30. M. Radhakrishna Sarma, *Temples of Telingana* Hyderabad, 1972, pp. 101-102.
31. *Ibid.*, pp. 103-104.
32. *Ibid.*, pp. 119-120.
33. *Ibid.*, pp. 139-140.
34. N. Ravi, 'Thousand Pillar Temple of Hanamkonda A Trikūtachala form' *Cultural Heritage* of the *Kākatīyas*, 30-31.
35. *Corpus* No. 38.
36. M. Radhakrishna Sarma. *op. cit.*, p. 137.
37. E. Śivanagi Reḍḍi and B. Subrahmanyan 'Kākatīyas Kāla Śidhilālu' *Āradhana* (Telugu monthly) Department of Endowments, Govt. of A.P. Sept. 1987 pp. 26-28.
38. M. Radhakrishna Sarma *op. cit.*, p. 137.
39. N. Ravi, *op. cit.*, p. 46.
40. *Ibid.*, p. 46.
41. B. Subrahmanyan and E. Śivanagi Reḍḍi. *op. cit.*, 48-49.
42. Ch, Prasada Rao. *Kākatīya Sculpture*, Hyderabad, 1987, p. 38.
43. *Ibid.*, pp. 53-54.
44. *Ibid.*, p. 48.
45. M. Radhakrishna Sarma. *op. cit.*, p. 267.
46. Ch, Prasada Rao, *op. cit.*, p. 49.
47. M. Radhakrishna Sarma. *op. cit.*, pp. 267-268.
48. Ch, Prasada Rao. *op. cit.*, p. 48.
49. *Ibid.*, p. 48.
50. *Ibid.*,
51. *Ibid.*, pp. 49-52.

Chatper-VII

CONCLUSION

The Kākatīyas ruled over a vast area, comprising of a major part of the present Andhra Pradesh except the three extreme northern circar districts and also some places in the present Karṇataka and Tamilnāḍu districts. It embraces the area from Drāksharāmam to Pīṭapuram in the north and Kāñchi in the south. It also included Bidar and Raichur districts and some places in the present Kolar district in Karṇāṭaka.

The Teleṅgāṇa region lying between the river Krishṇa and the Godavari formed the central zone or nucleus of the metropolitan state, with three peripheral areas, viz., the coastal region, and region from the river Krishna to the river Godavari along the coast, comprising of Vēngi *Manḍala*, and the third from Kōṭagiri on the river Manjeera to the Kaivaram Kōṭa in the Chintamani Taluq of Kolar district. There is also a twilight zone or contact zone lying between the river Krishṇa and Gundlakamma and extending in the west to Śrīśailam, and Kurnool and still beyond upto Raichur doab and Kolar. Of the eleven subordinates rulers under investigation, the Recherla, Malyāla, Viriyāla, Natavāḍi, Cheruku and Velamas were the subordiantes of the Kākatīyas in the central zone. The second peripheral zone was shared by Indulūri chiefs and the Chālukyas of Niḍadavole, while the entire third perpheral zone and some part of twilight zone were under the sway of Gona chiefs and the Kōṭa chiefs. Thus large tracts of land were under the control of the subordiante chiefs. Most of the subordiante chiefs were located in the central zone while large tracts of land were under the command of Kāyastha chiefs. Perhaps this was one of the reason for the Kāyastha chief Ambadeva to rebel against his overlord Rudramadevi. This assumption is strengthened by the fact that while none of the other feudatories had either the resources, or the advantage of the geographical factors, the Kāyastha chiefs had advantages both material and physical to assert their independence. The geographical locals paved way for the Kāyastha chief Ambadeva to rebel against his ovelord, which also prompted Pratāpa Rudra to lead a three pronged attack to subdue the rebel.

The geographical locals of the central zone which was mostly under the direct rule of the Kākatīya emperor exposed him to direct attack with no buffer zone to absorb the shock waves of the Muslims onslaught. Once the Sēuṇas were vanquished, Pratāpa Rudra was exposed to attack. His valour and determination however enabled him to withstand no less than seven expeditions against his Kingdom. Political history of the subordiante chiefs was reconstructed after analysing all the available information widely scattered, which helped to assess the contribution of subordiante chiefs to the kindom. There have been some missing links which have not been hither to connected to arrive at a complete picture of the genealogical tables of the subordinate chiefs. In the study an attempt was made to fill the gaps. There also have been mistaken identites which are resolve in the study.

The Viṛiyāla chiefs were one of the earliest associates of the Kākatīya rulers. Kāmavasāni, wife of Eṛṛanripa took up the cause of young Kākati Garaḍa Beta and secured for him the Anumakoṇḍa *vishaya* from the Chālukyan emperor. In this connection an attempt is made to corraborate the epigraphical evidence with the chronicles *Śri Siddhēśvara Charitramu* and *Pratāpa Chartramu*. The association of Viriyāla and Kākatīya dates back to the times when they were the subordiante chiefs of the Rāshṭrakūṭas and then the Western Chālukays. There were marital relations between these families (as is seen in the case of Kāmavasāni) and the alliance continued from the period of Kākati Guṇḍa IV to that of Rudramadevi.

The epigraphial evidence proves that the Natavāḍi belonged to the caste of the *chaturtha kula*. The identification of Rudra I is also satisfactorily explained on the basis of epigraphical evidence. Rudra I and Rudra II are not one and the same person, but two sons of Budha. Rudra I and Rudra II, married the daughters of

Kākatī Mahadeva or the sister of Gaṇpatideva namely Kundāmba and Mailāmbika respectively. By these matrimonial relations. Budha became a close relatives of Kākatīyas. As we donot hear of Natavāḍi chiefs after 1259 A.D, it is surmised that the teṛṛitories ruled bythe chiefs were merged with the Kākatīya Kingdom after Gaṇapatideva's reign.

The history of the Recherla chiefs is an in coherent and unconnected story. They ruled over the principalities of Elkurti and Āmanagallu and served the Kākatīya rulers with unfailing loyalty. Of the several members of the family Rudrasēnani was the greatest and acclaimed as the restorer of the Kākatīya kingdom and was endearingly described as *Sanmantri*, *Kākati-rājya Samartha* and *Kākatī-rājya bhāra dhourēyunḍu*. In recognition of his services his sovereign Gaṇapatideva gave him a throne and the paraphernalia of a *mānḍalika*.

The Cheruku chiefs who began their career by the humble grant of Cheruku-12 from Kākati Beta rose to the highest position of *mahāsāmantas*. One of the important members of the family Bolli Reḍḍi described as *Jammulūru Puravarēśvara*, was very close to Gaṇapatideva and as one of his generals participated in his expedition against Diviseema, Nellore, Velanāḍu, Choḷa, Vaidumba, Pānḍya and Yādava Kings. Because of the services of Bolli Reḍḍi the family attained the status of *mahāsāmanta* by securing the principality of Amarabad Vanguruseema and Veluru of Kurnool *Manḍala*. Veluri Bolla of this family seems to have changed his loyalty to Kāyastha Ambadeva and came closer to him by accepting the hand of Ambadeva's daughter to his son Rajarudra, he lost his life espousing the cause of his ally. But Pratāparudra who remembered the services of Bolli Reḍḍi and his brothers pardoned him, as is attested by the Goruvankapalli copper plate inscription. But this incident suggests the fact that already rivalry for political power assumed series proportion between the Velama and Reḍḍi chiefs and finally this became one of the causes of the down fall of Kākatīyas as several historions believe it as one of the causes. The rivalry between the Reḍḍi and Padmanāyaka families also led to mutual destruction. The Reḍḍi generals deeply resented the appointment of the Velama chiefs to high position in milatary organisations and turned against their masters. Since the Reḍḍi chiefs did not support the Kākatīyas in the hour of crisis during the Muslim invasions, Pratāparuda was over powered and captured.

Soma mantri was an illustrious member of the Indulūri family who successfully affected the subjugation of Vēngi. Gaṇapatideva in appreciation of his services made him the lord of Kolanuseema. This enabled Gaṇapatideva to acquire strong control over Velanāḍu. Afte the death of Gangaya *Sāhini*, Indulūri Gannaya was made the *Bāhattara niyōgādhipati* by Gaṇapatidevi. Kolani Rudra, another important member of the family enjoyed the position of *Bāhattari Durganāyaka* during the reign of Pratāparudra.

The Malyāla chiefs had matrimonial relations with other chiefs like Viriyāla, and served the Kākatīyas as commanders. One of the illustrious members of the family Chaunḍa *senani*, married Mailama the daughter of Viriyāla Annaya. Thus the two families became close and strengthened the hands of Kākati Gaṇapatideva. The title *Gaṇapati Mahipāla Sēna-abhibharturḥ* indicates that was the commander in chief of the Kākatīya forces. Gaṇapatideva pleased with the valorous achievements of Chounḍasenapati conferred on him the titles *Divi Churakara* and *Dvipi luṁṭaka* (the plunderer of the *dvīpa* or island). Another prominent member of the family was Gunḍa *Danḍadhīsa* who served Gaṇapatideva and Rudramadevi. He married Kuppāmbika, daughter of Buddhaya of Gona family, the renowed author of *Ranganāth Rāmāyana*. This feudatory family which played an important part in the early part of the Kākatīya rule appear to have lost interest during the reign of Rudramadevi. Although Malyāla Gunḍa, who had been a general under Rudramadevi was alive until 1274 A.D., he seems to have been living in retirement taking no part in the stirring events which shook the kingdom to its foundations during the first decade of the queen's regin. His sons and other members of the family were probably more interested in the construction of temples and the excavation of irrigation tanks in their own fief than in the political affairs at the centre.

The Kōṭa chiefs ruled over the area called *Shatsahasra,* the Velanāḍu six thousand country. It was during the reign of Bhima II that Kōṭa chiefs confronted with the Kākatīya rulers. Kākati Rudradeva's expedition against Dhanyavati resulted in the death of the Kōṭa chief Bhima. Though victorious Rudradeva did not annex his kingdom and gave it back to Keta II, son of Bhima II on the condition that he ruled it as the vassal of the Kākatīyas. Keta II expressed his loyalty and unity by maintaining matrimonial relations with the Kākatīyas. The Kōṭa desa was later partitioned between his son Bhima and Rudra; while Bhima ruled from Dhānyavati. Rudra made Yanamadala his seat of power. Rudra's son was Beta, who married Gaṇapāmba, daughter of Kākati Gaṇapatideva. On the death of her husband Gaṇapāmba had taken over the responsibility of governing the kingdom.

Of all the subordinate chiefs, the Kāyasthas, a class of warrior immigrants were the most powerful rulers. The Kāyastha armies, along with the Kākatīyas, successfully marched into the teṛṛitories now comprising Guntur, Kurnool, North Arcot and Cuddapah districts and the impact of the Kāyastha power was also felt by the neighbouring kingdoms. Gangaya sāhini, the earliest member of the family accepted the overlordship of Gaṇapatideva and participated in several battles on behalf of the king. Ambadeva the most powerful and illustious chief of the family was an able general with great political ambition. He defeated all the chiefs who were allies of Rudramadevi and indirectly weakened her position. The Sēuṇas and Pānḍyas were always at logger heads with the Kākatīyas. The power intoxicated Kāyastha chief ultimately revolted against the Kākatīya in A.D. 1290. However, his rise and fail indicate the short sightedness of the Kākatīya overlords to allow him to grow too powerful and setup the standard of rebellion. It is surprising that Gaṇapatideva and Rudrama never thought of securing the goodwill and loyalty of the Kāyastha chiefs by matrimonial alliances which they had contracted with most of the other feudatory chiefs.

The Valama chiefs distinguished themselves as the most faithful and competent generals. Of the chiefs of the family Prasādatiya was an illustrious general. When the succession of Rudrama to the throne of her father was threatened by other nobles, it was Prasaditya who helped Rudrama to ascend the throne by his unswerving loyalty and military prowess. Prasaditya rightly deserved the title *Kākatīya Rājya Sthāpana chārya* and *Rāya Pitamahānka*. In recognition of his services he was elevated to the prestigious position of *Bāhattara niyōgādhipati*. Prasāditya was credited with the introduction of *Nāyaṁkara* system in the Kākatiya administration, according to which the defence of the kingdom was entrusted to seventy two *nāyakas*. It is pertinent to observe in this connection that the Vijayanagara rulers also adopted the *nāyaṅkara* system in their administration. This suggests that the founders of the Vijayanagara kingdom had their roots in the Kākatīya kingdom and promoted Kākatīya pattern of administration. We notice a well organized system of military administration from the period of Rudramadevi. Another Velama chief was Eṟṟa Dācha, who after gaining victory over the Pāṇḍyas obtained the title *Pāṇḍya rāya gajakēsari*. By the time of Rudramadevi, the Velama chiefs became more influential and got a preferential treatment at the hands of Rudrama and later Pratāparudra. The Velama chiefs were loyal to the end and survived the onslaught of the Muslims. They later made Rāchakoṇḍa and Dēvarakoṇḍa in the Nalgonda district as their seats of power and weilded consideration authority in the post Kākatīya period. The important role during the Vijayanagara period and that of the *Sūryavaṁśa* Gajapatis.

The Gona chiefs ruled over the area around Raichur with capital at Vardhamānapura. Gona Buddha Reḍḍi and Gona Ganna Reḍḍi were more famous members of the family. The fact Ganna occupied supreme place among the Kākatīya feudatories and generals is attested by the epithets be bore *Kākatīya Kataka Sennaha* and *Rudradēva dakshina bhaja daṇḍa*. It appears that Ganna's politcal victories were achieved during the closing years of Rudrama's reign and with the passing away of Rudrama, the Gona chiefs lost their importance and political significance.

Gaṇapatideva secured the loyalty of the Chālukya chiefs of Nidadavole by offering the hand of his daughter Rudrama to Virabhadra, son of *Māṇḍalika* Induśekhara. Virabhadra's brother Mahadeva and his son Indusekara II served Rudrama and Pratāparudra as governers of Niḍadavole province.

The Political history of the subordiante chiefs point to the fact that most of them lost their prominence by the time of Rudramadevi and Pratāparudra was left with only a few. The Recherla, Viriyāla, Malyāla, Natavāḍi, Kāyastha and the Gonas who served their overlords with unswerving loyalty have faded out of the political scene and even if a few members of these families remained they were not much interested in political affairs of the kingdom. Only the Kōṭa, Cheruku, Velama, Indulūri and the Chālukyas of Niḍadavole were active in politics. Even of the remaining five subordiante chiefs, the well known caste factor between the Reḍḍis and Velama chiefs worked at cross purposes. No such dissensions could be seen during the period of Gaṇapatideva and with all his subordiante chiefs serving loyally, the Kākatīya kingdom reached the zenith of power. Slowly one after the cther the loyal chiefs faded out of the scene by the time of Rudramadevi: though she retained the earlier glory, the process of disintegration has set in.

The Kākatīya rulers knew the importance of the subordinate chiefs as the props of the empire. They never exercised autocratic that any policy involving autocracy would certainly lead to a conflict with most of the *māndḷikas* who might form a confederacy against them. So they continued their liberal policy even after attaining sovereign power. They were successful in the novel experiment but with the lone exception of Ambadeva. They did not differntiate between their allies and subordinates in following a liberal policy.

In the course of the rise of Kākatīya rulers to power different chiefs came under their subordination in different ways. The chiefs may be classified under four categories: Associates- The Viriyāla and Natavāḍi who were the supporting pillers of Kākatīya rulers during the initial stages of their rise come under this category;

Appointees- the Recherla, Malyāla, Cheruku Reḍḍi, Kāyastha, Indulūri, Velama and the Gona come under this class for they were granted principalities in recognition of their military prowess and acumen in the administration of the kingdom. Under the category of vanquished vassals, the lone example was that of the Kōṭa chiefs who were partdoned and regranted kingdom after their defeat in the battle field; and the last category of vassals who became feudatories by matrimony the example of the Chālukaya chiefs of Niḍadavole family.

Of the eleven subordiante chiefs the Gona, Indulūri and Velama held the *sāmanta* position, while the Cheruku and Malyāla chiefs were *mahāsāmantas*; Recherla, Viriyala and Natavāḍi held the status of *māndalika* and the *mahāmānḍalika* status higher than that of *mānḍalika* was held by the Kōṭa, the Kāyastha and the Chālukya chiefs of Niḍadavole. Though it is difficult to clearly define and explain the position, status, previleges and functions of each feudatory the fact that every family what ever their heirarchial status was greatly honoured and rewarded by the Kākatīyas. This fact is well substantiated to these titles since they themselves did not assume a higher title than that of *mahā manḍalēśwara*.

Though these chiefs came into the service of the Kakatīya rulers by their military prowess, some of the chiefs were drafted for administrative duties as well. Of them, the members of the Indulūri family were prominent. The chiefs had different appellations suggesting their military status and all the chiefs were participants of military enterprise. But once they became chiefs they gradually renounced the appellations since they denoted as inferior position to that of *mahāsāmanta*, *mandalika* etc.

The *Nāyaṅkara* system which was an important aspect of the administrative organization of the Kākatīya rulers was indeed a bold and novel experiment. The system came into existence due to the ingenuity and innovative mind of Prasāditya, the Velama Chiefs who guided Rudramadevi in framing and implementing the system. The significant aspect was the participation of the feduatories in the military organization of the Kākatīya rulers by way of supplying contingents of elephants, horses and foot soldiers. The feudatories were granted lands on condition of rendering military service to the king. But the possession of land was not a permanent feature and liable to the terminated in case of non compliance of the terms by the *Nāyaṅkara*. Though provincial governors, ministers and *leṅkas* were also appointed as *Nāyaṅkaras*, it appear the most of the *Nāyaṅkaras* were feudatories. The *Nāyakas* collected taxes of a military nature like *Baṁtala-āyamu* in addition to land revenue and taxes on industries in the fiefs under their jurisdiction. The intent and content of the *Nāyaṅkara* institution is primarily military service. The high office of *bāhattara-niyōgādhipati* or the president of the 72 *niyogas* or branches of administration was generally bestowed on the subordinate chiefs who were *nāyakas*. Thus the feudatories were bound to the king by strong bonds of military service as well as administrative responsibilities. No wonder such a mighty and significant institution was later adopted by the Vijayanagara rulers. This itself was an appreciation of the *Nāyaṅkara* system a brain child of the Kākatīya rulers, by the great Vijayanagara rulers.

We do have not much evidence to speak of civil and military functions of these subordiante chiefs. However, it is possible that these subordiante chiefs. However, it is possible that these subordiante chiefs ruled their fiefs on the same lines as that of their overlords since we come across several ministers and commanders engaged by the subordinates to look after the administrative and military affairs in their principalities.

As in other parts of the Kākatīya kingdom, the four fold Hindu varna institution survived despite occasional attacks on it by Vīra Śiavism. The subordiante chiefs also upheld the varṇa system enjoined in the scriptures. The Brāhmiṇ still retained his earlier status in educational sphere and religious affairs. The subordinate chiefs donated *agrahāras* to the Brahmins. Though normally the Brahmin was expected to be a teacher, a *purōhit* or a priest, there were instance where they took to sword, and held administrative positions, the Indulūri chiefs being the illustrious example. The Vaisyas carried on traditional occupations of trade and commerce. The trade guilds played an important role in shaping the economic life of the country. The emergence of the *Śūdras* as the ruling class is a unique characteristic of society in medieval Andhradesa. Most of the ruling families of the period belonged to *chaturthakula* or sudra caste. However, there was a process of upward movement of the Śūdra rulers who not only styled themselves Kshatriyas but also drew mythical and semi mythical ancestry to strengthen their borrowed claim. However, the fact remains that Varṇa system was not rigid, atleast among ruling classes. Examples are galore to show that matrimonial alliances were affected between the Śūdras: Śūdras and Kshatriyas and sudras and Brahmins: These inter marriages saw horizontal and vertical mobility in the Varṇa divided society of medieval Andhradesa. The social mobility largely improved the actual social status of the sudras.

Though the foundations of society were based on patriarchal pinciples, women of the age enjoyed equal status with men. Still ideal womanhood was *Grihalaxmi* and *ardhāngi*. Some women occupied high administrative posts and played key role in political life as is evidenced by Kāmavasāni, Nāgasāni, Gaṇapama Devi, Rudrama devi etc. They were not lagging behind men in serving the cause of people; we have a number of royal women who built tanks, temples etc., and made munificient grants. The social evil of *sati* was in vogue. There were instances of the practice of *Sati*, but they were voluntary. We have a number of instances of women who did not commit *sati* on the funeral fire of their husbands like Rudramadevi, Ganapamadevi, Viriyāla Nāgasāni, Viriyāla Kāmavasāni, Malyāla Kuppāmbika etc., The practice of employing girls in the service of god was in vogue and they were called *Sānis*. The word *sāni* had not the derogatory meaning amounting to a prostitute as is now. It is a term of respect as is evidenced by the names of the royal ladies of the time. The *sānis* of the time conducted *aṅga raṅga bhōga* and other types of services to the gods and were organised into guilds like guild organisations of trade and commerce. The guilds of the sānis administered the endowments kept under their trust by donors and played a very important role in propagating *bhakthi* among devotees through their music and dance performances. Because of the these temples became centres of social and cultural life.

The important centres of learning during the period were the *ghatikas, brahmapurīs*, *agrahāras*, temples and *maṭhas* which received gifts and donations from royal personages and common people for their maintenance. The *Vēdas, vedāngas, smiritis*, purānas, *āgamās, mīmāmsa,* astronomy and medicine were taught in these institutions. Generally *maṭhas* and temples and *maṭhas* for the maintenance of hospitals. Temples situated at Śrīśailam, Tripurantakam, Eleśvaram, Drākshārāmam, Ālampuram etc. located near forest areas became famous medical centres in those days.

There was as much economic prosperity in the fiefs of the subordiante chiefs as in the territories of their overlords. Agriculture was the main occupation of the people. Population was not so dense in medieval times at present. The Telengana region comprised of rocky soil and other areas were thick with dense forests. So the twin tasks before the rulers were land reclamation by clearing jungles and poviding irrigation facilities by digging wells and tanks. The Gona chiefs were primarily employed by Kākatīya rulers to clear the forests and reclaim land for cultivation. The subordinate chiefs like their overlords paid much attention to irrigation facilties for the purpose of agriculture. A net work of tanks or reservoirs to catch the rain water and store it was established. Every village in the country had one or more tanks. However, the State took no direct responsibility for the construction and maintenance of irrigation works. The construction of a tank was regarded as an act of charity which would accrue great religious merit being one of the *saptasantānas*. So the kings and *sāmantas*, nobles and officials, religious leaders and merchants and wealthy men paid attention to the construction of tanks. Canals were excavated from rivers to provide irrigation facilities. Lift irrigation was also in vogue employing *ratanas*.

The basic proprietary ship of the land rested with the king. While the individual possessed only secondary ownership. For the sake of peaceful administration the king never disturbed the cultivators so long as he got his taxes regularly. While the king was the primary owner of the land the subordinate chiefs got the deputised rights over the land.

The main source of income of the feudatories was land revenue and next to it came the taxes levied on trade and industry. For the purpose of taxation land was categorised into dry and wet lands, fallow land etc. Taxes in kind were collected in two instalments during the two main crop seasons. The officers of the king or subordinate chiefs went round the villages to collect the government's share of grain. Merchant guilds collected taxes on merchandise and paid a fixed sum of the government. How the king and subordinate chiefs shared the state income is not known. The subordiante chiefs might have engaged their officials to collect taxes and retained their share and sent the rest to the king.

In religious matters Buddhism and Jainism lost their popularity. The worship of Budha continued in Andhra till about the close of 12th century A.D. The last below at the remnants of Jainism in Andhra was delivered by Śaivism. From the time of Prola II, the Kākatīyas took advantage of the weakness of their Chālukyan overlords and made a bid to build an empire. Their ambition necessitated the ruthless destruction of all elements that were a part of the culture of the Western Chālukyas. The policy resulted in the destruction of Jainism. Its well known that many of the Jain temples including the famous Padmākshi temple at Hanamkonda were converted into Śaivite shrines. Like the Kākatīya rulers their feudatories never became religious fanaties.

Śaivism was at its zenith during the Kākatīyas period. Many of the subordiante chiefs were Śaivites. The Recherla, Natavāḍi, Kōṭa, Kāyastha, Indulūri, the Chālukyas of Niḍadavole were all Śaivites and built several temples for lord Śiva. The Chruku chiefs though Śaivites were tolerant towards other sects and built and endowed lands to Śaiva and Vaishnava temples. The Velama chiefs were Śaivites initially falling in line with their Kākatīya overlords and later adopted Vaishṇavism. Kālāmukha Śaivism found favour and spread through out Andhra. But during the reign of

Gaṇapatideva, the Pāsupata Śaivas belonging to *Gōḷakhimaṭha* in Dahala country gained popularity among the masses as well as rulers. However, the *Gōḷakhimaṭha* which received patronage from Gaṇapatideva and Rudrama was also in favour of compromise with Brahminism as was evidenced by their anxiety to uphold caste system and frequent mention 18 *samayas* etc.

In spite of their obvious preference for Śaivism, the Kākatīyas were in no way opposed to Vaishṇavism. The subordinate chiefs belonging to Viriyāla, Malyāla and Gona families were Vaishṇavites. However, the fact is that the sectarian conflict between Vīra Śaivas and other faiths did not develop into religious conflicts as in Karṇāṭaka during that period.

The subordinate chiefs were patrons of art and letters. Several sanskrit scholars and poets like Īśvara Sūri, Bāla Bhārata kavi etc. have flourished in the court of subordinate chiefs, through their works are not available. Among the works on grammer belonging to the period, the grammatical work of Kolani Rudradeva, is worth mentioning. It is a commentary on *Slōka Vārtika* and is called *Slōka Vārtika Vyākhya* or *Rāju rudrīya* after the author. Literary activity in the field of Telugu, though not much did not completely cease. There were Talugu schoḷars and poets like Harihararāya, Evatūri Somana, Manchirāju of Bālāsarasvati, Pradakshinamu Mahadēvamanchi, Somamantri, Sutradhāri Kommoju, Īśvara Sūri, Bālābharata kavi, Bhimaya panda, Nandamiya etc., who flourished in the courts of the subordiante chiefs. Gona Budha Reḍḍi and his son Kācha and Vithala were the authors of the famous of *Ranganātha Rāmāyana*, considered to be the best of the Telugu *dvipada* poems. Buddha was the first among Telugu poets to have made major, but significant changes in the main story.

Painting, though was on the decline did not die out completely in Andhra. The ramnant examples at the temples of Tripurantakam and Pillalamarri attest to this fact.

Following the Western Chāḷukyan architectural traditions, the Kākatīyas as well as their feudatories carried on the construction of temples. Following the footsteps of their overlords, the subordiante chiefs as well embarked upon liberal construction of different temples forms invariably associated with water tanks thus realising the twin objectives of *puṇya* and *purushārtha*. These temples partake of the forms of *Ekakūta*, *Dwikūta*, *Trikuta*, *Manḍapa* and *Panchakūta*, depending upon the number of shrines put together on a common plinth with a *raṅga manḍapa*. Of these *Ekakūta* and *trikūta* temples were well popularised during this period. The temples at Pillalamarri, Pālampet and Nāgulapāḍu etc., examples of *Ekakūta* or single shrine are rich in decorative art and figurative sculpture. The *Trikutas* or triple shrine temples at Pillalamarri, Nidigonda, Kondparti, Pushpagiri and Nāgulapāḍu are the finest forms of this type of architecture, and figurative arts. The Kākatīya sculptors adopted several flora and fauna motifs to decorate their artistic works. The figurative sculpture reached its zenith in Rāmappa temple.

Thus subordinate rulers played an important role in the consolidation of Kākatīya kingdom. They were great generals and good administrators. They patronised arts and letters like their overlords and left their imprints in the form of monuments, water tanks etc.

BIBLIOGRAPHY

ORIGINAL SOURCES

Epigraphical

Andhra Pradesh Government Annual Report on Epigraphy, 1965, 1966 and 1967, Hyderabad.

Annual Report of Indian Epigraphy.

Annual Report of South Indian Epigraphy.

Corpus of Telengana Inscriptions.

Copperplate Inscriptions of Hyderabad Museums, vol. I and II, Hyderabad, 1962, 1970.

Epigraphia Andhrica.

Epigraphia Indica.

Indian Antiquary.

Inscriptions of Andhra Pradesh: Cuddapah District. Vol. I and II.

Inscriptions of Andhra Pradesh: Karimnagar District.

Inscriptions of Andhra Pradesh: Nalgonda District, Vol. I and II.

Inscriptions of Andhra Pradesh: Warangal District.

Nellore District Inscriptions. 3 vols. Madras, 1905.

Peruru Inscriptiomns. Hyderabad, 1973.

Śasana Samputi, Vol. II (ed) B.N. Sastry, Hyderabad, 1973.

Select Epigraphs of Andhra Pradesh, Hyderabad.

Studies in Indian Epigraphy.

South Indian Inscriptions (Texts).

LITERATURE

Sanskrit

Nrittaratnāvaḷi by Jāyapa Sēnāni. (ed) R. Ananth Krishna Sarma, Hyderabad, 1969.

Pratāparudra Yashobhūshanam by Vidyanatha (ed) Vavilla and Sons, Madras, 1954.

Telugu

Basavapurānamu by Pālkurki Somanatha (ed) N. Venkat Rao, Madras, 1952.

Kreeḍābhiramamu by Vinukonda Vallabharaya (ed) B. Tammayya, Madras, 1960. *Palnāti Veeracharitra* by Srinatha, Vijayawada, 1961.

Pratāpa Charitra by Ekamranatha (ed) C.V. Ramachandra Rao, Hyderabad, 1984.

Ranganātha Rāmāyana by Gona Buddha Reḍḍi, (ed) Vavilla and Sons, Madras, 1960.

Siddhēśwara Charitra by Kāse Sarvappa, (ed) K. Lakshimi ranjanam, Hyderabad, 1960.

Sri *Pandithādhya Charitra* by Pālkurki Somanatha, (ed) C. Narayana Rao, Madras, 1936.

MODERN WORKS

Books

Acharya P.K. *An Encyclopedia of Hindu Architecture*, Manasara Series, London, 1946.

Adinarayana Shastry, M. *Rāyalaseema Telugu Śāsanāla Sāmkritika Adhyanam*, Anantapuram, 1995.

Arudra, *Samagrāndhra Sāhityam* (Tel) (Kākatīya Yugamu) Madras, 1965.

Alteker A.S. *Rāshtrakūṭas and their times*, Poona, 1932.

Alteker A.S. *State and Government in Ancient India*, Delhi, 1958.

Appa Dorai, *Social and Economic conditions in South India*, Madras.

App Rao V, (Ed). *Reḍḍi Saṁchika*, Hyderabad, 1991.

Basavaraja. K.R. *Administration Under the Chālukyas of Kalyāna*, Madras, 1983.

———, *History and Culture of Karṇāṭaka*, Dharwad, 1984.

Bawa V.K. (Ed), *Aspects of Deccan History*, Hyderabad, 1963.

Basham. A.L. *The Wonder that was India*, London, 1954.

Beni Prasad, *The State in Ancient India*, Allahabad, 1928.

Brown. Percy, *Indian Architecture, Buḍhist* and *Hindu Periods*, Bombay, 1959.

Bhandarkar. D.R. *Some Aspects of Ancient Hindu Policy*, Banaras, 1928.

Bhandarkar. R.G., *Early History of Deccan*, Calcutta, 1920.

Buchi Nayana, *Padmanāyaka Charitra* (Tel) Waltair, 1979.

Burton Stein, *Peasant State and Society in Medieval South India*. Delhi. 1985.

Chenchaiah. P. and Bhujanga Rao, *A History of Telugu Literature*, Calcutta, 1030.

Collis, Maurice, *Marcopolo*, London, 1959.

Desai Dinakar, *Mahāmanḍalēśvara* under the Chālukyas of Kalyāṇi, Bombay, 1951.

Gopal Chari. K., *Early History of Andhra Country*, Madras. 1941.

Gopala Krishna murthy. S, *The Śculpture of the Kākatīyas*, Hyderabad, 1964.

———, *Jain Vestiges* in Andhra, Hyderabad, 1963.

Gopal Reddy. Y, *The Ghanpur Group of Temples*, Hyderabad, 1985.

Gopinatharao. T.A, *Elements Hindu Iconography* 2, Vols. Madras, 1941.

Guha Amalendu, *Feudalism in Early Medieval India some comments*, Aligarh, 1968.

Gurumurthi. A, Sculpture and Iconography Cuddapah District Temples, Madras 1990.

———, *Temple of Cuddapah District*. Madras, 1990.

Hanumantha Rao B.S.L., *Andhrula Charitra* (Tel) Guntur, 1984.

———, *Religion in Andhra*, Hyderabad. 1993.

Isvaradutt Kundurti, *Prācheenāndhra Charitraka Bhūgolamu* (Tel), Hyderabad, 1962.

———, Inscriptional *Glossary of Andhra Pradesh*, (Tel) Hyderabad. 1967.

Jawaharlal. G., *Jainism in Andhra*, Hyderabad, 1994.

Kanakadurga. P.S., *Gaṇapati Deva's and Times* (A.D. 1199-1262) Unpulished Thesis, Nagarjuna University, Nagarjuna Nagar, 1985.

———, *Kākatīyula Kālamunāṭi Sāmājika Jeevanam*, Vijayawada. 1992.

Kramrish Stella, *The Hindu Temple*, Calcutta, 1946.

Krishna Kumari, M., *History of Medieval Andhradeśa*. Delhi, 1989.

———, *Social and Cultural life in Medieval Andhra*, New Delhi, 1990.

Lakshmiranjanam, K., *Kākatīya Yugamu* (Tel) Hyderabad 1975.

Malaya Sri, *Kākatīyula Kālamanāṭi Sāmājika Jeevitham*, Hyderabad, 1990.

Mangalam, S.J., *Historical Geography and Toponamy of Andhra Pradesh*, New Delhi. 1986.

Mahalingam, T.V., *South Indian Polity*, Madras, 1955.

Meister Michael, W. and Dhaky. M.A. (eds.) *Encyclopaedia of Indian Temple Architecture*, Delhi, 1986.

Nagabhushan Rao, S. (ed)., *Cultural Heritage of the Kākatīyas*, Warangal, 1993.

Narasimha Murthi, A.V., *The Sēvuṇas of Devagiri*, Mysore, 1971.

Narasimha Rao, R., *Corporate life in Medieval Andhradesa*, Hyderabad. 1967.

Neelakantha Sastri, K.A., *A History of South India*, Madras, 1992.

———, *Development of religion in South India*, Madras, 1963.

———, *Studies in Choḷa History and Administration*, Madras, 1992.

Nigam. M.L., *Sculptural Art of Andhras*, Delhi, 1980.

Prasada Rao, Ch., *Kākatīya Śilpamu*, Hyderabad. 1987.

Pratapa Reddy, S., *Andhrula Sānghika Charitra* (Tel) Hyderabad, 1950.

Rajendra Prasad, B., *Art of South India, Andhra Pradesh,* Delhi, 1983.

———, *Temple Sculpture of Andhra Pradesh*, Hyderabad, Hyderabad, 1978.

Rama Krishna Gopal, B., *Early History of the Deccan*, Delhi, 1985.

Rama Rao, M., *Andhra Through the Ages*, Guntur, 1958.

———, *Buddhism in Andhradesa*, Hyderabad, 1956.

———, (ed) *Kākatīya Sanchika*.(Tel). Rajahmundry. 1935.

———, *Select Kākatīyas Temples. T*irupati. 1966.

———, *The Kākatīyas of Warangal*. Hyderabad, 1952.

Ritt, S.H., The *Sēuṇas of Devagiri*, Dharwar. 1972.

Sarojinidevi, K., *Religion in Vijayanagara Empire,* Delhi, 1990.

Sastry B.N., *Andhrula Sānghika Charitra*, (Tel) Hyderabad,

———, *Andhradeśa Charitra Samskriti*, (Tel) part II, Hyderabad, 1992.

———, *Cheruku Vamśa Charitra śāsanamulu*, (Tel) Hyderabad, 1989.

———- *Kāyastha rājulu*, (Tel) Hyderabad, 1991.

———, *Recherla Reḍḍi vamśa Charitra Śāsanamulu*, (Tel) Hyderabad,

———, *Recherla Padmanāyakulu*, (Tel) Hyderabad, 1991.

———, *Śasana Samputi* (Tel) Part I and II, Hyderabad, 1973.

———, *Tripurantaka Dēvālaya Śasanamulu* (Tel), Hyderabad, 1984.

Sastry, K.A.N. and Venkataramanayya N., *Further sources of Vijayanagara History*, Madras, 1936.

Sastry, P.V.P., *Kākatīyas Charitra*, (Tel) Hyderabad, 1977.

———, *Kākatiya Coins and Measures*, Hyderabad, 1975.

———, *Kākatiya Śāsana Sāhityamu* (Tel), Hyderabad, 198

———, *The Kākatīyas of Warangal*, Hyderabad, 1978.

Satyanarayana, K., *A Study of the History and Culture of the Andhras*, Vol. II New Delhi, 1983.

Sewell, Robert, *A forgotten empire*, New Delhi, 1970.

Sharma, M.R.K., *Temples of Telingana*, Hyderabad, 1972.

Sharma, R.S., *Indian Feudalism* C. 300-1200, Calcutta, 1965.

Sivanagi Reddy, E, *Evoluation of Building technology in early Andhradesa*, (upto 14th Century A.D.) Unpublished Thesis, University of Hyderabad, 1994.

Sivarama Murthi, *Indian Sculpture*, New Delhi, 1961.

Soma Reddy. R., *Hindu and Muslim Religious Institutions of Andhradeśa* (A.D. 1300-1600) Madras 1984.

Soma Sekhara sarma, M.A. *Forgotten Chapter of Andhra Ḥistory*, Madras. 1945.

———, *History of Reḍḍy Kingdoms.* Waltair. 1948.

Soundara Rajan K., *Indian Temple Styles*, New Delhi. 1972.

Srinivasachar, P. *Rāmappa and other Temples at Pālampet*, Hyderabad, 1953.

Sundara, K., *Studies in Economic and Social Conditions of Medieval Andhra*, Waltair, 1979.

Suryanarayana. K. *History of the Minor Chālukya Families in Medieval Andhra deśa*, Delhi, 1986.

Vaidehi Krishnamurthy, *Temples of Medieval Andhra*, Hyderabad, 1956.

———, *Social and Economic conditions in Eastern Deccan*, (from A.D. 1000- A.D. 1250), Secunderabad, 1970.

Venkata Ramanayya, N., *Early Muslim Expansion in South India*, Madras, 1942.

———, (ed) *Velugoṭivāri Vamśāvali*, (Tel) Madras, 1939.

Veerabhadra Rao, C., *Kākatīyāndhrarājayuga Charitramu*. (Tel)Rajamachendravaram, 1936.

Yashodadevi, V. *The History of Andhra Country* (1000 A.D.- 1500 A.D.) New Delhi, 1993.

Yazdani (Ed)., *The Early History of the Deccan*, 2 vols. Oxford, 1960.

Articles

Cynthia talbot., Political Intermediaries in Kākatīyas Andhra, 1175-1325 *The Indian Economic and Social History Review*, Delhi 31-3-1994. pp. 261-289.

Ganapati- R., Nagulapāḍu Dēvālayalu Vāstu Śilpalu (Tel) *Telugu Vaijnanika Māsa Patrika, Telugu* Akademy Hyderabad, Feb. 1993.

———, Subordiante chiefs of the Kākatīyas -A study, P.A.P.H.C., Gunturu, 1996, pp. 79-81.

Gopal Reddy. Y. Agriculture under the Kākatīyas of Warangal, *Itihas*-I, Hyderabad, 1973.

———Kākatīya Gaṇapati Deva and the Yādavas of Devagiri. *J.A.H.R.S.*, XXX (Part I-IV), 1965.

———, Varna in Relation to Policy and Justice under the Kākatīyas of Warangal. *A.H.R.S.*, 38 pt II, Hyderabad, 1986.

———The Pillars in the Kākatīya Architecture and Art. *The Journal of Archaeology*, V, Hyderabad, 1984.

———The Exterior Architectural and Artistic Embellishment of the Kākatīyan Temples, *Itihas, VIII*, I, Hyderabad, 1980.

———, Ghanpur Group of Temples, J.A.H.R.S., XXIX, 1-2, 1963.

———, Ganapati Deva's Conquest of Kalinga, *Itihas*, III-2, pp. 19-28, Hyderabad, 1976.

Kanakadurga, P.S., Nakara in Medieval Andhra, P.A.P.H.C., Kakinada, 1984.

———, Inter State Trading during the Kakatiya Period. (A.D. 1000-1300)

Quartarly Journal of Mythic Society, LXXVII-1986

———, Golaki Matha- Andhradesa. *Quartarly Journal of Mythic Society* 78- 1987.

Krishna Kumari, M., Kota Ganapama Devi Rājya Pālanākālamu -Oka Parishilanamu, *Bharati*, August, 1984.

———Sanis (The Temple Girls) of Medieval Andhra, *Itihas,* XIV-2, Hyderabad, 1988.

Laxma Reddy, R., The Causes for the Fall of Kākatīyas of Warangal, A New Interpretation. *J.A.H.R.S*, XXXIX, Hyderabad, 1995.

Nagi Reddy, E.S & Subrahmanyam. B. Kākatīya Kala Śidhilalu *Āradhana*, Hyderabad, Sept., 1987.

Prasad, P.R.K., The Art of Painting in Kākatīya Times. A Paper presented at the National Seminor on *Kākatīya Art* and *Architecture*. Telugu University, Srisailam, 1991, (Cyclostyled)

Ramachandra Rao, C.V., The Kākatīya Polity, Economy, Society; A few considerations. (The Kakatiya State as a Metropolition State) *P.A.P.H.C.*, XIV, p. 63.

Sastry, P.V.P., Anumakonda Inscription of Kākati Rudra Deva,- A Review, *J.A.H.R.S.*, XXXVI,-I, Hyderabad, 1975.

———, Autocracy on the decline under the Kākatīyas *A.H.R.S.*, 3- II, Hyderabad, 1986.

Yasoda Devi. V. Agrarian Relations in Andhra during Medieval Period *J.A.H.R.S.*, XXXIX, Hyderabad, 1995.

Journals

Andhra Sāhitya Parishad Patrika

Bhārti (Telugu Monthly), Vijayawada.

Deccan Geographer, Hyderabad.

Indian Historical Quarterly, Calcutta.

Itihas, Journal of A.P. State Archieves and Research Institute, Hyderabad.

Journal of the Epigraphical Society of India.

Journal of Telugu Studies, Hyderabad.

Journal of Andhra Historical Research Society, Rajahmundry.

Journal of Andhra History and Culture, Guntur.

Journal of the Hyderabad Archaeological Society, Hyderabad.

Journal of Indian History, Trivendrum.

Oriental Journal, Tirupati.
Proceedings of Andhra Pradesh History Congress.
Proceedings of Indian History Congress.
Proceedings of South Indian History Congress.
Quarterly Journal of Mythic Society.
Telugu Vaijnanika Masa Patrika, Hyderabad.
The Journal of Oriental Research, Madras.
The Journal of Archaeology, Hyderabad.
The Indian Economic and Social History Review, New Delhi.

◊◊◊